THE

Eight Million

JOURNAL OF A NEW YORK CORRESPONDENT

THE
Eight Million

JOURNAL OF A NEW YORK CORRESPONDENT

by Meyer Berger

ILLUSTRATED BY
Henry Berger

1983

Columbia University Press

New York

Copyright 1942 by Meyer Berger

Library of Congress Cataloging in Publication Data

Berger, Meyer, 1898–1960.
　The eight million.

　　Reprint. Originally published: New York: Simon and Schuster, 1942.
　　1. New York (N.Y.)—Social life and customs—Addresses, essays, lectures.　I. Title.
　　F128.5.B48　1983　　　974.7′1　　　82-22212
　　ISBN 0-231-05710-5
　　ISBN 0-231-05711-3 (pbk.)

Reprinted by arrangement with Simon and Schuster, Inc.
Columbia University Press Morningside Edition 1983

Columbia University Press
New York

Clothbound editions of Columbia University Press books are Smyth-sewn and printed on permanent and durable acid-free paper.

Printed in U.S.A.

To Mae
who deserves better

Contents

Introduction

*When I was eleven years old I got a night job in the Brook-
lyn Office of* The New York Morning World. *I ran advertising and editorial copy to the main building which
now squats, dusty and desolate, in Park Row hard by
Brooklyn Bridge.*

*When there was no copy I ran hot coffee and hot bean
sandwiches from Dirty Smith's, or, sometimes, cold pints
from Dixon's. On winter nights I'd hold the sandwiches
against my chest so the heat would come through the paper
and warm me. On hot nights I'd linger outside the office
door the longer to cool my hands on the tin growler.*

*Best of all, when the copy was in, I could stand near the
long copy table in the cavernous old* World *office and
watch the poker games. Here I absorbed all the legends
of the craft, ancient and contemporary. I contracted news-
print fever in this way, by a kind of osmosis. Here I
learned, I think, a sounder journalism than is taught in
graver halls of learning.*

*The men from whom I caught this fever have, for the
greater part, long since died of it. They didn't know, but
they were my faculty. I was their sole student. For the
things in this volume they are indirectly to blame.*

Wherever they are—Big Bob McNamara, Arthur Curtis,

Old Major Clowes, Louis Hart, Arthur Meyer, Charles McCarthy, and Buck Moran—whether getting out editions on asbestos or on tablets of samite and gold, I hope their reviews will not be too unkind.

The papers in this book are mostly about the queer, the quaint, and the quizzical in New York City; fragments and sketches of people I have met or of places I have visited in journalistic wandering in the avenues and side streets.

These papers were not written with an eye to book publication. No one was more astonished than I when the idea of a book was suggested. If the pieces gain any favor I shall count myself a fortunate fellow. If they meet only indifference it will not be too difficult to make believe it never happened.

M. B.

Acknowledgments

THE author and publishers of *The Eight Million* are grateful to the editors of THE NEW YORKER, LIFE, and THE NEW YORK TIMES for permission to reprint material that originally appeared in their pages.

PART ONE

Apprentice Days

I Cover the Water Front

A BEERY man with hoary chin stubble approached an applecart at Fulton Ferry in Brooklyn at ten o'clock one morning about thirty years ago. He said to the peddler, "Will you let me eat all the apples I can for a quarter?" Apples then sold at twenty for twenty-five cents—more than most men could eat—and it seemed a shame to take the money. Perhaps the apple vendor had no conscience. Anyway, he took the twenty-five cents and the customer dug into the heap.

At two o'clock that afternoon someone called the Brooklyn office of *The Morning World*. The beery man was still eating apples. The city editor had no reporters in the office. They would not come for another hour. He called the new office boy.

"Go down to Fulton Ferry and learn what you can about some fellow eating apples," he said. "Get all the names and addresses and listen to what people say."

The ferry was a good mile's walk from the office, but it was October and the sky was blue. The office boy walked through the latticed shadow under the old Fulton Street El. He was puzzled. What matter if a man ate apples? Most people ate apples. They didn't get their names and addresses in *The Morning World* for doing it, did they? When I get home, the office boy thought, and tell them I went to see a man eating apples, they will say, "Are they crazy to pay a boy to watch a man eating apples?"

Down by the river, smoke was rising from chuffy tugs and heat waves shimmered from the towboat stacks like webby curtains in a breeze. Off the barge slip some two hundred stevedores and water-front loafers milled about the apple vendor's cart. The apple mound that had been four feet high at ten o'clock that morning was now a valley between the low pushcart walls. The face of the beery man was very flushed but he munched steadily.

Silver and grimy banknotes swapped hands. A little man with dirt ingrained in his facial seams kept tabs. Each time an apple was reduced to core, he marked the cobblestone pavement with a piece of white chalk. At six o'clock, when the sun roofed Manhattan on the opposite riverbank with autumnal red and gold, the count was two hundred and fifty. The watchers hoarsely cheered this news. The poor apple peddler was crushed.

"I got to go now," he said.

He put his hands to the cart handles. The stevedores made rumbling noises in their throats. The cart did not move.

Night filtered its first layer of dusty powder on the river. Lights came on in Manhattan's graying towers. Trolley cars and El trains blossomed with weak yellow incandescents. They moved like toys through the spider-web structure of Brooklyn Bridge. The river darkened and turned gelid black. The beery man continued to munch stubbornly.

It was full night when the cart was emptied. Brittle stars quivered over the river. The bridge, an arc of glow-

ing dots, reproduced itself on the onyx waters, as on a black mirror. River craft trailed serpentine reflections, red and green, in their own ripples.

Two hundred and fifty-seven apples. The stevedores and the loafers noisily and triumphantly bore the bloated champion across the cobbled drayway toward a water-front saloon.

The poor apple man moved off in the dark. His empty cart rattled on the cobblestones and the street lamp distorted his image in long and melancholy shadow. I wondered what he would tell his wife and children when he got home. "I sold two hundred and fifty-seven apples for twenty-five cents," he would say. Twenty-five cents was a day's cart hire.

I hurried back to the office. I had it all on copypaper: the count, the names, the addresses, what the men had said. I had careful notes about the changing lights and sights on the river; enough, I recall, for a 10,000-word thesis on apple eating.

The city editor was white-haired and very wise.

"No," he said gently. "Not a column. Try to keep it in ten lines."

Ten lines? How could that be? I had been down by the river for five hours. Many exciting things had happened. The wise old man said yes, he knew, but in the same five hours other things had happened in other parts of the world. He picked up a copy of the paper and pointed at date lines, some quite remote from Fulton Ferry.

I forgot the beery man's name long ago. I do not remember now how much was wagered on his apple eating. I have even forgotten how he did away with two hundred and fifty-seven apples, except that I vaguely recall he left the cart several times to visit one of the creaking barges while the anguished apple vender was held captive by the stevedores.

In *The Morning World*, next day, my ten lines were reduced to four or five. They seemed quite changed but my heart tried to escape through my ribs when I found them.

All this, as I have told you, was long ago. I had caught ink fever and I never got over it. I was to devote my life to searching out the odd fish and the unfortunates in a city of several millions. Two hundred and fifty-seven apples had shaped my career. When I grew older I realized this was not strange. Think—so I would console myself— what damage was done in paradise by only one apple.

Lady in a Canopied Bed

THE WISE old man who sent me on my first assignment was Major Norris A. Clowes. When he died, a few years ago, he was past eighty. In his youth he had enjoyed the confidence of Joseph Pulitzer, who founded *The World*. In winter he wore a fur-lined greatcoat. "Joe Pulitzer gave me that," the Major would say. It was a reward for exceptional reporting. On Sunday mornings, the Major wore a high silk hat.

He was florid and paunchy, with bags under his eyes. His hair was pure white and his mustache was lush and long and curled at the ends. It was an off-shade orange. The Major chewed Virgin Leaf. He wore celluloid collars less than an inch high, with starched white string bow ties. The only place that stocked these collars and ties was a dusty little shop under the El down near the river.

When the Major came in, or left the office, he would pound the tiled floor with a knobby walking stick. You could tell the Major's moods by the vigor of the cane tap. When he came from The Hole in the Wall in Pierrepont Street, the tapping was apt to be extremely vigorous and hearty. A keen ear could gauge by the force behind the thrusts whether the Major had had seven Haig and Haigs, or only three.

The staff could always tell when the Major was working himself into the mood for a snort. He would wash one hand with the other several times in anticipatory gesture before he reached for the lower right-hand desk drawer where he kept his bottle. There would be another dry hand wash after the drink was down. This was ritual.

Some odd duties went with the job of office boy to the Major. Mrs. Clowes was bedridden. She was a tremendous woman, somewhere around three hundred pounds. When you brought the evening newspapers to the house in quiet Pierrepont Street you would be ushered into Mrs. Clowes' bedchamber. She would be sitting up in her canopied old bed and there would be from six to eight fox terriers on the counterpane, on the hills, and in the valleys made by the contour of her body. Mrs. Clowes' hands always blazed with diamonds, tremendous stones that spat fire in the gaslight. Some fingers would have three or four big rings.

Once a week an open carriage would roll up to the brownstone stoop. The Major would get a telephone call and I would be instructed to hurry over to help two maidservants and two house men get Mrs. Clowes down the brownstone stoop and into the carriage. I would be called again when the carriage returned.

On bad days, Mrs. Clowes would have the Major send me over to sit at the foot of her bed with the terriers. The room was always dark because the gaslights were weak. Mrs. Clowes would say, "Sit down, boy, I am going to talk." Mostly she talked about when she was a belle in Baltimore, and how spry she was then. She would make mincing gestures that shook the old bed and stirred up the terriers. They would roll their eyes at her in mute rebuke and snuggle into position again.

Some days Mrs. Clowes' temper was extremely short. She would scream for the servants. When a girl—or both girls—got near the bed she would lash clumsily at them with her cane. The girls were used to this. "Yes, ma'am," they would say, and stand just beyond stick's reach. It was a kind of game. I grinned the first time it happened and had to slide off the counterpane when the stick lashed at me. "Go about your silly business," Mrs. Clowes screamed. "Get out!"

One rainy Saturday night—it was late fall, I remember —the Major put down the telephone and called me.

"You are going to a concert," he said.

I stole a glance at the office clock. It was time to go home.

"I don't think I care much for concerts," I parried.

The Major looked very tired.

"I know," he said grimly, "but its *her* concert. She's made up her mind it won't start until you get there."

It was one of those nights when soot seemed mixed with the rain. I mounted the brownstone steps, filled with resentment. Odd noises came from inside the house, noises that might come from a pigpen, deep grunts and little squeals. The dark-faced maid who let me in pinned me against the vestibule wall and shook with suppressed laughter.

"You're going to love this," she said. "This beats all."

The living room was brilliant with gaslight. The squat old table lamps with fat rose paintings were aglow. Gold wall brackets, turned up high, splashed the papered walls with light. On the overstuffed sofas and tremendous armchairs, in various degrees of discomfort, sat twelve red-faced musicians, members of an itinerant German band. Mrs. Clowes had heard them down the street, from her bedroom, and had sent a maid to fetch them.

The terriers were restless. Mrs. Clowes, astonishingly bulky in a shiny green silk dressing gown gaudy with red and yellow flowers, held them captive in her broad arms in the canopied bed. Her cheeks were high-rouged and flushed with excitement. Diamonds dripped fire from her ears and on her broad chest. She held the wriggling pups tightly. They did not like the musicians or the tuning brasses. They yelped and wailed.

Mrs. Clowes' eyes widened when I stepped into the room.

"You're holding up the grandest concert," she shouted. "I want you to meet my musicians."

The fat German band leader stood up and bowed a most courtly bow.

"It iss a bleasure," he said.

He had a big brown mustache and very rosy cheeks. So did the others. Except for height, they seemed turned out of one mold. I went around shaking hands. I had to reach around tubas and French horns to do it.

"That's fine," Mrs. Clowes shouted happily. "That's fine."

The first number was "Dixie." Mrs. Clowes picked it out of loyalty to Baltimore. Gold-framed paintings shivered on the walls. Vases shook on the marble mantel. It was deafening. Mrs. Clowes beat time with her walking stick and screamed rebel yells. The terriers yowled dismally. They ran excitedly up and down the Clowes hills and valleys. In the corridor the maids stifled their laughter.

The concert lasted two hours. It rocked the staid old brownstone mansion. People stopped in the rain and stared up at the windows. An outraged patrician somewhere upstreet called the police, but the Major telephoned to the station house from the office, and nothing came of the complaint. Mrs. Clowes arranged to have a concert every Saturday night. Each musician got two dollars, the leader one dollar more.

I grimly attended these deafening musicales for two years. The songs were always the same: "Swannee River," "Dixie," "Carry Me Back to Ole Virginny," some German numbers, romantic pieces like "Love's Old Sweet Song," and "Flow Gently, Sweet Afton." I still wince when I hear a brass band.

Second Floor, Left

ONE DAY while I was still an office boy a postcard came to the city desk. It said, "If you will send a reporter to (I have forgotten the house number, but I know it was on Jefferson Avenue in Brooklyn) you will get an unusual story. Try to get your man into the apartment left-hand side, second floor, coming upstairs." No name was signed.

Today, such a card might go into the wastebasket, but the world was more leisurely then. There was time to look into little things, time to turn up amusing or tragic incidents in individual lives. The accent had not switched to the international theme. You took more thought to near neighbors.

The postcard assignment went to Joseph Henry Appelgate, Jr. I went along to fetch any pictures that might turn up. On the way, Appelgate stopped in the neighborhood precinct and a detective joined us. This gave the mission high flavor. This was better than watching a man eat a mound of apples.

The house in Jefferson Avenue was an old brownstone, a type almost vanished now. The street was quiet and lined with whispering trees. The sunlight through the leaves made shaky patterns on the flagstones. I was disappointed. This promised no great excitement.

Appelgate jerked the bell handle and we heard a muffled tinkle, far off down the dark hall. An old lady opened the door and peered up. The detective showed his gold shield.

"Who is the tenant on the second floor, left?" he asked.

"I don't know their name," the old lady said. "They moved in two years ago, but I don't know their name. No one knows their name. They never come out. They have never put their name in the letter box."

"They couldn't be up there two years and never come out," Appelgate argued. He was becoming excited. "How do they get their food? They go out for food, don't they?"

"Sometimes a man came late at night and left a box of food at the door," the little old lady said. "He came every two or three weeks, but no one ever saw him up close. It's very mysterious."

Appelgate and the detective went up the carpeted stairs. Second floor, left. The detective knocked several times. No one answered. The detective put his ear against the dark wooden door panel. He whispered, "I don't hear anything."

I shuddered with excitement.

The old lady called to us from the foot of the stairs.

"They're up there," she said. "I heard them early this morning. They were moving around."

The detective hit the panel with his shoulder. The door creaked under his weight. A thin voice behind the panel said, "Go away. Go away." It was an old woman's voice, weak and quavery. I trembled as with ague.

After some more pushing the door was forced. Just across the threshold sat a startling creature. Not old, only seemingly so. Her hair, gray and matted, was a greasy ball on her head. Strings of it were down over her eyes and mouth. She covered her face with her hand to shut us from her sight. She kept repeating, "Go away, go away, go away." It was a chant.

In both corners, at the far end of the room, indistinct in the thin-barred light that struggled through dark-green shutters, were two other strange creatures. They were girls, one about sixteen, one about twenty. Their hair was matted, too, and let down like slick ropes over their eyes. They stared at us but made no sound.

The detective was bewildered.

"Jesus!" he said. "What is this?"

He shook the woman, but she tightened the protective grip that hid her face. The table where she sat, only a foot or two from the door, was cluttered with food fragments, bottles, and paper, as if untidy people had eaten there for years but had never bothered to clean after meals. There was an open bottle of Father John's medicine. Later we found a dozen such bottles, as if the nostrum had been used as a food instead of as medication. The detective called downstairs to the old woman who had let us in.

"Get an ambulance," he said.

The girls made animal noises in their throats, something between a sob and a whimper. The woman, on the chair, talked through her fingers.

"Go away," she kept saying. "Go away."

Appelgate and the detective went through the apartment. There were four other rooms, large rooms with high ceilings, all in deep shadow because the shutters were to, front and rear, all filled with furniture that had not been unwrapped. Appelgate noticed the dates on the newspaper wrappings.

"These are *Brooklyn Daily Eagles*," he announced. "All going back two years or more."

It turned out the women had lost all track of time.

They had tried to keep up with it, when they first moved in. They had made a crude calendar, thirty penciled boxes on the back of an old cake carton. They had checked off the days. After a few months they gave this up.

An ambulance from Kings County Hospital pulled up in the street and neighbors came out of other brownstone houses in the block to murmur and stare. The intern looked at the three women.

"Mental cases," he said.

He had the driver herd them together. The girls had to be pulled up from their squatting positions in the corners of the room. The old lady was lifted out of the chair. Their dresses stuck to them. They sat on the floor in the ambulance as it moved through a lane of gabbling neighbors.

In the flat, Appelgate and the detective found papers that bore the name of a Park Department employee. The police picked this man up and brought him to the brownstone house in Jefferson Avenue. He was short and round and dough-faced with fear. His collar was wilted. The round little man would not talk at first. He just dabbed at his forehead and at the back of his neck. His little eyes roved over the rooms and the shrouded furnishings.

"Good God," he kept saying. "Good God."

Finally, though, he told the story. He seemed too roly-poly for romance but he had acquired a mistress. She was jealous of his wife and two daughters. She wanted him to leave them and set up a permanent home for her.

"I couldn't do that," he explained earnestly. "I have a city job. They'd throw me out of my job."

Instead, the little man moved his wife and daughters out of their old home in Flatbush and into the Jefferson Avenue brownstone. He seemed harmless enough as he stood before the detective, wilted and with his eyes rolling, but somehow he had managed to scare his family into believing he would kill them if they left their new lodgings.

He fetched them food at early morning hours, renewed his threats. Sometimes he beat his wife when she cried out against his cruelty. In a few months he had her spirit broken, and the children's with it. They would shrink if he came inside the door.

It seemed fantastic. Why didn't they break out and appeal to neighbors? Why didn't they just lean from the windows and call to some passing policeman? Appelgate asked the neighbors about this. They had never heard a sound from the shuttered second floor, left.

Joe Appelgate had imagination. He always figured hypnotism might have been the answer. At the hospital they shaved the women's heads to the bone, washed them, and gave them medical attention, but they were mental cases.

The little fat man got ten years.

When I got home that night my mother knew by my suppressed excitement that something extraordinary had happened. My brother did, too.

"Was it apples again?" he wanted to know.

This time, though, I had a thriller. I told it at dinner. Later my mother took me next door and had me tell it to the Polish lady who lived there. She crossed herself. My mother took me upstairs to Mrs. Costello's flat and I told the story again. Mrs. Costello rolled her eyes.

"Jesus, Mary, and Joseph," she murmured. "Such goings on. That couldn't happen anywhere but New York."

The End of the World

IT CAME to pass after a few years that I was graduated from apple and animal stories to bigger pieces, including an earthquake, floods, an eclipse (total), divers homicides, and "The End of the World." By some curious twist of the mind, the details of the first apple assignment have stayed with me, fresh and green, while the first homicide has long ago been washed away as the tide washes footprints from a lonely beach.

Sometimes I puzzle over the reason for this, but I reflect that you are not apt to meet during a lifetime more than one man who can, or who will even try to, do away with two hundred and fifty-seven apples at a sitting. Murder, on the other hand, is distressingly commonplace in a city of more than seven millions and a man might easily lose track of one.

The End of the World crept up rather quietly in 1927. The first signs, little paragraphs no larger than a man's hand, came from a woman correspondent near Patchogue on Long Island. With a minimum of encouragement from the city desk, this lady had written tirelessly for years, in a round childish hand, about the first robin in Patchogue, about the rosebush that grew buds in December, journal-

17

istic ephemera that sometimes made the paper, but not often.

Suddenly the Patchogue correspondent discovered the machine age. She obtained an old Oliver typewriter and increased her literary output. In her new prolific mood she added broader human interest to her items about perennial robin arrivals and out-of-season rosebuds.

The fruit of the Oliver, one quiet day, was an assortment of short pieces about plant and animal life in and around Patchogue and, at the end, a casual paragraph about one Robert Reidt, a house painter, who was disposing of his possessions in anticipation of the end of the world.

I called the correspondent and learned that the house painter was a solemn fellow, with a flaxen-haired wife, three flaxen-haired kids, and a half-dozen flaxen-haired disciples, moony folk who read and reread the Bible with him for clues to Earth's and Mankind's destruction.

Our correspondent had forgotten to mention in her piece that Robert Reidt had at last come upon the fearsome message in Revelations, that he had, in fact, figured it down to razor edge. "Prepare," he was telling neighbors sepulchrally, "for the End of the World at six A.M., March seventh." Wherever he spread this dismal word the flaxen-haired disciples grouped behind him, echoed the prophecy in melancholy chorus.

With these additional details, Robert Reidt and his preparations for Doomsday made a sizable story. Within a fortnight the eyes of the world were focused on Patchogue and the Prophet. Staff men from metropolitan dailies swarmed to his humble cottage. Photographers took pictures that showed the Prophet with his finger on the fatal passage in the Scripture.

The Prophet left his pastoral surroundings to preach the

Gospel of Doom in Times Square. The secret of World's End, which might have been confined to Patchogue, was broadcast to the far corners of the land over press-association wires. The Lady of the Oliver, incidentally, vanished from the picture at this point.

At four o'clock on the morning appointed for the End of the World, our staff man called excitedly on the telephone. He seemed slightly hysterical. He had gone into the village with the other reporters to take a few drinks against The Hour. He had left the Prophet and his earnest disciples awaiting Doom's crack on the lawn before the Prophet's cottage. The reporters stayed overlong at the tavern. Eventually they were turned out. The innkeeper reminded them that they had a rendezvous with Eternity on Robert Reidt's hilltop. They left the taproom with alcoholic uncertainty and staggered toward Reidt's cottage in the dark. The stars looked coldly down on their sinful progress.

A half mile from the cottage the reporters froze to the road, startled. From the general direction of the Prophet's cottage, eerie green flame shot up against the sky. It happened again and again, each time plunging the world in deeper darkness. The reporters stared silently at one another. They seemed a little shaken. All were struck with the same thought at the same moment. Could this be The Sign? They ran toward the Reidt cottage.

Our staff man said, "The green flame came from photographer's flash powder. "We found that out when he got near the lawn." He sounded relieved. "It had me sweating."

It is a practice in newspaper offices, when great events are expected, for rewrite men to prepare alternate leads for a story. This saves time getting copy to the composition room when the event occurs or doesn't come off. It is done most often in big jury cases, where the alternatives of the event are pretty well narrowed down to guilty and acquitted. I had alternate leads ready for this one.

The first said: "Patchogue, L. I., March 7—Robert Reidt, Prophet of Doom, surrounded by crestfallen disciples, waited in vain here at daybreak today for the End of the World."

The alternate lead read: "Patchogue, L. I., March 7—The World ended at 6 A.M. today."

East Side

The Tombs

FOUR days after the Tombs, our city jail, opened on June 15, 1838, James Gordon Bennett, the excitable editor of the *Herald,* suggested that it be torn down. The new prison on Centre Street was, he said, "a loathsome and dreary charnel house." The rather unimaginative gentlemen who comprised the New York City Common Council disagreed. For one thing, they had just spent $430,000, a large sum for the eighteen thirties, putting up the loathsome place. For another, they were very proud of having patterned the building on a steel engraving of what they considered an esthetic, if melancholy, Egyptian tomb in a popular contemporary travel book by a man named John Stevens, of Hoboken. This same Mr. Stevens was an ancestor of the Mrs. Frances Stevens Hall whose clerical spouse, almost a century later, figured as one of the corpses in the Hall-Mills murder in DeRussey's Lane, near New Brunswick, New Jersey. The Common Council optimistically named the jail the Halls of Justice, but no one ever called it that.

"The Halls of Justice," Bennett wrote in the *Herald,* "will never deserve the name unless . . . the architect who designed it and the jackasses that fixed on the location shall have been sentenced for life in one of the dreary cells of their own contriving." The prison was an all too convincing copy of Mr. Stevens' Egyptian mausoleum. The public immediately took to speaking of it as the Tombs, and the name stuck. Actually, as few present-day New Yorkers know, there have been two buildings known as the Tombs. The first was torn down in 1897 and three years later was replaced, on the same site, by a gray, brooding, chateaulike structure which was formally named the City Prison but which deserved to inherit the name of the Tombs, and did. It is this second Tombs which will in its turn be given over to the wreckers. Before that, our municipal prisoners were moved into the new city jail, a cheerful, modern, twelve-story building directly across Centre Street from the old quarters. It, too, is named the City Prison, but already the newspapers have begun to refer to it as "the new $18,000,000 Tombs," and the chances are that the traditional name will not be easily shaken off.

The Common Council fiddled over the idea of putting up the first Tombs for more than twenty years before getting around to it. New York then had two prisons, both on the Common. One was Old Bridewell, erected between Broadway and the present City Hall about 1775. The other was a stone jail built on the northeastern end of the Common in 1756. Both were British prisons managed by the sadistic Provost Cunningham during the American Revolution. Old Bridewell finally came down, and the contractor who built the Tombs saved a few dollars by using some of the stones salvaged from the wreckage. When, sixty years later, the first Tombs was torn down, some of these same stones were salvaged again and went into a wall in Central Park. Just where these stones are today, no one seems to know. The stone jail at the end of the Common was converted into a hall of records and did not come down until 1903, when the first New York subway was built. This prison stood about where the subway kiosk in City Hall Park is now.

Mayor Philip Hone found both old prisons offensive and in the early years of the nineteenth century frequently wrote nasty pieces about them in his diary. George P. Morris, fastidious editor of the original *Mirror* and a close friend of Washington Irving, abandoned temporarily the composition of lacy essays on literature and the fine arts to demand the "removal of these foul excrescences." The *Post,* with characteristic chilliness, wanted to know whether the two old jails were kept as "a sort of snuffbox for Their Honors," meaning the members of the Council, and demanded a new prison "somewhere up around the Five Points, or some other place out of sight." Fashionable society lived far downtown, mostly below Chambers Street, and the *Post* wanted the prison planted in the slums. When, in the eighteen twenties, the complaints got noisy enough, the Council grudgingly appointed a committee to find a new site.

New York was then a grimy and untidy town of three- and four-story houses, principally below Canal Street. To the north lay meadows and country roads. Fat pigs, scarred from fights with wandering dog packs, slopped and grunted through Broadway mud, rooting for dainties. The prison committee, after a half-dozen excursions into the upper sections of the city, triumphantly brought in their recommendations. Their first choice was the site of Old Brewery, a rookery just east of Centre Street, crawling with unfortunates in extreme stages of mental and physical decay. It was generally agreed that no place in the world matched Old Brewery for crime, disease, and diversified sin. Around it, in muddy lanes and crooked alleys, sprawled rows of sagging wooden shacks, incredibly overcrowded with the poor and the wanton. This was the Five Points district. The Council decided that it could not approve this site. "The Five Points," it reported in April, 1829, "produces a great rent on account of being a good location for small retailers of liquor who have extensively located themselves in this vicinity and what may be considered a nuisance has in reality increased the value of this property."

Finally, the Council approved another spot picked by the committee, the block bounded by Lafayette, Centre, Leonard, and Franklin Streets, which had once been Collect Pond. The pond has been filled in in 1808 by jobless seamen and other unemployed of the time. This group had threatened, on a mass visit to City Hall, to tear the Council members apart if it didn't get jobs, so the Council hastily set up a sort of WPA and, for want of something else to give them to do, had them level the hills that looked down on the pond from Broadway on the west and from Chambers Street on the south. The hills were dumped into the pond. When, in 1938, WPA workers began to clear the ground for the newest Tombs, which, like its predecessors, stands on the bed of Collect Pond, they had to remove the hills deposited by the earlier WPA a hundred and thirty years before. They even found some of the nineteenth-century WPA shovels.

In 1836, workmen started digging a foundation for the first Tombs. A few feet down they struck the pond. The contractor laid down a huge raft of hemlock logs in the mudding ground and built the Tombs on a floating foundation. After the prison was completed, two years later, there were recurrent rumors that its weight was squeezing the water of the pond into the cellars of houses in the Five Points and that the Five Points might be undermined. Then the Tombs itself began to sag. Within five months after it opened it had sunk several inches, warping all the cells. A firm of locksmiths reset the doors and locks and put in a bill for $489.26 for the job. Carpenters and masons were forever rushing into the jail to jack things up or to mend new breaks. Nervous prisoners, distressed by the noises the structure made as it settled, were apt to scream that the Tombs was caving in, but it never did.

Looking over the Tombs police records, or blotters, dating back to the opening of the first prison, you gather that the watch—as the police force was called then—tried, perhaps overconscientiously, to fill all two hundred of the prison's cells as soon as possible. The very first prisoner registered was Catherine Hagerman, a lady of the town, brought in from a brothel in the fabulously evil Five Points section. She got six months for vagrancy. The next arrests were Bill Stubbins and Hannah Varon, picked up by the watch for stealing secondhand clothes in the Five Points, and then came Jake Prout and James Corrigan, accused of leering at females. The day's haul came to around thirty prisoners, mostly drunken draggletails and young Negro girls caught in minor shoplifting.

A fortnight after the Tombs opened, Tom Hyer, a butcher by trade and a bare-knuckles fight champion on the side, was brought in. He had cut off a friend's nose during a political dispute in a tavern at Chatham and Pearl Streets. In the jail Hyer complained about his accommodations and demonstrated his sincerity by beating up the jailer, a Mr. Coggeshall. "Mr. Coggeshall," Bennett's *Herald* cheerfully noted, "was thrashed within an inch of his life, night before last, by Tom Hyer. Hyer

fell upon him and beat him in such a dreadful manner
that he was carried away in a state of insensibility." A
week later Bennett published a footnote to this incident.
"The Keeper of the Halls of Justice," he told his readers,
"just apprised us, to our inexpressible joy, that his brains
have not been bashed out against the stone walls in the
Tombs by Tom Hyer, as stated."

Nine tenths of the early prisoners came from the Five
Points, Paradise Square, and Cow Bay, all districts bogged
down in the mud just east of the Tombs. This area
teemed with giant cartmen, truculent pugilists, and bull-
throated street brawlers, white and black. The watch
followed a discreet policy of not interfering with the homicidal element. Though murder was a routine activity in
the Five Points, the watch seldom caught up with the
murderers. Its first catch was Edward Coleman, a ragged
Negro. Coleman, it seems, slipped up behind his wife on
Saturday morning, July 28, 1838, as she was panhandling
near Jollie's Music Shop on Broadway at Walker Street,
squeezed her head to his chest, and all but cut it off with
a razor. He threw the razor in the mud and, dazed, waited
for the watch to come for him. "I done it," he told his
captors, and was lugged to the Tombs. "It appears," the
Sun reported, "that the horrible deed resulted from Coleman's belief in her infidelity and if the statements of their
acquaintances are correct his belief was not without cause."
Coleman was hanged the following January, the first of
some fifty murderers executed in the Tombs yard.

Mainly, the Tombs was crammed with streetwalkers
and petty thieves, with a sprinkling of young sporting fops.
On the blotters you come upon entries like "Patrick Brady,
stealing cider," "Andrew Jackson, stealing pig," and
"James Hadley, run-off apprentice." Bonded apprentices

ran away with considerable regularity. There were also an astonishing number of arrests for "bastardy." Pigtailed sailors in glazed hats were frequently herded into Tombs cells in batches when they got out of hand while "strolling in search of the lions," which was the watch's nice-Nellie way of saying they were frequenting brothels. An early entry tells about Officers Baker and McManus bringing in "two young larks whom they found acting in a very disorderly manner in a house kept by Maria Adams at No. 3 Franklin Street." The two young gentlemen— a Mr. Augustus Hutchens and a Mr. George Fredericks— had spat tobacco juice on Maria Adams' carpet and "otherwise destroyed furnishings." Next morning a Justice Osborne severely scolded these giddy fellows in Tombs Court, where minor cases in the Tombs district were arraigned daily, and fined them ten dollars apiece.

There were four tiers of cells. Convicted prisoners had the ground floor and those awaiting trial had the other three; murderers occupied the second, burglars and arsonists the third, and minor offenders the fourth. Homeless children seven and eight years old were thrown into cells with prostitutes, alcoholics, and cutpurses. The Common Council voted that debtors also be confined in the Tombs. These prisoners, who had been kept in one of the old jails on the Common, petitioned the Council to reconsider this order, asking that "a little discrimination be made" and that they be kept apart from common criminals. The Council refused them. Members of the Hoboken Turtle Club, a group of sporting gentlemen, promptly showed their sympathy for the debtors by sending them a large kettle of hot turtle soup.

Prisoners without money were apt to be forgotten in Tombs cells for months when judges and attorneys lost interest in them or when some careless clerk mislaid commitments. On October 17, 1839, for example, Officer Hanlon of the watch found Will Kitcheman sleeping off a drunk on Dover Street pier. He loaded the toper into a wheelbarrow and dumped him into "The Hole," a little stone building in the Tombs yard, used mostly for truculent prisoners. Nobody remembered Kitcheman until his body was found there, quite by accident, one morning four months later. He had been eaten by rats.

In the early days of the Tombs, corrupt guards charged prisoners a dollar a week for blankets they should have had for nothing and collaborated with the shyster lawyers who operated in the prison to milk prisoners to the limit. Wardens short-changed the city on fees collected from those prisoners who could afford to pay seventy-five cents a day for their keep. The wardens and the guards worked another fat little graft. "One prisoner," a *Herald* reporter once wrathfully wrote, "was obliged to give one of these pale-faced pimps a quarter of a dollar for bringing in a pitcher of beer that some kindhearted visitor had furnished." Toward the end of his article the reporter was evidently overcome by literary hysteria. "Down with the Bastille!" he scribbled frantically. "*À la Lanterne* with the supporters of it!"

Most of the early Tombs wardens were good Democrats. Their training for prison management consisted chiefly in rounding up the Five Points vote, including the graveyard poll. It was common knowledge that the wardens and other prison employees were corrupt, but, except for editorial protests in the newspapers and magazines, there was almost no public indignation. Prison corruption was considered respectable and went unpunished. The merriest of the Centre Street jailers was

Malachi Fallon, a saddler by trade, who ran the Tombs with informality through the lively eighteen forties. A sporting gentleman, he kept fighting cocks, bred pit dogs in the prison yard, and maintained a cote of carrier pigeons on the roof. Warden Fallon, for a consideration, would allow rich murderers, thriving abortionists, and other important prisoners certain privileges. By paying the warden a proper sum, for example, an influential boarder was permitted to give his cell a few homey touches, like singing canaries, a Kidderminster carpet, or fancy wallpaper. For an especially openhanded inmate Fallon would have the Tombs carpenter put up a few hanging shelves, build in a clothes closet, or throw together some small tables to hold books, pipes, and tobacco. He farmed out to Phineas T. Barnum the exclusive right to make death masks of notorious pirates, murderers, and highwaymen confined there and to buy the clothing which these prisoners had worn when nabbed. The masks and the clothing were put on exhibition in Barnum's Museum on lower Broadway. Later wardens made similar arrangements with Barnum. One of them, Charles Sutton, dickered with Barnum, who wanted to make a death mask and buy the clothing of Albert E. Hicks, a pirate who had killed the captain of an oyster sloop and two of his own shipmates with an ax. The deal was made shortly after Hicks was sentenced to the gallows. Barnum paid Sutton twenty-five dollars for the privilege and generously gave the pirate, who wasn't in on the transaction, two boxes of cigars. Barnum also gave him a new suit to die in. The day before he was hanged, he complained to the warden that Barnum had cheated him. "This suit I got in exchange for my own," he told the jailer bitterly, "is shoddy. It won't last." The warden, at the city's expense,

got him a suit of blue cottonade with gilt buttons and
needlework anchors to wear at the hanging, and the pirate
felt better.

Warden Fallon kept open house for celebrities of the
day and was always ready to put the jail at the disposal of
distinguished citizens who might wish to use it as a setting
for a practical joke. If an alderman or a rich merchant
wanted a drunken friend jugged, just for amusement,
Fallon would willingly arrange it. Junius Brutus Booth
the elder, the great tragedian, frequently went to the
Tombs on unofficial, and usually alcoholic, visits. Even
when sober, Booth enjoyed talking to murderers, and
Fallon didn't discourage him. Booth's favorite murderer
was known only as "Dave Babe." There was a rumor
that Babe was the black-sheep son of an Episcopal bishop.
He was in the Tombs from July, 1843, to May, 1846, having been convicted in a Federal court of piracy and murdering the mate of the schooner *Sarah Lavinia*. He was
reprieved from the gallows seven times before President
Polk gave him a pardon.

One afternoon Booth was let into Dave Babe's cell.
Like all Tombs murderers, the pirate was chained to the
stone floor. "Strike the gyves and fetters from that unfortunate youth!" Booth hoarsely declaimed. He assumed
a theatrical pose and tears rolled down his cheeks. "Secure
me in his stead!" he screamed, and beat his breast. The
guards talked Booth out of making this dramatic sacrifice.
Before they got him out of the cell, quite overcome by his
unselfish impulse, he unwrapped a dozen black cigars he
was carrying in a silk handkerchief and handed them to
the pirate. Farther down the corridor Booth impetuously
gave a Negro strangler a twenty-dollar banknote. The

Negro tried to swallow the bill on the justifiable assumption that the keepers would take it away from him if he didn't, but Warden Fallon got his strong fingers around the strangler's throat and made him disgorge it. By now Fallon had tired of Booth's whimsicalities and ordered the guards to hustle him into a vacant cell in Murderers' Row. Booth indignantly shook the bars and harangued the tier of cells about this desecration of liberty, but eventually fell asleep. An hour before curtain time at the Park Theatre, where Booth was playing, the guards, familiar with his routine, shook him out of his slumber, conveyed him past the taverns to his dressing room, and grimly stood by until he got into his make-up. A few minutes later, Booth, trembling from a hang-over, was on the boards as Richard III and knocking them in the aisles.

Early legend makers ignored the true story of how the Tombs got its name. While the jail was still new, its guards invented the story that it was called the Tombs because of the large number of suicides committed in its cells. They passed this version off on Charles Dickens when he was taken through the prison in 1842 and he recorded it in his *American Notes*. Dickens, as he told the story, wondered why inmates were allowed to scatter their clothes on the stone floors. He said to a guard, "Don't you oblige the prisoners to be orderly and put such things away? What do you say to hanging them up?" "When they had hooks," the guard told Dickens, "they would hang *themselves*, so they're taken out of every cell, and there's only the marks left where they used to be." Actually, the first man who hanged himself in the Tombs used a water pipe that ran along the ceiling of his cell. This suicide was Frederick Smith, a Philadelphia horse thief, picked up on Broadway as a fugitive a few days before the Tombs was opened. Smith used his neckerchief for a noose.

The most sensational suicide in the history of the Tombs, however, was the result not of a hanging at all but of a simple knife wound, and it had contemporary journalists panting for weeks. The principal was John C. Colt, whose brother Samuel Colt, six years before, had invented the revolver, which was the basis of the great Colt fortune. One mild September afternoon in 1841, John Colt, it seems, won a dispute with Sam Adams, a printer—something about a small debt Colt owed—by bashing in Adams' head with a hammer in Colt's office at Broadway and Chambers Street. Colt stuffed the corpse into a packing case and had a drayman cart it to the schooner *Kalamazoo,* which was taking on cargo for New Orleans at the foot of Maiden Lane. When blood began to leak out of the case aboard ship, the body was found. Investigation led to the discovery that Adams had last been seen alive in Colt's office.

Asa Wheeler, a penmanship teacher with an office across the hall from Colt's, one of those remarkable people who forever keep turning up as surprise witnesses in murder cases, had, after hearing a noise, seen the killing through a keyhole. Colt was found guilty of murder and was sentenced to be hanged in the Tombs yard November 18, 1842. His brother persuaded Warden Fallon, with a generous fee, to wallpaper his cell in Murderers' Row and to add a few knickknacks to make the place cozy. Before noon of the day set for the hanging, John Colt decided to make an honest woman of Caroline Henshaw, with whom he had spent leisure hours before he took a hammer to Sam Adams. They were married in his cell in the presence of some of the town's most prominent people—David Graham, Robert Emmett, Justice Merritt, and John Howard Payne, who wrote "Home, Sweet Home." This was the first wedding in the Tombs.

Down in the yard, meanwhile, carpenters were erecting the gallows. About two o'clock in the afternoon, a couple of hours before the hanging was to take place, one of the keepers found John Colt stretched out on his cot, dead, with a knife in his heart. At the same moment keepers and prisoners started crying, with reason, "Fire!" The new cupola on the Tombs, which conveniently housed a fire bell, was aflame. Not until after the fire was put out was the news of Colt's death made public. The *Herald* hinted that one of the important gentlemen who had been at the prison wedding must have provided the knife. Knowing fellows let on that they had information that the corpse in the cell wasn't Colt's at all but one fetched up from the morgue, and that the fire was started to cover the hammer man's escape. For years afterward there were recurrent stories that John Colt and Caroline Henshaw were living in California under Spanish names. No one has ever proved or disproved the story. It is probable, however, that the body in the cell was Colt's. The Reverend Dr. Anthon of St. Mark's Church, who performed the prison wedding ceremony, swore that John Colt was buried in St. Mark's churchyard. Most people took his word for it.

In the winter of 1844, a man named George Wilkes, the crusading and talented editor of the *Police Gazette,* who had been convicted of libel and given a thirty-day sentence, was thrown into the Tombs. It was then customary to arrest all witnesses as well as offenders, and sometimes criminals got bailed out while witnesses, lacking bail, stayed in.

The papers had crusaded against this extraordinary working of justice for a long time, but nothing was done to
change it. Wilkes, in editorials, had taken up the cause
and kept jabbing at indifferent Tombs magistrates, as well
as shyster lawyers who hung around the jail, until he was
imprisoned. While in the Tombs he kept a diary, which
was later published as a one-shilling pamphlet entitled
"Mysteries of the Tombs." In the opening chapter a
reader gets the impression that the charge of libel may not
have been altogether unjustified. This nineteenth-century
muckraker described, for example, the police court in the
Tombs as a place "where four magistrates and some forty
or fifty tributary devils consisting chiefly of bullheaded,
hatchet-faced, hawk-eyed, pot-bellied, hook-nosed, long-
fingered fellows who carry gilt staves on public occasions
out of a foolish pride of office and who go secretly provided
with dark lanterns, burglars' tools, India-rubber shoes, to
be prepared for all emergencies, wait their opportunity for
daily plunder." Wilkes wrote further, "It is a favorite
amusement with them to indulge in the harmless practical
joke of sounding the pockets of everyone that comes within
their reach and of thrusting them playfully into cells in
case they object to these operations or be criminal enough
to be penniless." Wilkes found the Tombs doctor "a mild,
amiable, harmless young man apparently of vegetable ori-
gin who condenses the whole science of medicine into an
invariable prescription of Dover's Powders."

On hot days, Wilkes wrote, the prison reeked with damp.
Water condensed on the ceilings and dripped on the inmates. It ran in rivulets down the stone walls and formed
pools on the stone floors. On cold nights, the guards, if
they were sober, ran a little hot water through the cell pipes
to provide at least token heating, but the pipes were not

always equal even to this. They sometimes burst and scalded prisoners. If a man was scalded and screamed, others in his tier would rattle their tin cups or beat on the pipes in futile protest. The pipes, incidentally, served another purpose. Prisoners could talk through them—how, Wilkes did not record. Some nights anyone who was interested could listen in on a debate. Wilkes, in his diary, told about hearing a discussion between a burglar and a forger about President John Tyler's stand on the Oregon question. The forger lost out orally, but won the debate physically the next day when he caught up with the burglar in a corridor and broke his nose with one well-aimed punch.

At this time, thirty prisoners, mostly streetwalkers and petty thieves, ran the Tombs kitchens and worked as house staff. Wilkes wrote that "Whitewash here is the universal panacea for everything in the shape of dirt; no sooner does a quid fall or a pool of spittle spread its stain, than a sooty genii armed with brush and pail appears and slicks it over with two or three dabs of the brush and then as suddenly vanishes." The prisoners' menu consisted almost entirely of pallid stews and coffee made of burnt rye steeped in hot water. The only variant was an occasional ration of pale tea. The food was lugged from cell to cell in big buckets and ladled through the bars. Affluent murderers had their meals brought in from the best hotels: things like ortolans, game *patés*, wines, cognac, coffee, and cigars. When supper was done, the inmates, according to Wilkes, had to provide their own entertainment. There was a Tombs library, the gift of missionaries, but it afforded a rather cheerless selection of reading matter. Among the books were *The Sinner's Friend, Practical Piety, Perceval on Apostolical Succession, Speech of John McKeon on the Ashburton Treaty,*

Gift for Children of Sorrow, Essays by the Reverend Cotton
Mather, and *Argument in Favor of Infant Baptism.* Not
much reading was done at the Tombs, Wilkes indicated.
Through the night, the inmates sang bawdy ballads or river
songs, like "The Boatman's Dance" and "Will, the Bold
Smuggler." Some nights, the whole prison would join in.
It was in the Tombs kitchens, however, that prisoners
had the most fun. Several of Warden Fallon's narrow-
minded predecessors had made a practice of running the
kitchen help into their cells as soon as the evening chores
were done. Fallon, on the other hand, seemed amused
when the scullions put on a show one night. An entry in
the Wilkes diary tells all about it. First, a giant blackamoor named Williams stuck a series of pugilistic poses as
a demonstration of the art of self-defense. "Brilliant,"
Wilkes observed, "but spasmodic." Then Ben Gaunt, another Negro kitchen hand, took Williams on for a go. The
rest of the staff formed a ring and whooped until the fight
ended with Williams knocking Gaunt over an empty flour
barrel.

Two nights later, the Tombs scullions held a cotillion.
The ladies were prostitutes from the Five Points. There
were Mag Madden, a tall, angular harridan; Boy Jack ("a
short, stumpy blossom," Wilkes called her, "with a sharp
chin embedded in fat"), the Dark-Eyed One, whose dancing
partner was a Dutch shoe thief called Heel Taps; and Mrs.
Dickens.

Mrs. Dickens was, according to Wilkes, an extraordinary
blowze, "a lazy-looking, ill-jointed slavey with a languid
smile, a profusion of straggling dust-colored hair, a Roman
nose, a very moist lower lip with a perpetual crimp, or plait,
in it." She assumed the name of Mrs. Charles Dickens
when she was booked by the police on the thin excuse that

when Dickens was guided through the Five Points he actually looked at her as he passed. Wilkes said that she "frequently evinced her devotion to her transatlantic chevalier by kissing her hand affectionately across the water." The ladies had a high night of it in the kitchens. Ben Gaunt beat time and played "Dandy Jim" on a jew's-harp. The crowd screamed and laughed, and everybody got drunk on cheap liquor. A game of blindman's buff was organized. Williams, the pugilistic Negro, was blindman. He was annoyed because a giggling, fat little Irishwoman kept just beyond his reach. Finally, he got his hands on her and, in sheer vexation, picked her up and sat her down on top of a hot stove. The fat little woman hollered, and Warden Fallon somewhat regretfully broke up the party.

In a corner of the men's washroom in the sheriff's office in the Hall of Records on Chambers Street, visitors are likely to notice a peculiar, dusty little stand, something like a rack for croquet mallets. In it are thirteen staves carved like banister rails. They have gilded spear tips, and wrapped around the middle of each stave is a strip of worn red velvet. Most of the sheriff's staff don't know what the staves are, or how they became a part of the office, but old-timers know and keep muttering that they ought to be in a museum. The same could be said for an old sword that hangs in a tarnished scabbard on the wall in the sheriff's office.

The sword and the staves are relics of the first Tombs, which stood on Centre Street from 1838 to 1897. Since the last Tombs hanging took place in 1889, no one was ever hanged, except by himself, in the second Tombs, which went up in 1902 and has only recently been put in the hands of the wreckers. Public hangings were one of the chores of the sheriff of New York County. City holidays

were proclaimed for them, and on these occasions the
sheriff carried the sword and his deputies, usually forty in
number, brought up behind him with the staves, holding
them by the red velvet grips. These formalities were a
hang-over from medieval days, but the New York City
Common Council never bothered to do away with them,
probably on the theory that the sheriff and his halberdiers,
mostly Tammany ward heelers, seemed to buck up condemned men as they were escorted to the Tombs gibbet.
It was good theater, too.

The most important man at the executions was the
Tombs hangman, and the most famous executioner of all
was Joseph—Little Joe, prisoners called him—Atkinson,
a Brooklyn carpenter who began his gruesome career in
1852. He hanged forty of the fifty murderers who died in
the Tombs yard. "I kind of eased into this business," he
used to say modestly. "I guess I just had the knack."
Atkinson learned the rudiments of his trade when a man
named George Isaacs was city executioner. Isaacs came to
Atkinson's carpenter shop in Brooklyn one day to have
some gallows timbers cut and persuaded Atkinson to rig
the scaffold for a few executions. Later Isaacs taught
Atkinson the technique of tying a hangman's knot. Little
Joe succeeded Isaacs when Isaacs died toward the end of
1852. His first assignment was a double-header, a matter
of pride with him to the end of his career. On January 28,
1853, he finished off William Saul and Nicholas Howlett,
two river thieves who had killed a watchman on the
schooner *William Watson,* off James Slip. Three hundred
persons saw this hanging, including such personages as the
pugilists Tom Hyer and Bill Poole. "I done perfect,"
Atkinson would say happily to his friends when he recalled
the event. He had only one other hanging in 1853, only

one in 1854, and no more until 1857. "Business was dull them years," he later remarked.

Little Joe was in the hanging business thirty-six years, including his period of apprenticeship. He did a job on Albert Hicks, the pirate, which was never surpassed for color. Hicks was a Federal prisoner and had to be hanged on Federal property, so Bedloe's Island was chosen. Early on the morning of Friday, July 13, 1860—about twenty-five years before the Statue of Liberty was put up there—Hicks, Little Joe, the sheriff, the forty deputies, and about fifteen hundred of the city's prominent citizens set out from the foot of Canal Street in the steamer *Red Jacket*. It was a pleasant day and someone proposed that the party first go up the river a bit for a look at the steamship *Great Eastern,* which was at anchor off West Eleventh Street. Both Hicks and Little Joe were asked if they minded. Any delay, it seems, was all right with Hicks. The *Red Jacket* accordingly set off on the side trip. When, two hours later, Little Joe went to work on Hicks, more than ten thousand persons watched him. They dotted the harbor in all manner of craft. Concessionaires on awning-covered barges sold great quantities of cold pop and lager. Atkinson never had so large an audience again. He considered this hanging one of the high spots of his career.

Atkinson always regretted that he didn't get Edward S. Stokes, who, on January 6, 1872, shot and killed the millionaire Colonel Jim Fisk on the grand staircase of what is now the Broadway Central Hotel. This was the classiest killing of the period and Joe confided to friends that he was figuring on something special for Stokes. He grew worried when word got around that the Ninth Regiment, which Colonel Fisk had commanded, was marching on the Tombs to take Stokes out and lynch him. Police Chief Kelso threw five hundred men around the prison, but the Ninth never showed up. Stokes was tried three times; finally he got four years for manslaughter.

Atkinson thought that his masterpiece was a quadruple hanging in the Tombs yard on August 23, 1888. His professional pride had been hurt, however, when Warden Osborne called on Jake Van Hise, who did hangings in Newark, to stand by. Atkinson indignantly sat the rival hangman on the sidelines, rigged a double scaffold with the help of his son and some Bowery idlers, and announced that he was ready. The victims were Patrick Pakenham, who had slit his wife's throat with a razor; Ferdinand Carolin, who had killed a lady of his acquaintance with a hatchet; Black Jack Lewis, a Negro who had shot and killed another lady; and James Nolan, who had shot and killed a third lady. A few minutes before being hanged, Carolin, who was a carpenter, embarrassed Little Joe. He stopped at the foot of the scaffold, took hold of the timbers, and shook them. "Wobbly," he commented. "I could do a better job." Lewis and Carolin went first, then Pakenham and Nolan. "The hangman did his work well," the *Times* said next day. "There was no bungling."

The last man hanged in the Tombs was Harry Carlton, an East Side rowdy who killed a policeman in a beery free-for-all on Third Avenue. He went to the scaffold the morning of December 5, 1889. "Atkinson," one of the papers reported, "was quite jolly. He sized up Carlton as a man who would swing easily." Next morning Atkinson went to the Raymond Street Jail in Brooklyn, where he did away with an obscure murderer named John Greenwald. This was the last hanging in New York City.

In January, 1890, the machine age caught up with Little Joe; the electric chair replaced the gallows and the state took over all executions. The first man ever to die in the electric chair was William Kemmler, who killed Tillie Ziegler with an ax in Buffalo. He was put to death by means of the new device at Auburn Prison on August 6, 1890. Little Joe bravely sneered when he heard about this. "It's a novelty," he assured reporters. "It won't last." He glumly retired after the first few experimental electric-chair jobs, which were done by an up-to-date executioner with a feeling for electricity, had turned out all right. Several years later, when Little Joe was moving from his home on Evergreen Avenue, Brooklyn, one of the moving men dropped a wooden chest he was lugging to the van. The cover flew open and Little Joe's neighbors were startled to see a lot of black hoods spill out on the street. These were the caps worn by condemned men at their executions. There were also a few nooses and a piece of the Tombs gallows crossbeam. Little Joe had kept them out of sentiment.

Few of the thousands of criminals who passed through the Tombs in its early years were distinguished. Murderers were predominantly of the ax and bludgeon types and lacked subtlety. A number of women were brought to the Tombs on murder charges, but early nineteenth-century jurors, like today's crop, were squeamish when it came to convicting women. No woman was ever hanged in the Tombs yard, though outspoken journals of the eighteen forties insisted that some of them should have been. Mary Bodine, an acid-tongued hussy of Staten Island, for example, celebrated Christmas Eve of 1843 by taking a hatchet to Emeline Houseman, an oysterman's wife, and to Mrs. Houseman's infant child. She was tried for the crimes, but, in spite of what seemed overwhelming evidence against her, was set free. Having spent some uncomfortable weeks in the Tombs, she sat down and wrote a sharp note to the city officials demanding a rebate on the money she had put out for painting and wallpapering her cell.

One of the most notorious women inmates of the Tombs in its first few years was a Mrs. Weatherwax, alias Madame Costello. Mrs. Weatherwax was an abortionist; a "surgical assassin," the newspapers called her. Like Mary Bodine, Mrs. Weatherwax had her cell done up with feminine frippery—red carpet, wallpaper, and lace curtains—and had all her food sent in. She was eventually sent to Blackwell's Island to pick oakum. It was Mrs. Weatherwax who was popularly supposed to be the murderer of Mary Rogers, a pretty clerk in a Broadway tobacco shop. The body of Miss Rogers, who waited on such customers as Fenimore Cooper, Washington Irving, and Edgar Allan Poe, was found in the North River late in July of 1841. The cause of her death was never fixed, though amateur detectives as well as the police worked hard on the case. Even Poe took a crack at it, in his *Mystery of Marie Roget*.

No other murderer, probably, lent as much cachet to the Tombs as did Lee Ah Bow, its first Chinese prisoner. In the summer of 1840, two years after the Tombs went up, the Chinese junk *Ki Ying*, run by its English owners as a kind of showboat, anchored in the East River. The citizens, most of whom had never seen a Chinese, paid to come aboard and watch Chinese artisans at work in stalls below decks. The junk burned one night and the promoters disappeared. The stranded artisans settled on Mott Street, between Chatham and Pell, and so started New York's Chinatown. The Chinese are a quiet, philosophical lot, who seem to produce astonishingly few criminals. When they do turn one out, though, he is likely to be something extraordinary, like Lee Ah Bow, who somehow got into the police records as Quimby Appo, probably because the New York cops were as weak on names then as they are now. Careless historians have written that he was the first Chinese in New York, but he was not. He came to the city's Chinatown at least seven years after the *Ki Ying* colony arrived. He was brought to the West Coast by American slavers who worked the Chinese ports for laborers to sell in towns that sprang up in California after the gold rush began.

Lee was a small, brown man with enormous arms and a short temper. He served four terms in the Tombs for murder and did several other stretches for assault with intent to kill. The guards seemed to tolerate his nasty moods because he was something of a freak, an oddity to show important visitors. The missionary ladies all but pulled one another apart in their eagerness to convert Lee Ah Bow to whatever faith they represented, and he didn't seem to mind so long as they left him presents. He was quite willing to swing from one religion to another for as small a temptation as a roast chicken or a good cigar.

On March 9, 1859, Lee Ah Bow entered his flat at 49 Oliver Street from the cold, raw outdoors somewhat out of sorts. Catherine Fitzpatrick, with whom he lived, was suffering from a bad case of beer hiccups and was late with dinner. In the midst of the ensuing argument she pushed the choleric little man up against the hot stove. He bit her, and she hollered for help. Mary Fletcher, a neighbor, rushed into the kitchen. Lee Ah Bow stabbed Miss Fletcher to the heart with a dirk. As he tried to escape down the stairs, another neighbor, a Mrs. Gaffney, blocked him on the stairs by turning her broad back. This was a mistake. Lee Ah Bow planted the dirk, not fatally, in Mrs. Gaffney, and proceeded down the stairs. Eventually he was caught and sentenced to be hanged in the Tombs yard. The missionaries got the sentence commuted, and he was released after he had served seven years.

A few weeks later, he stabbed a Miss Lizzie Williams, a Bowery landlady with whom he was boarding, but again the missionaries got him a good lawyer and he was released. In 1872, in an alcoholic pet, Lee dug a cobblestone out of a street and caved in the head of a laboring man named John Linkowski. Linkowski died. Lee Ah Bow did three years for this performance. By now the newspapers called him "Devil Appo" and "Chinese Devilman," but the lady missionaries refused to believe they couldn't make a good Christian of the fierce little man. Often Lee would throw himself on the floor of his cell, gnash his teeth, and try to bite the hands of trusties who shoved his stew through the bars, but the ladies were not discouraged.

In 1875, Lee Ah Bow took a dirk to Cork Mag, a Bowery Jezebel, but no one paid much attention to the incident. Cork Mag pulled out of it all right. On the night of October 21, 1876, Lee, who fancied himself as a draughts player, lost a game to a derelict named John Kelly in the Howe Lodging House at 192 Chatham Street. The Devilman's pride was hurt, and, in an effort to salve it, he resorted to the dirk again. Kelly died in a few minutes of multiple stab wounds. The police caught up with Lee and once again he was home in the Tombs. Coroner Woltman, at this point, got tired of Lee Ah Bow's fatal moodiness. He suggested that the small Chinaman's mind might be unbalanced. This was Lee Ah Bow's last stay in the Tombs. Soon he took up permanent residence at Matteawan, the state prison for the insane. The records of this institution note his growing hallucinations, which were usually poetic. When the Hudson River night boat

steamed up the river, playing its searchlight,˙Lee Ah Bow
would beat the bars of his cell with his hands and scream,
"Here comes my diamond." "He believes," says one asylum report, "that he has grand hotels, palaces, servants, and
horses outside the asylum; that he is King of the World and
Omnipotent; the Second God; commands the Wind and
the Sun; that Tom Sharkey and General Coxey are his
military staff and that he must suffer for Ireland." The
doctors figured that Lee Ah Bow was around ninety-eight
years old when he died on June 23, 1912. He was buried
in the asylum grounds.

The Tombs had some odd tenants in the latter part of
the nineteenth century. One of these was Ameer Ben Ali,
a short, sooty Algerian with large eyes and a woolly black
beard who was picked up for the murder of Carrie Brown,
a water-front slattern known to nautical customers, for no
apparent reason, as old Shakespeare. Old Shakespeare was
found dead in the morning of April 24, 1891, in the East
River Hotel, a mariners' hangout. She had been untidily
mutilated, somewhat after the manner of Jack the Ripper's
victims in the Whitechapel district of London. Because
the Ripper was still a lively topic, the Old Shakespeare
case excited great interest. Ben Ali, who was jugged in the
Tombs while he awaited trial, was convicted of murder in
the second degree and sent to Sing Sing. Thomas Byrnes,
Superintendent of Police at the time, kept hinting that the
Algerian had been in London when some of the Ripper
murders were committed and that he probably *was* Jack
the Ripper. Romantic Tombs guards were inclined to
believe this. "See that cell?" they would tell visitors, after
Ben Ali had been shipped out. "That's where we had Jack
the Ripper." Visitors were always deeply impressed.

Another odd fish in the Tombs was George Francis

Train, a wealthy, long-haired, publicity-loving old duffer who wrote pamphlets and made speeches defending the naughty Claflin sisters, Vickie and Tennie, in the eighteen seventies. These sprightly ladies startled the town with their advanced views on sex and the marriage tie, and, after publishing a pamphlet attacking the Reverend Henry Ward Beecher of Plymouth Church in Brooklyn, landed in the Ludlow Street jail on a charge of libel. Train made a soapbox speech on Wall Street, taking the side of the Claflins against Beecher. Anthony Comstock, who was Virtue's right arm at the time, set out after Train and, to Train's supreme delight, had him thrown into the Tombs on a charge of public indecency. "Take me to the Bastille!" Train shouted contentedly when the cops came. "Away with me to the donjon!"

As time went on and Train's case did not come to trial, the warden and the guards got weary of their tenant's incessant oratory. They took him from his moderately comfortable cell and tried to freeze his martyr complex in a cold one, but Train wrapped himself in a traveling rug and grew even noisier. "I'll raise hell in this Egyptian sepulcher!" he yelled repeatedly. His harangues kept other prisoners awake. At last the warden tried to coax him to leave the Tombs on bail, but he indignantly refused. The guards then hustled him to Murderers' Row. They had an idea that this might frighten him, but the move was merely tartar steak to Train. He organized the Murderers' Club, with himself as president, and laughed boisterously whenever the newspapers mentioned the organization. Finally, the warden moved him into solitary confinement, where there was no one within earshot of his magniloquent speeches. It turned out that Train could stand anything but isolation. He arranged for bail and moved out of the

Tombs to his mansion on Murray Hill, mumbling that he had been done out of what he called "my mission." The courts soon freed him, and he went to Paris to become an expatriate.

Many Tombs tenants didn't feel about prison the way George Francis Train did; they were forever figuring ways to break out. Some fifty of them have succeeded between 1838 and the present, but they have been chiefly criminal small fry and ordinarily no great fuss has been made. John Mahony, a rather indifferent thief but an artist at jail-breaking, established the record for getting out of the Tombs. He escaped four times, by picking locks and other methods. He made his first break in 1860, when he was sixteen years old and apprenticed to Italian Dave, a kind of Neapolitan Fagin; his last was in 1880. He made a career of jail-breaking, in fact; he found his way out of Sing Sing, Rikers Island Penitentiary, an army guardhouse on the Potomac, a jail in Washington, D. C., and Police Headquarters in Philadelphia. He also once got away from his guards on a moving train upstate. When news of Mahony's fourth escape from the Tombs got around among the prisoners, they cheered. Mahony wasn't so good, though, at keeping out, once he got out. He died, eventually, in Clinton Prison at Dannemora.

The most important prisoner to escape from the first Tombs was William J. Sharkey, a foppish fellow who graduated from pocket-picking to a district leadership under Tweed. During an argument in The Place, a Hudson Street grog shop, where he had stopped on Sunday afternoon, September 1, 1872, on his way home from a politician's funeral, Sharkey shot and killed Bob Dunn, a political crony who dealt faro in a West Side saloon and worked on the side in the City Comptroller's office. Sharkey was

b. 1845 NYC

found guilty and sentenced to be hanged in the Tombs on August 15 of the following year. What with appeals and other legalistic stalling, he was still in Murderers' Row on the morning of November 23, 1873.

He had two visitors that day—Maggie Jourdan, a lady he had known some years, and Mrs. Wesley Allen, the wife of a West Side burglar. One by one, late that afternoon, the Tombs visitors, none of whom could leave without giving up his visitor's ticket, departed. Mrs. Allen turned up at the gate after all the others had checked out and every ticket had been accounted for. She said that she must have lost hers. Guards hastily searched the cells. In Sharkey's —No. 40 in Murderers' Row—they found the politician's clothes and, on a shelf, the remains of his black mustache, creamy with lather. One of the keepers belatedly remembered that a rather queer-looking figure had gone out—a woman wearing an Alpine hat, a heavy green veil, a black wool dress, and a thick black cloak. This, it was discovered, was Sharkey. He later turned up in Ireland, where he lived the rest of his life. The cops couldn't pin anything on Mrs. Allen and, although Maggie Jourdan was brought to trial on a charge of aiding the escape, the jury wouldn't convict her. Four Tombs keepers, however, were discharged for their carelessness.

More than 500,000 men and women prisoners passed through the first Tombs before the city got around to ordering it torn down, in 1897. One day in February, just before the demolition began, Lillian Russell made a charitable visit to the place with Mrs. Beekman de Peyster of the Prison Guild. Miss Russell wore Persian lamb trimmed with ermine, a small bonnet of primroses and feathers, and a profusion of lace and violets. Her perfume left Murderers' Row giddy, but the unfortunates in the women's

McKenna, a small-time tough, and Hyman Amberg, who had killed a jeweler, had one pistol each. They killed Jeremiah Murphy and Dan O'Connor, the first two guards to take after them. Peter J. Mallon, the Tombs warden, was shot in the lungs and abdomen and died a few hours later. He was the only chief jailer in the history of the Tombs who died at his post. While the fight was on, downtown New York sounded like a battlefield. Judges and court attendants watched the battle from the windows of the Criminal Courts Building. Clerks and stenographers in near-by office buildings were also able to look down upon it. Detectives were out on fire escapes, at windows, and on the roofs of the Tombs itself, armed with rifles and machine guns. J. Allen Steadwell, assistant superintendent of the New York Life Insurance Building, who was standing in an eighth-floor window of the Conklin Building, opposite the Tombs on Lafayette Street, was wounded by a shot from Berg's pistol.

The first outside assistance to arrive in the Tombs yard was Detective Johnny Broderick, who later developed into a sort of Paul Bunyan of the force. Just as Broderick came in, Patrick M. Kelly, a laborer who had hidden in the ditch in the yard where he was working when the three gunmen darted behind the coal pile, raised his shovel over his head to find out if it was safe to show himself. Broderick shot it out of his hand. Kelly decided to wait. Broderick then ran behind the coal pile, shooting, but the three gunmen were already dying. Each man had turned his gun on himself.

After this episode a flood of fresh invective was let loose against the Tombs and its administration. It was discovered by the State Prison Commission that the guards were charging for blankets and cots, just as the first Tombs guards had done almost a hundred years before. Murderers and other felons were allowed out of their cells for evening poker and for dice games in which thousands of dollars were wagered. Someone sounded a buzzer when the warden left the building as a signal to open the cells of privileged prisoners who wanted to play poker. Two buzzes warned of the warden's return. Hyman Amberg had paid a hundred dollars two nights a week for the privilege of entertaining women in his cell. "The visiting room," the State Prison Commission reported, "is a delirium of screaming men and women. How the officer in charge stands this bedlam is a mystery." It also turned out that guards were depriving imprisoned drug addicts of their daily narcotics ration of four and one-eighth grains and were selling it to other prisoners, and that additional drugs were getting into the Tombs under stamps on letters, in visitors' hatbands, and even taped behind Red Cross lapel buttons. In 1928 the New York County Grand Jury bellowed the familiar cry, "The Tombs is obsolete and inadequate." The State Commissioner of Correction called it a "breeding place for crime." The uproar grew until, on October 18, 1938, upon order of the Board of Aldermen, a gigantic "For Sale" sign was posted outside the Tombs and work was started on a new, $18,000,000, twelve-story prison, directly across Centre Street from the old place.

City tax appraisers figured that the land on which the Tombs stood was worth around $1,000,000, and that the building was worth $850,000, but real-estate people, possibly because they knew that the playful Collect Pond still lurked below ground, didn't even nibble. The city therefore decided to raze the building. In laying the foundation for the new prison, the contractors made up their minds to deal firmly with Collect Pond. They sunk steel building caissons into the ground and hired two former United States navy divers, John Kelly and Jim Graham, to go down inside them until they found bedrock. Air locks were built into the caissons, and the two men, wearing diving suits and helmets, used them as taking-off points for their explorations until the caissons reached through the bed of the pond to bedrock. Bedrock, in some spots, was a hundred and forty feet down. The caissons were filled with concrete and became a part of the foundation. They are the world's deepest building caissons. The cost of the foundation alone came to something like $2,000,000.

Prisoners in the new Tombs can be pretty sure of one thing, now. The place is not apt to cave in on them.

Rooftops and Higgles

GROUPS of active, screaming children blocked the sidewalk in front of the house on Avenue B. The broad woman at the door stared at me when I asked about the man who raises eagles.

"Higgles?" she said, puzzled.

"Birds," I explained, and her face brightened.

"Hopstairs," she said. "In the poolroom is higgles."

At the second landing, I opened a battered metal door. A German shepherd dog, big as a yearling, sniffed at my coat. Pool balls clicked through banks of stale tobacco smoke in the dark loft. At the lower end of the room, near windows roughly painted red and green, eighteen or twenty men were grouped around two tables. Yellow light from two drop lamps, thrown up from the green cloth, etched the men's faces in deep shadow. A collarless chap, broad and chunky, face deeply pitted, came to the door.

"The guy you want is Harry," he said. He turned and called hoarsely across a partition down the room. "Hey, Harry! There's a man here about them eagles."

The pool games stopped. Players and watchers looked up. A dozen or more trailed behind Harry when he emerged from behind the partition. Harry was a little man. Thin, coarse black hair combed back, but at this moment dropped in disorderly locks on his forehead. His thin hands were jammed in the side pockets of his black sweater. Like the chunky chap, he was collarless. As he faced me the pool-game kibitzers formed round him in a semicircle. Harry seemed uneasy, perhaps out of modesty. He said eagles were his hobby—eagles, hawks, and pigeons.

"Kind of an East Side Audubon?" I suggested.

Harry shrugged. His eyes darted to a picture frame on one of the walls. Newspaper clippings in the frame told how Harry Leiner's eagles had escaped into Tompkins Square one September day and how the lower East Side had been thrown into a hubbub over it. The photographs showed Harry holding one of the birds.

"That's Harry's picture in the papers," one of the customers explained. "He got lots of publicity out of them eagles."

Mr. Leiner squirmed, out of sheer modesty. He had a friend, he said, who was a seaman on a tramp steamer.

"Right now this guy is in Africa," he said. "If he sees any good buys in wild birds he gets them for me. I raise 'em, but only for a hobby."

One of the customers urged him to tell about the hawks the seaman brought home a year ago.

"I don't know for sure," Harry said, "but I think those were chippy hawks. I raised them on raw meat, upstairs, in the empty loft. In several months they was eating like brewery horses. I gave them to a guy up in Throgs Neck."

The eagles, it seems, came in with the seaman seven months earlier. Like the hawks, they were turned loose in the upstairs loft. Like the hawks, they gobbled fresh meat. Their wingspread increased enormously. Mr. Leiner did not know how they broke out.

"It was spite woik," said one of the customers.

Harry hunched his thin shoulders. However it was, the birds got out. Children, coming from school, filled Avenue B as the eagles flew from tenement roof to tenement roof. Men and women leaned from windows and screamed to the children to get into hallways. Pushcart men ducked for cover. Someone telephoned for the police emergency. The pool hall emptied, and Harry formed hunting squads. He took one group, and Henny Worsena took the other. Worsena got one of the birds in a yard in Tenth Street, where a woman keeps pigeons.

"A guy had a holt of him," said Mr. Worsena, "and he was clawin' the pants off this guy until I grabbed him."

Harry, the pale Audubon, got the second bird on a fire escape near Christadora House.

"He didn't fight," said Harry, "because he was used to me. He knew I was the guy that was feeding him. They would have come back anyway, only they were excited. They was stiff and in no shape to fly."

He had to give the birds away, though. The neighbors didn't want eagles around.

"Brazilian eagles, these was," said Harry, "not American eagles."

He gave one of the birds to the Zoo on Staten Island, one to the New York Zoo. One of the customers said he bet the zoos were glad to get these Brazilian eagles. "They gave Harry a certificate for the eagles," this customer added. The pool players grew impatient. They could stand so much ornithology and no more.

"Hey, Harry," one said, "why don't you get this guy away from here? He's breaking up the game."

Harry seemed nervous. He delegated one of his helpers to lead me to the roof. I climbed three flights of dark iron stairs with a queue of pool-hall kibitzers behind me.

pen shrilly criticized her getup. Miss Russell sang several numbers for the inmates, who applauded by hammering the bars with tin basins.

The second Tombs, which was erected on the same site, did not formally open until September 29, 1902. Actually, the building was opened in sections, so it was possible to transfer the prisoners gradually as the old building came down. At the dedication of the New Tombs, the City Fathers said almost exactly what the Common Council had said sixty-five years before—that a new day was dawning. The second Tombs, like the first, disobligingly started to bog down in the subterranean Collect Pond almost immediately, and plumbers, masons, and carpenters were kept busy repairing cracks caused by the constant settling of the foundations.

As the first Tombs was making way for the second, the most celebrated prisoner was Roland Burnham Molineux, man about town and son of General Molineux, a Civil War army officer. He was accused of having sent, at Christmastime in 1898, a gift of some cyanide of mercury, labeled Bromo-Seltzer, in a silver container to a man with whom he had quarreled, Harry Cornish, athletic director of the Knickerbocker Athletic Club. The cyanide killed Mrs. Katherine Adams, the physical director's housekeeper, and made Cornish violently but not fatally ill. After a short stay in the Tombs, Molineux was convicted of murder and sent to the Sing Sing death house, but he was later retried and turned loose. He died in a madhouse. *- 1917*

Molineux, a literary fellow, wrote extensively about his prison experiences. He did one piece on old John Curran, unofficial sightseers' guide in the Tombs through the seventies, eighties, and nineties, who glibly made up many legends about the jail and the prisoners. From fees for the tours and the sale of what he claimed were "pieces from the gallows on which fifty were hanged," Curran piled up a modest fortune. Actually, the samples came from any lumber Curran could find. Molineux once related that he heard Curran tell visitors that a distinguished-looking minister they saw in the corridor of Murderers' Row had just thrown his mother-in-law out of a third-story window in a fit of unchristian temper. The dominie was one of the city's most esteemed, and mildest, churchmen. He was Molineux's spiritual adviser.

Curran vanished after the second Tombs opened. No one ever saw or heard of him again. There were vague rumors that he had bought a farm in some remote spot in Maine and that he had died there. His offices were taken over by Billy Gallagher, an untutored understudy who had been a sort of messenger around the Tombs. Gallagher knew most of Curran's patter by heart, but he wasn't the inventive type. He kept on selling bogus bits of gallows and drank up everything he earned. He was found dead of gas poisoning at the age of eighty-six, on the morning of December 16, 1927, in a grimy room in one of the ancient brick houses on Centre Street, across the way from the Tombs.

Another character around the second Tombs in the early years of the century was Freddy the Waiter. He ran beer and water to the cells, and brought in special food and carried messages for prisoners. He had no official standing, but he did quite well on tips. He also had another sideline. He was a peddler of talismans. Whenever a new murderer was brought in, Freddy the Waiter subtly high-pressured him into buying a rabbit's foot from a rabbit guaranteed killed in a graveyard in the dark of the moon. His customers included Harry K. Thaw, Lieutenant

Becker, and the four gunmen who were hired by Becker to murder Herman Rosenthal. Lieutenant Becker and the four gunmen died in the electric chair, as most of Freddy the Waiter's patrons did, but this didn't seem to hurt sales. They were steady up to the day fifteen years ago when Freddy, like old John Curran, quietly vanished from the Tombs.

There existed, around 1910, a journalistic weakness for applying the term "angel" to any woman engaged in welfare work in the Tombs, but only two women seem to have worked hard or earnestly enough to deserve the rating. One was Mary Xavier McCaffrey, a Sister of Mercy, whose brother was a member of the district attorney's staff. One man in Murderers' Row was said to have constantly cursed at Sister Xavier when she visited him. She serenely persevered with him, however, and one day dug up a witness who won him a new trial and saved him from the electric chair. Sister Xavier died in 1923.

The other woman was Rebecca Salome Foster, the widow of a Civil War general. Even District Attorney William Travers Jerome, who was no sentimentalist, called her a saint, and a plaque was erected in the Tombs to her memory after she was burned to death in a fire which destroyed the Park Avenue Hotel in February, 1902. Among the mourners were Marie Barberi, who had done time in the Criminal Courts Building for murdering a faithless lover; George Appo, son of the Tombs' first Chinese prisoner, Devil Appo; and an assemblage of dissolute women Mrs. Foster had befriended in the jail.

The second Tombs, formidable as it looked from the outside, was as vulnerable to breaks as the first. On July 24, 1907, about four years after it was opened, Frank Schneider, a Yorkville sneak thief, got out over the wall.

A wide-eyed urchin named Tommy Martin saw him drop down on Franklin Street. "Don't you say nothing, sonny," Schneider advised him. He patted the boy's head and walked off. He was caught within a fortnight.

A break that caused even greater excitement occurred on September 2, 1912. The prisoner was Reynold Forsbrey, generally referred to as "the pale little man," who was in the Tombs for two holdup murders, one in Brooklyn and one on the lower East Side. Both murders were the result of the pale little man's desire to get together enough cash to buy a decent wedding ring for Mary Ryan, a Brooklyn girl. One night she smuggled some small saws and a phial of muriatic acid into the Tombs by hiding them in her high pompadour. He was caught with these objects and put in solitary confinement. The guard who was assigned to sit outside his cell door had been up late the night before at a Democratic clambake and soon fell asleep. Forsbrey upended his cot against the wall of his cell, worked some rusted screws out of a ventilator, and wriggled through the hole. Using his sheet as a rope, he let himself down twenty feet into the carpenter shop. Here he picked up a nail-studded joist, made his way to the yard, and got over the outside wall by climbing up the joist. He was found several months later living with Mary Ryan in the Bronx. Subsequently she helped Forsbrey escape from Auburn Prison and from Clinton Prison, but he was caught each time and brought back.

Easily the most tumultuous and bloodiest day the Tombs ever saw was November 3, 1926. That afternoon, around three o'clock, three prisoners eluded their guards and got behind a coal pile in the yard, armed with revolvers that had been smuggled in to them. Robert Berg, of the Whittemore gang in Chicago, had two pistols; Michael

McKenna, a small-time tough, and Hyman Amberg, who had killed a jeweler, had one pistol each. They killed Jeremiah Murphy and Dan O'Connor, the first two guards to take after them. Peter J. Mallon, the Tombs warden, was shot in the lungs and abdomen and died a few hours later. He was the only chief jailer in the history of the Tombs who died at his post. While the fight was on, downtown New York sounded like a battlefield. Judges and court attendants watched the battle from the windows of the Criminal Courts Building. Clerks and stenographers in near-by office buildings were also able to look down upon it. Detectives were out on fire escapes, at windows, and on the roofs of the Tombs itself, armed with rifles and machine guns. J. Allen Steadwell, assistant superintendent of the New York Life Insurance Building, who was standing in an eighth-floor window of the Conklin Building, opposite the Tombs on Lafayette Street, was wounded by a shot from Berg's pistol.

The first outside assistance to arrive in the Tombs yard was Detective Johnny Broderick, who later developed into a sort of Paul Bunyan of the force. Just as Broderick came in, Patrick M. Kelly, a laborer who had hidden in the ditch in the yard where he was working when the three gunmen darted behind the coal pile, raised his shovel over his head to find out if it was safe to show himself. Broderick shot it out of his hand. Kelly decided to wait. Broderick then ran behind the coal pile, shooting, but the three gunmen were already dying. Each man had turned his gun on himself.

After this episode a flood of fresh invective was let loose against the Tombs and its administration. It was discovered by the State Prison Commission that the guards were charging for blankets and cots, just as the first Tombs guards had done almost a hundred years before. Murderers and other felons were allowed out of their cells for evening poker and for dice games in which thousands of dollars were wagered. Someone sounded a buzzer when the warden left the building as a signal to open the cells of privileged prisoners who wanted to play poker. Two buzzes warned of the warden's return. Hyman Amberg had paid a hundred dollars two nights a week for the privilege of entertaining women in his cell. "The visiting room," the State Prison Commission reported, "is a delirium of screaming men and women. How the officer in charge stands this bedlam is a mystery." It also turned out that guards were depriving imprisoned drug addicts of their daily narcotics ration of four and one-eighth grains and were selling it to other prisoners, and that additional drugs were getting into the Tombs under stamps on letters, in visitors' hatbands, and even taped behind Red Cross lapel buttons. In 1928 the New York County Grand Jury bellowed the familiar cry, "The Tombs is obsolete and inadequate." The State Commissioner of Correction called it a "breeding place for crime." The uproar grew until, on October 18, 1938, upon order of the Board of Aldermen, a gigantic "For Sale" sign was posted outside the Tombs and work was started on a new, $18,000,000, twelve-story prison, directly across Centre Street from the old place.

City tax appraisers figured that the land on which the Tombs stood was worth around $1,000,000, and that the building was worth $850,000, but real-estate people, possibly because they knew that the playful Collect Pond still lurked below ground, didn't even nibble. The city therefore decided to raze the building. In laying the foundation for the new prison, the contractors made up their minds to deal firmly with Collect Pond. They sunk steel building caissons into the ground and hired two former United States navy divers, John Kelly and Jim Graham, to go down inside them until they found bedrock. Air locks were built into the caissons, and the two men, wearing diving suits and helmets, used them as taking-off points for their explorations until the caissons reached through the bed of the pond to bedrock. Bedrock, in some spots, was a hundred and forty feet down. The caissons were filled with concrete and became a part of the foundation. They are the world's deepest building caissons. The cost of the foundation alone came to something like $2,000,000.

Prisoners in the new Tombs can be pretty sure of one thing, now. The place is not apt to cave in on them.

Rooftops and Higgles

.GROUPS of active, screaming children blocked the sidewalk in front of the house on Avenue B. The broad woman at the door stared at me when I asked about the man who raises eagles.

"Higgles?" she said, puzzled.

"Birds," I explained, and her face brightened.

"Hopstairs," she said. "In the poolroom is higgles."

At the second landing, I opened a battered metal door. A German shepherd dog, big as a yearling, sniffed at my coat. Pool balls clicked through banks of stale tobacco smoke in the dark loft. At the lower end of the room, near windows roughly painted red and green, eighteen or twenty men were grouped around two tables. Yellow light from two drop lamps, thrown up from the green cloth, etched the men's faces in deep shadow. A collarless chap, broad and chunky, face deeply pitted, came to the door.

"The guy you want is Harry," he said. He turned and called hoarsely across a partition down the room. "Hey, Harry! There's a man here about them eagles."

The pool games stopped. Players and watchers looked up. A dozen or more trailed behind Harry when he emerged from behind the partition. Harry was a little man. Thin, coarse black hair combed back, but at this moment dropped in disorderly locks on his forehead. His thin hands were jammed in the side pockets of his black sweater. Like the chunky chap, he was collarless. As he faced me the pool-game kibitzers formed round him in a semicircle. Harry seemed uneasy, perhaps out of modesty. He said eagles were his hobby—eagles, hawks, and pigeons.

"Kind of an East Side Audubon?" I suggested.

Harry shrugged. His eyes darted to a picture frame on one of the walls. Newspaper clippings in the frame told how Harry Leiner's eagles had escaped into Tompkins Square one September day and how the lower East Side had been thrown into a hubbub over it. The photographs showed Harry holding one of the birds.

"That's Harry's picture in the papers," one of the customers explained. "He got lots of publicity out of them eagles."

Mr. Leiner squirmed, out of sheer modesty. He had a friend, he said, who was a seaman on a tramp steamer.

"Right now this guy is in Africa," he said. "If he sees any good buys in wild birds he gets them for me. I raise 'em, but only for a hobby."

One of the customers urged him to tell about the hawks the seaman brought home a year ago.

"I don't know for sure," Harry said, "but I think those were chippy hawks. I raised them on raw meat, upstairs, in the empty loft. In several months they was eating like brewery horses. I gave them to a guy up in Throgs Neck."

The eagles, it seems, came in with the seaman seven months earlier. Like the hawks, they were turned loose in the upstairs loft. Like the hawks, they gobbled fresh meat. Their wingspread increased enormously. Mr. Leiner did not know how they broke out.

"It was spite woik," said one of the customers.

Harry hunched his thin shoulders. However it was, the
birds got out. Children, coming from school, filled Avenue
B as the eagles flew from tenement roof to tenement roof.
Men and women leaned from windows and screamed to the
children to get into hallways. Pushcart men ducked for
cover. Someone telephoned for the police emergency.
The pool hall emptied, and Harry formed hunting squads.
He took one group, and Henny Worsena took the other.
Worsena got one of the birds in a yard in Tenth Street,
where a woman keeps pigeons.

"A guy had a holt of him," said Mr. Worsena, "and he
was clawin' the pants off this guy until I grabbed him."

Harry, the pale Audubon, got the second bird on a fire
escape near Christadora House.

"He didn't fight," said Harry, "because he was used to
me. He knew I was the guy that was feeding him. They
would have come back anyway, only they were excited.
They was stiff and in no shape to fly."

He had to give the birds away, though. The neighbors
didn't want eagles around.

"Brazilian eagles, these was," said Harry, "not American
eagles."

He gave one of the birds to the Zoo on Staten Island, one
to the New York Zoo. One of the customers said he bet the
zoos were glad to get these Brazilian eagles. "They gave
Harry a certificate for the eagles," this customer added.
The pool players grew impatient. They could stand so
much ornithology and no more.

"Hey, Harry," one said, "why don't you get this guy
away from here? He's breaking up the game."

Harry seemed nervous. He delegated one of his helpers
to lead me to the roof. I climbed three flights of dark iron
stairs with a queue of pool-hall kibitzers behind me.

On the roof the sun was bright. The air was clean and crisp. One of the men pulled a latch string and assorted pigeons—Chinese dun owls, Russian high-fliers, two homing birds, some model bronzes, and some tumblers— whirred out of the coop. They organized over Avenue B, swung out over Tompkins Square Park, and circled over my head. One of the men climbed into the coop and came out with a fresh pigeon's egg. He put it in my hand.

"It's good if you drop it in a malted milk," he earnestly assured me, but I gave it back.

A tall, thin youth with hollow cheeks reached for it, broke the shell against the chicken wire, and drained the contents. This youth, one of the kibitzers whispered, is known on Avenue B as The Scholar.

"He's smart," my informant said. He turned to the thin one. "Give him a debate, Scholar," he urged, but The Scholar was not in the mood. He leaned against the scabrous roof wall, in silence.

I learned about "hit-outs," birds which flop to a near-by roof and refused to budge; about "clucks," birds which blunder into aerial wires and other roof obstructions; how the birds follow wind currents, and about the hawks which live in the towers of the Brooklyn, Williamsburg, and Manhattan Bridges in winter and come out to prey on the pigeon flocks.

Overhead, almost out of sight, the flock spiraled in the sun. The birds were visible only now and then in momentary glints of white, as they wheeled in formation.

"That's what we call 'pin-high,' or 'in the marble,'" one of the bird fanciers explained. "It means they look small as a pin, or tiny like a marble."

I stayed a while, looking down into the narrow, crowded East Side streets; at the scaly-brick walls and cluttered roofs around us and at Tompkins Square Park, a lone patch of bronze green in a great area of slums. Skyscrapers were misty at the skyline.

As I passed the pool-hall landing on my way down, one of the customers brought me the "certificate" Harry received for his "eagles." It was on a letterhead of the New York Zoological Society.

"My dear Mr. Leiner," it said. "Please deliver to bearer one South American Turkey Vulture for which this letter will serve as receipt."

Wind on the River

THE CAR shuddered in the river blast when I came to the exposed waste on the city's rim where Cherry, Grand, and East Streets meet. Rivulets, thick as mineral oil, raced down the windshield. I caught the full slap of the storm when I got out to flounder through rain pools to Victor's Auto Repair Shop, a huddle of lean-tos typical of careless water-front architecture. An electric light over the warped door threw golden beads in the rain sheets, crowded the long yard with grotesque shadows of old wrecks and bulky motor parts. The door slammed behind me, pushed by the wind. At the littered desk a brawny man with tired eyes looked up.

"I came to find out about the fishing," I said. "I understand the fish are back in the East River."

The man ran a fat hand through his rumpled hair.

"Turn to the right just outside this door," he said. "There's a shack. Knock on the door and ask for Frank Leighton. He knows more about it."

I stepped back into the windy blackness. Off East Street dock the fireboat *George McClellan* bobbed on the whipped-up tide. Off to the left Williamsburg Bridge was a black arch over the restless water. Across the river high stacks and derrick skeletons marked the location of the navy yard in Brooklyn. Not a soul in sight in this rain-swept desolation, but blue smoke, blown by the gale, poured thickly from a rusty garbage can under the lone street lamp. A very wet black-and-white cat darted from the nightmare shadows in the auto yard and streaked across the blackened pier planks, lightly vaulting rain puddles. To the right, directly on the water front, towered the wet ruins of "Home of Hecker's Flour," of old Fidelity Warehouse, and the abandoned Corn Products plant. Wreckers had broken the walls away. This night the structures looked like the ruins at Ypres.

I knocked on the crude door of the little shack facing the river. There was no light inside; no sound. I stood there awhile, hearing the wind's wail and the tide's suck at the bulkheads, watching the riffles in the water puddles. The door opened six inches and a steamy, damp odor corrupted the street air. A man in an old army overcoat looked out, a red-faced, middle-aged man with a stubble of beard.

"Frank's in here," he said. "Come on in."

The shack was pungent with stale body smells, exaggerated by the river damp and the rain. Frank was a hoarse voice off to my left. He said it was true; the East River, since pollution abated several years ago, had been yielding tommies, blue-claw crabs, and eels.

The man who had let me in, I sensed in the dark, was standing with his back to the door. On my right still another shack dweller was fussing with a kerosene lamp.

"Tell him, Frankie," he said. "Tell him about the two striped bass we got."

"We got two striped bass," said Frankie. "One was around a pound; one run around a half a pound."

The lamp wick blossomed into feeble, yellow flame. It brought out, on the board walls, the shadowed shapes of limp old shirts, grimy pictures framed and unframed. Frank Leighton was a gray-haired man, quite ruddy, lying on a bulgy cot. He was covered with a coarse blanket. His head rested on locked fingers. He stared at the low roof.

Frank Leighton was born on the East River water front at Jackson Street sixty-four years ago. Hoarsely, and with a definite Irish brogue, he recalled his childhood on the docks, how he used to wear a pair of Kentuckys and go barefoot.

"Kentuckys," he said, "was a kind of blue overhauls. You wore them with a jumper and you was all dressed up. You was, indeed. All along the docks there was only low shacks with mostly Irish and Germans in them. Now it's all changed."

Frank, in his boyhood, was one of the Border Gang, mostly kids from Jackson Street. The traditional enemy, he remembered, was the Hook Gang farther down the docks at Corlears Hook. They fought with slingshots, with cobblestones, and with their fists.

"We was great for makin' bonfires in them days," he said hoarsely. "Every night we'd have big fires on the docks."

They caught lafayettes, bass, eels, and blue-claws; sometimes flounder, weaks, drums, and even lobsters. Farther up the river, among the rocks, sometimes they got blackfish.

"They'll all be comin' back, now the river's gettin' clean again," he predicted. "On the eleven-o'clock tide, the other night, we must have struck sixty or seventy eels.

The man who had lighted the lamp, a short, pinch-faced fellow with dark, unshaved cheeks, asked Frank to tell about the two-pounders Dukie got.

"They was fine," the pinch-faced man said eagerly, "wasn't they, Frankie?"

Frank figured the red-nosed tommies were about due. Winter tommies he called them.

"They run twelve to fourteen inches," he said, out of the dark.

One of the shack's tin walls slatted and popped under the wind's pressure. The wall boards trembled.

"Tell him about the old fella, Frank," said the man at the door.

I could barely make out his figure and had forgotten he was there.

"They's an old fella—he must be in his seventies," Frank said, "who comes down every night. He comes along with his old sister. She's older than him and bent over. She fishes, too."

He didn't know the old fisherman's name.

The little lamp tender said you must get down to the bulkheads early on good nights to get your spot. Some nights he and Frank go out in their skiff and get under the docks.

"That's where you go for the blue-claws," he told me. "You knock 'em off the logs with a stick. They're fine eatin', them blue-claws. You boil them and they turn red in the water. When they turn up red they're good eatin', hey, Frank?"

They talked about the old sugar house that once stood where the shack is now. Frank said when he was a boy there was a story that it was haunted.

"Musta been somethin' to it," he told me, "because when this place come down they found a skeleton."

I thanked them and bade them good night. The little pinch-faced man took the lantern and led me out onto the bulkheads. How lonely it looked! The black-and-white cat showed up again. She pattered behind the lantern bearer. I could almost lean on the wind as it snapped the rain at my face. The lantern bearer went out to the edge and showed me Frank's skiff, where it heaved frantically off the dock in the sleek water. He said the river, here, took seventy-five feet of line. I went back to the corner and stood on the glistening cobblestones for one awkward moment.

"I'll be going in, now," said the pinched-faced man. "This wind'd blow the hair off your head."

He blew out the lantern, vanished into the darkness in the little shack. I got back in the car and started uptown through the rain, the sound of my motor disturbing the water-front silence.

By Altar Tapers

I STOOD a while on the high brownstone stoop in East Twenty-ninth Street before I put my finger to the bell. The block was dark and quiet. In Fifth Avenue, on my right, a few cars passed without breaking the stillness. In Madison Avenue there was no traffic.

The latch clicked and I stepped into a high vestibule. I stared at the warm old woodwork, at the high ceiling, and at the colored tiles in the floor. A tiny grilled window opened at my right and a black-robed nun smiled through it.

She said, "Come right in."

From a tall door on the left came the Mother Superior. She wore a white habit, blue scapular, and a pale-blue veil. Her soft features were framed in white linen. The linen enfolded the neck and came down in a guimpe, like the Puritan collar.

She led me through a long room, down a few steps, into St. Leo's Church, to a chair by a gold-railed choir, facing the white altar.

Thursday-evening service was closing. Held by the gleaming white altar tapers, by banks of dancing votive candles, and row upon row of novena lights that were steady flames in tall ruby lamps, I fell thrall to the organ tones, to the clear-voiced invisible choir. The music came from somewhere deep in the church, as from some place remote.

Inside the golden choir enclosure knelt the Sisters of the Society of Mary Reparatrix. Four rows of them, in long pews. White cloak and veil fell in soft folds round their faces. Some sat with hands meekly folded, some with their hands in the sleeves of their habits. The lights from the altar touched all their features with faint, rosy color. They were motionless. The scene was one for the brush of some medieval master. Only the soft pealing notes of the organ, the hidden choir's song after benediction, edged it with life.

Father Courtney had told me about this old church. Back in the eighties, when it was founded, Father Tom Ducey had in this parish the Iselins, the Lees, Clarence Mackay, John McCormack, Delmonico—the wealthy families on Madison Square and Madison and Fifth Avenues. All these have gone. Now the church is in debt. In 1909, when Father Ducey died, Cardinal Farley turned the edifice over to the Sisters of the Society of Mary Reparatrix.

Each Thursday night, after the regular service, the sisters, in pale blue and white with the white cloak and veil, begin adoration and continue into the evening on Friday. Two at a time, inside the golden enclosure, with only the light from the altar, they pray. Fifteen minutes before each hour two other nuns leave their beds and dress to relieve them, and thus the shifts change, hour after hour.

On other days of the week, the sisters kneel before the Blessed Sacrament at seven o'clock in the morning and change, the same way, until time for the benediction at five o'clock in the evening.

On the night of my visit we watched the congregation

departing. Father Courtney had told me they came from all parts of the city and New Jersey. When all but a few had gone we moved far back in the church. In pews, here and there, a few women lingered. Behind us, and off to our right, a young girl in mourning leaned on the pew rail, her eyes steadfast on the altar, rosary beads in her white fingers.

A nun in a black habit—these sisters combine work with prayer—came through the pews collecting the hymnbooks. She switched off the lights in the nave, one by one, leaving behind her great banks of shadow. Now only the candles' gleam stood in the darkness; the votive candles' red glow. The tall altar tapers faintly lighted the golden grille round the altar. Deep quiet fell, a quiet that seemed to press on the ears. The far-off wail of a radio car came dimly through, then died away into silence.

The sister in black had done with her duties. A door in the rear of the church caught the distant light from the candles, lost it again, and the sister had vanished. Somewhere in the church the muted clock chimes strummed the time through the dark—9:30 P.M. Down by the altar rail a white-mantled sister, upon her knees, was a statuelike figure, head bowed in deep adoration. Another white-mantled form sat just behind her, patiently waiting.

I sat a long time, held by the spell. I knew the soft high lights on the altar frame. I stared upon the altar's whiteness till it blurred, until the tapers' gleam shifted, or seemed to shift. No sound intruded here. This might have been a dream. Time seemed suspended, but again the chimes trembled out of the shadow and it was ten o'clock. I left the pew and tiptoed out into the room through which the Mother Superior had led me.

The Mother Superior sat and talked with me a while.

There were thirty-six sisters in the convent, she told me. They did not leave the enclosure. The black-robed sisters moved about, but not the choir religious, the nuns in the white and pale blue. People of all faiths came to the church to witness the ceremony of adoration. Many came from far places. The society had sixty houses throughout the world, but only one in New York.

I stood, at last, at the door, looking again on Twenty-ninth Street. The Mother Superior, smiling, held the knob.

"Good night," she said, gently. "God bless you."

Mr. Caro and the Lonely Hearts

ONE SATURDAY night, when a storm was over the town and thunder rolled over the roof, I took up, quite by chance, a copy of *The Villager*. Among the public notices I read:

"Lonely on Saturday night? Young composer pianist welcomes you to his studio to partake in social activities and make new friends. Refreshments served, but no drinking. Subscription $1. Call after 5 P.M."

The telephone was in the Regent exchange. The voice that answered was crisp and businesslike, but extremely polite. I seized my stick and wraprascal, had the doorman whistle up a cab, and splashed my way uptown.

The address was a few doors off Madison Avenue in Eighty-sixth Street. I pressed the button alongside the name, "Mr. Caro," and waited in the dim-lit vestibule. Presently I heard my name, thin and metallic, in the speaking tube.

"Take the elevator at your left, sir," it said. "Get off at the fourth floor."

The lift gave onto a narrow corridor. There were two doors. I waited awhile, but no one came. I tapped lightly on the panels behind which I heard the confused sounds of muted revelry. The door opened and I stared at a slender young woman cased in black velvet. She had a high hair-do and a high white collar.

"Your cloak, sir," she said.

She slid into a little room off to one side and put the garment on a hanger, beside other hats and coats. The counter for the hat-check room, I noticed, was an ironing board, covered with dark cloth.

Mr. Caro was a little man in his early thirties. Extremely neat, with hard collar; hair slick and right to the last strand. He shook hands, warmly.

"Come in, sir," he said. "All here are friends."

I moved up a narrow little hall into the studio. The windows were closed against the storm and it was warm. A little electric fan, set under the old grand piano, bravely murmured against the smoke and humidity with no appreciable effect. Blue candles burned on a marble mantle against one wall. Pink candles flickered gently on a table across the room. Three young couples shuffled dreamily in the narrow floor space—eight by ten, I figured—and a big girl played for them at the piano.

There were some eighteen or twenty young men and women in the studio and another five or six in a tiny room giving off the studio. They stared at me. I stared at them. A young Spaniard, earnestly talking to two heavy Irish girls about how the Castilians gave their best blood to Erin, stopped long enough to invite me to have a seat. Mr. Caro had popped off; vanished behind the great doors of a kitchenette. I heard him rattling glasses and bottles. The big girl at the piano played, "Somebody Stole My Gal" and "I Kiss Your Hand, Madame." Mr. Caro bustled out, clapped his hands, and announced refreshments. The dancers retired to divans on the edge of the studio. Mr. Caro set up a bridge table and piled it with tiny sandwiches and a glass bowl of melancholy-looking punch. The young men got up and carried sandwiches and punch. Mr. Caro seemed delighted.

"That's the spirit," he kept repeating. "That's the proper spirit." He stopped at my side with a glass of punch. It looked purple in the candlelight. "Very stimulating," he assured me, in his crisp way. "Fruit punch. Half pint of rum."

I sipped the stuff and studied the rampant blue horse in a water color on the wall. Two blonde girls at my elbow got to talking about psychology. If a girl strikes her matches sideways, one said very earnestly, she has masculine traits. Girls usually strike their matches upward, she insisted, if they're truly feminine. No one argued the point. Mr. Caro took the piano seat while the big girl went at the sandwich pile.

"Have you any special requests," he asked eagerly, "or shall I just improvise?"

He improvised. He rolled the heavy notes, smoothly and expertly; gradually shaded off to a lighter motif, till the music was as of mice racing on broken glass.

"It is something expressive of the evening," said Mr. Caro.

He left the piano and the big girl went back. She played, "Parlez-moi d'Amour," pulling all the sad stops. A dark-haired girl sat down beside me. She was shy at first, but voluntarily unfolded her story. She lived on Ninety-fifth Street. She was two years out of Germany. She came to the party to improve her English, but didn't seem to be talking very much.

"I listen," she said. "I like to listen."

More young people arrived. They stared awkwardly across the room in the candlelight, found seats, and entered hesitantly into conversation with their neighbors. A tow-haired stripling, not more than twenty-two, squeezed in between the dark girl and me.

"How I came here," he said. "I had a date with a New York girl in front of the Capitol. I'm from New Jersey. This girl stood me up. I bought a copy of *Cue* to see where to go, and I saw about this place. I like it here. This is real congenial."

Mr. Caro stopped by again. He told me how he got the idea for his Saturday-night parties. Mr. Caro had been in the city ten years. He worked downtown in a food house. He knew what it was to be lonely in a city of more than 7,000,000 people. So he started his parties. His friends and the newspaper ads have filled the studio every Saturday night. On Sunday afternoons he gives one-dollar parties for elderly people.

"They sit and they knit," he said, "and I play soft music."

A week before, at the Saturday party, he invited one of his friends, a former U-boat commander. The commander held the guests spellbound with stories about the *Untersseboten* in the Great War.

After midnight Mr. Caro vanished again behind the kitchenette doors. He came out, slightly dotted with perspiration, but neat as ever, bearing a china teapot. It breathed clouds of live steam. Everybody had tea and Mr. Caro seemed beside himself with delight. He clasped his hands nervously.

"That's the spirit," he murmured. "That's the proper spirit. Cream or lemon?"

The party broke up at one A.M. All the guests (who, incidentally, had signed a copybook register on entering) filed out. I left with a blonde girl and two young men.

"Nice man, Mr. Caro," the young men said.

I dropped one of the young men in Eighty-sixth Street, West; the girl and the other young man in Gramercy Square. I went home and tossed the rest of the night. I dreamed of Mr. Caro, fussing with teapots and sandwiches for lonely people. He kept saying: "That's the spirit. That's the proper spirit!"

Hero — Twenty-two Years After

SOMEONE on the city desk handed up the invitation. It said: "308th Infantry Reunion Dinner, 1940, Saturday evening, Feb. 3, at 7 P.M. Hotel Governor Clinton."

"There was a little fella," the city editor mused "Kroto, Krotoshy, or some such name. I think he was in the 308th. He was the little barber, if I have it straight, who carried back the message that saved the Lost Battalion. Wonder if he's still around."

Pages in *The Lost Battalion* by Thomas Johnson and Fletcher Pratt told the story of the beleaguered unit. Pocketed at Charlevaux Brook, Argonne Forest. Thirty runners dead or wounded. Carrier pigeons downed. Water gone. Food gone. Five days of this. Then, October 7, 1918, 8 A.M. The major, sick with seeing more and more of his men die under the Seventy-seventh Division's own cannon, asked the captain for another volunteer runner. The captain called, "Abe!"

"A little stoop-shouldered Polish Jew slithered over to them," the book says, "his uniform more than unusually untidy. Pale, a long, hooked nose, not very exact posture . . ."

I closed the book and went over to station F of the United States post office, on Thirty-fourth Street between

Second and Third Avenues. It was late afternoon and the rotunda was gray with winter sun's decline. The personnel man had said: "You'll find him at the Inquiry Window." The man at the window, though, was tall and dark.

"Krotoshinsky?" he said. He turned and called into the gloomy post-office interior. Behind him, through the grille, I could see mailbags piled high. "Abe!" he shouted. "Abe!"

A little stoop-shouldered Polish Jew slithered from behind the pile of mailbags. His garb was more than unusually untidy. He was pale and had a long, hooked nose. His posture was far from good.

"What you want?" he said.

His pale hands fumbled at his lips. He squinted through gold-rimmed spectacles. He could have stood a shave. I showed him the invitation. Abraham Krotoshinsky narrowed reddened lids to focus on the printed card. His sleeves were raveled. The collar of his blue coat was askew.

"You got it wrong," he said. "The T'ree Hundred Ate is not my outfit. I am Company K, T'ree Hundred Seven. I was on li-ais-on detail in Charlevaux with the T'ree Hundred Ate."

He came from behind the grille. He leaned against the desk in the center of the rotunda, a shabby, undistinguished little man.

"Mostly I forgot already," he said. "I don't talk so much about it no more." He stared into Thirty-fourth Street. He said: "It is more than twenty years. It is twenty-two years already."

The voice, like the man, was colorless. The thin, sandy hair was all but gone from his head. His face was lined.

He fumbled at his mouth. Prodding brought out fragmentary details.

"Some clippings I still got," he said. "I got a D.S.C. from Gen'ral Pershin'. I got a Conspicuous Service Cross. Victory Medal. The medals, I don't bother no more. My kids they take them out. My uniform I don't wear no more, only for affairs."

Abraham Krotoshinsky could not recall the names of the other men who went out with him that morning. His brow wrinkled. His manner was that of a man perplexed, apologetic, uncomfortable.

"It is more than twenty-two years," he murmured. "One of the other fellas is a replacement fella. His name I do not remember. The other is a Irish fella. He has a Irish name."

The book had said: "Two of the men came back, one with a smashed shoulder." One of them had told the captain: "Abe? We lost track of him. Killed, I guess."

I asked him about that. Abe stared into the street. The white fingers were at his lips again.

"Hmm," he said. "From these things I don't know." The details of how he crawled out of Charlevaux pocket to a trench in the rear were vague now in Abe's mind. "The machine-gun bullets shake the bushes," he said as he tried to remember. 8 A.M. to 7 P.M. He heard American voices. I asked if he recalled what he said. "I said 'Hello!' " he said. "I did not know the signal. To the officer? To him I said, 'You should come right away.' " He remembered the hot coffee, though. And the bully beef. "The bully beef then is better," he paused to find a fitting contrast, "better, even, than turkey from the present day."

Someone called from behind the grille: "Abe!"

He turned to go. I held him for a moment with my hand. I wanted to know if he liked war movies.

"Please, I got to go back," he said. He moved off. "I don't like such movies. It makes me all upset."

He vanished into the gloom behind the grille.

The Barge Folk

THE CANAL barges were tied up for the winter off Coenties Slip on the South Street water front. They would ride the bay tide now, until the ice broke up in the Hudson and in the Lakes. Canal barge women would get in their winter knitting and crocheting. They had packed their unwilling moppets off to city schools and they would spend most of their days and nights in their tiny barge cabins, gently rocking with the tide and with the wash of passing tugs and ferries. There would be visits from one barge to another, long nights of listening to the battery radio or hugging the "Mascot" wood stoves in the galley with their numerous pets about their feet. The men would loll in their chairs and swap fresh-water yarns about high adventure on the 525-mile stretch from South Street to Buffalo.

A latent envy for the barge folk, dating back to my first reading of *Huckleberry Finn*, urged me to South Street. In the subway rumbling southward from the Village I plagued myself with dreamy memories stored from that reading. I recalled Huck's heart-warming story; how he and Jim sprawled on their backs on the raft as it moved on the current; how the skies were speckled with stars, or streaked with shooting stars; how they would watch the candles in shore cabins wink out, one by one; how the towns slipped by in the dark, and how the Mississippi steamboats, all the way off to one side, would shower the night with sparks. Barge life, I figured, must be something like that.

It was coming on dusk; clear, crisp New York October twilight. The wind was sharp off the Bay. Shabby wretches, mostly in browning blue dungarees and thread-bare jackets scrounged in ancient rope-shop and chandlery doorways facing the water. Thinning sun diffused a kindly reddish gold on the little old buildings, filled with deep, ponderous shadow the clifflike rise of the Wall Street buildings massed beyond them. Brooklyn shore vanished slowly in crepuscular haze, with land lights dimly showing through the shimmer. On either side of the low concrete pier by the New York State Canal Terminal shed, the barges rose and fell, shoulder to shoulder, on the tide.

I climbed from the splintered stringpiece to the lifting deck of the nearest barge. A middle-aged man, huddled in a pea jacket with peaked cap down on his eyes, surveyed my approach through pipe smoke. Two dogs, a half-sized collie and a very soiled poodle, peered through an equally tangled hair screen and sniffed shyly at my pants. The barge man silently motioned to another chair against the low cabin wall and as silently heard my mission.

He didn't know Huck Finn but, from my eager sketch of the raft trip down to Cairo as Huck told it, he guessed barge life was "something like." I stared through the cabin window. A woman moved about inside in the weak yellow glow of a kerosene lamp. The smell of wood smoke and of cooking meat came downwind from the little tin chimney lashed to the cabin wall.

"About all them lights, and all," the barge man said, "we get all that. There's fifty-seven locks, and God knows how many towns, along the canals. We see them go dark like you said, and we see the towns by day."

He named the towns and the villages: Yonkers, Newburg, Kingston, Albany, Troy. He mentioned Cohoes, Waterford, Crescent, Amsterdam, Fultonville, St. Johnsville, Little Falls, Herkimer. Four days, in tow, from South Street to Troy, always in fleets of six, with a tug to pull the tow. All kinds of cargoes: grain, mostly, but sand, too, and iron, soda ash, coal. Take up to 2800 tons. The skipper is the only man aboard. He sees to loading and unloading.

"There's more to loading than you'd think," the skipper said. "Get it stowed wrong and a barge can buckle, even break in half."

He admitted, though, that he'd never seen one actually break in half; only heard of it.

Tows come at any time. If the woman and the kids happen to be away when a tow call comes, they come back to the slip and find their home is gone. They go to the barge owner, then, and find the tow's destination. Usually they can borrow train fare and catch the tow at Kingston or at Troy, where the Hudson connects with the Erie system. This happens fairly often. The barge owner, incidentally, furnishes kerosene for the cabin lamps, oilcloth for the cabin floor, and all cooking utensils.

"Oilcloth has to be worn through though," the skipper said, "before they'll honor a requisition."

Tugs pushed noisily by, off the far end of the dock, as the skipper talked. Gulls spiraled and dived with the fading sunlight warm on their breasts. The barges strained heavily at their ropes and groaned, when they rubbed together, like old men with rheumatism.

Barge folk, the skipper said, eat well; great ones for

meat. A skipper gets from $115 to $125 a month, depending on his worth and his record. Keep a wife and two or three kids on it, but never save a penny. The women shop on shore, Fourteenth Street, mostly, but sometimes in the uptown stores. They are just as fussy in their dress as city women are. Go to beauty parlors, sometimes, too.

It was dark now. Ferry blasts shattered and broke on the Wall Street skyscraper fronts. The harbor put on its diamonds. Brooklyn Bridge wore a string of pearls.

I went down three steps to the cabin. It was orderly and filled with the sweet scent of freshly baked chocolate cake. The whole room was no more than ten feet by ten feet. A row of three bunks was neatly made up. Cots, for the children, were ranged against one wall. A canary hopped in a battered cage and sang as if its throat might burst. The barge woman half curtsied when I was introduced. A towheaded boy, fussing with a damaged scooter, stared at me, round-eyed, from the floor.

The skipper explained about Huck Finn. The woman seemed puzzled at first, but finally caught on. January, the collie, sat at her feet and looked wistfully at the bubbling pot. The soiled poodle sank into a corner and drowsed with its head between its paws. The woman talked about parties on the different barges, about dancing in the crowded cabins or on deck, to the music of guitars and harmonicas. And she talked about the mountains and the woods and the country scenes along the Hudson and along the locks.

"People says," she shyly told me, "that you can't find no better scenery in the whole world, but after you've been going up and down with the tows for eleven years,

Bait

THE MAN behind the counter in Gus Walz' bait-and-tackle shop reminded me, somehow, of Christopher Nubbles in *Old Curiosity Shop*. His face had a rustic quality. Wonder started out of his blue eyes. His cheeks were ruddy and his hair was red where it showed under his cap.

"It's from the newspapers, Gus," he bawled, loudly but vaguely, toward the back of the shop.

I peered over his shoulder through a forest of fishing rods, but could not see Gus. There was a partition. Gus never came out. He sent his first assistant, a young Mr. Raby, who had been puttering around out in the shed where fishing rods are made to order. I told Mr. Raby I was interested mostly in bait. Where does the bait come from? How long does it last? How many kinds of bait are there?

"We'd like some information on the intimate home life of bait, if you have it," I told him.

The man who looked like Christopher Nubbles stared at me, then at Mr. Raby, and his eyes seemed to widen. Mr. Raby touched the fellow and gently shook him out of his daze.

"Bring out a couple trays of bait, Paul," he said. "I want to show this man."

86

like we have, it gets to be ordinary, sort of beautif
nary."

The woman looked very tired.

"If you seen her with rouge and jool'ry and lip
the skipper assured me, "you'd swear by heck she
city woman."

The woman shrugged but seemed pleased. She
her barge garden ivy, curly-leaf begonia, and ger
in window boxes.

"You see, everything shipshape," she said, "but
nights on Oneida Lake when you can't keep a pot
stove or a cup on the table." Barge life is heal
children, though, she told me. "My tykes is all
up," she said.

It was full dark when I stumbled onto the pier.
burned in all the barge windows. The air was sha
October wind and rank brine. I took one last, senti
look at the swaying craft. I headed uptown.

Paul shambled off into the back-store shadows and came back with a stack of five wooden trays. These were about two feet long, eighteen inches wide, and four inches deep. They were filled with seaweed. The man with the blue eyes stared at me across the stack. Mr. Raby lifted the top layer of weed and it was my turn to goggle. I had never seen such worms, nor dreamed they came this size. They seemed from ten inches to one foot in length. Mr. Raby said they came from the Maine coast, mostly. The man who looked like Christopher Nubbles sensed that I was amazed. His face widened in a slow grin. He took out two of the longest and dangled them in the unshielded brilliance of the electric drop light.

Mr. Raby explained that no one but members of the worm-diggers union can dig bait for the trade. It is a highly paid job, though he didn't know exactly how much diggers get. They work, as a rule, about nine months every year.

"These," he said, pointing to the monsters squirming in the expert hold of the man who looked like Little Nell's Kit, "are the very best sandworms. There's a trick to packing them so's they stand the trip down from the coast. They come in cardboard boxes of two hundred and feed off the algae in the weed."

Mr. Raby said Gus has some of the biggest people in the country as bait-and-tackle customers—President Roosevelt, Victor Moore, the actor, Guy Lombardo, the band leader, and E. F. Hutton, the financier. The store also sells worms to scientific laboratories. The shop is on the east side of Third Avenue, just below Fourteenth Street, at a point where Third Avenue still looks and smells like the Bowery. In a glass case on the store front Gus displays letters from his important patrons. He is proudest of a photostat of a check for $17.50, dated October 3, 1934. It was made out in the President's name by "M. A. LeHand, attorney."

Another letter of which the whole shop staff is proud is one on White House stationery, dated March 11, 1935. "I have received the box of bait," it says. "I think they are fine." This one is signed by Wilson Brown, Captain, U.S.N., naval aide to the President.

After I had inspected the testimonials to Gus' worms, I went inside the shop again and the man with the Christopher Nubbles face was delegated to tell me about hellgrammites and green crabs. These, it turned out, are his specialty. The man bent over a bushel basket and fetched up a wide fistful of little green crabs and sea grass. He held them out with a bashful grin.

"I trap 'em," he said, hoarsely. "I go out with this."

He reached to the counter and held up a wire basket with a wide mesh. He waits for low water at the beaches —at Rockaway, or out on Long Island—wades out with his traps and scoops the crabs in by the dozen and half dozen. They run from two inches to four inches in length. Speech seemed to come to Paul with difficulty. He held out the fistful of little crabs and intently watched their futile claw play.

"These are good for blackfish," he told me shyly. "Blackfish go for these."

He dropped the crabs back into the basket and carefully covered them. He sidled away. Mr. Raby, meanwhile, had wrapped some bait for a customer. He resumed his talk. The shop handles hellgrammites, in season, he said. These are caught under rotten logs, mostly. A lot of them come from Pennsylvania. They are especially good for fresh-water fish. Black bass like them.

Hellgrammites, I found out later from my Webster, are the larvae of long-winged insects.

Mr. Raby showed some night crawlers, long, dark worms that are found inland. Men go out with lanterns for these. They get the greatest numbers on damp nights, usually around old barns. They are best for fresh-water fishing.

"In the summer," he said, "we handle Indian stick worms. They are good for trout, but we're out of them today."

Gus, who had been napping, awoke behind the partition and I was escorted back to see him. He blinked up at me from an old army cot, a red-faced heavy man with gray hair. He had the weathered cheeks of a seafaring man.

Reclining, Gus talked of his boyhood in Corlears Hook on the East River. He looked well over sixty. A half century ago he caught all kinds of fish off the Hook. Big blackfish among the rocks off Ninth Street and giant lobsters. They vanished when big industry polluted the waters, but are coming back now. Gus told a long yarn about how he almost got his hook into a full-sized whale one day, twenty years ago, off Ambrose Light. He was on Captain Sorensen's fishing boat, the *Satellite,* at the time. The whale was only ten feet away, spouting.

"The skipper comes up to me," Gus related, sadly, "and he says: 'Gus, for God's sake don't hook that whale. If he gets mad he'll give us his tail and sink us.' I liked Sorensen, so I give in, but sometimes I think I was too bighearted. If I'd done what I'd a mind to, I guess Gus Walz would have been the only man in history who ever played a whale on a rod."

Stitch — the Bondsman

THE ORIGINAL Stitch McCarthy, a pug-nosed Irish boy who worked in the pressroom of the *Sun* back in 1895, has been one with the dust these many years. He was bantamweight champion of Jersey City.

But for forty-two tireless years until his death in 1937, the title was held by a wizened, cross-eyed little man who looked Irish, but wasn't by a good many miles. This Stitch McCarthy, a Rumanian Jew, was one of the shrewdest and most affluent bondsmen in the city, Mayor of Grand Street, Chief of the League of New York Locality Mayors, Inc., and Governor Emeritus of Barren Island. His real name, which appeared only on bail bonds, was Sam Rothberg.

The Rumanian Stitch and his brother Max, who was his senior by only five minutes, came through Castle Garden fifty years ago, when they were five years old. Next morning they were enrolled in the Five Points Mission School on Mulberry Bend, swapping punches with the Oliver Street micks; at least, Stitch was. Max took his lumps philosophically. He had no soul for heroics. He was destined for the fancy-poultry business.

Equipped only with a few strong profane phrases easily picked up in the schoolyard, Stitch began selling newspapers at Wall and Broad Streets. He got the corner by fighting for it. In due time he built up a trade that included such customers as Grover Cleveland, J. P. Morgan the elder, and Russell Sage. Stitch described Sage as "that philanthropede wit' th' big beezer." He had a genius for distorting words of more than one or two syllables. His entire vocabulary contained no more than six or eight hundred words, most of them vintage profanities; yet he managed to get the general drift of the "whereases" and other flub-dubberies of bail-bond phrasing, which was all he cared about.

The good Hibernian name engraved on Stitch's business cards and printed in large letters on the dusty windows of his dark little store opposite the Tombs was acquired in combat after he had knocked about Park Row, Mulberry Bend, and Wall Street for almost twelve years. Stitch never overlooked a chance to make some extra money. Besides drawing his salary on the *Sun*, he added to his savings by promoting boxing bouts between the pressroom boys and the carriers who worked with him. One night, in Woods' Hall in Jersey City, the carrier he had picked to fight the original Stitch McCarthy vanished from the dressing room, disturbed by the strength and number of McCarthy adherents.

"What could I do when that little bastard takes a sneak on me?" he would ask in later years. "I couldn' let all that dough get away. I collected my boy's end of the gate an' I went in there in his place."

After three rounds of bewildering eye- and footwork, he hung the pressroom champion on the ropes.

"I knocked his head off," Stitch would recall, "but his gang got sore on me."

He left Woods' Hall in his fighting trunks, with his

street clothes on his arm and a string of bloodthirsty customers trailing behind him. The original Stitch never came back to the *Sun*.

"I hear a few years later where he's dead," Stitch would say. "From then on they call *me* Stitch McCarthy."

Stitch quit the *Sun* when he was eighteen, soon after he broke the heart of the Jersey City champion. He opened a poolroom at 256 Grand Street, where his new name was one of his chief assets. He did so well that he had to move to larger quarters, at 83–85 Forsythe Street. He called his new establishment the Stitch McCarthy Apollo Saloon and Eagle Bowling Alleys. It adjoined the Forsythe Turkish Baths, where gangsters and gunmen from both the East and West Sides spent most of their nights. Stitch got all the bathhouse trade.

Lefty Louie, Gyp the Blood, Dago Frank, and Whitey Lewis, as well as Rosenthal, the gambler for whose death they went to the electric chair, were a few of Stitch's steady patrons. They behaved like gents, or went out on their ear. Stitch did his own bouncing, small as he was. Monk Eastman, Baldy Jack Rose, Limpy Farrell, Bugs Donlon, Kid Dropper, and Little Augie were customers too. All his customers, however, were not gangsters. Sam Rosoff, the millionaire subway builder, frequently slept on the billiard tables in his youth, as a house guest, and Al Woods, Sam H. Harris, and A. E. Lefcourt dropped in once in a while.

William Travers Jerome, when he was District Attorney, was a steady customer. It was not unusual to see him thundering the balls up one alley, with his shirt sleeves rolled up, while prospective subjects for prosecution perspired in the adjoining fairway. One night the District Attorney came in with a friend, a grave, distinguished person, whom he introduced to Stitch. The proprietor challenged the visitor to a game and beat him 290 to 260, Jerome keeping score. Stitch recalls that his solemn opponent was "the real goods in the book business," but he had to get out his collection of newspaper clippings to get his name. It was the author, Henry James.

Calvin Coolidge, before his election as Governor of Massachusetts, came in one day with Postmaster General Hitchcock. He acknowledged the introduction to Stitch, scowled at the nude paintings on the Apollo's walls, and left without taking a drink.

Stitch was Republican captain in "de Bloody Ate" Assembly District in the late nineties, powerful enough to bring troubled frowns to the august brows of Dick Croker, Big and Little Tim Sullivan, and crafty Charlie Engle. How he outsmarted the Tammany chiefs and elected Charlie Adler for Assembly is his favorite political story.

Rose (Rosenheim the lawyer), an active member of the Sullivan Democratic Club, hit on the brilliant idea of printing ten thousand circulars in Yiddish to let the East Side know what a sterling candidate they had in Adler's Tammany opponent. Stitch heard of it. He ordered ten thousand similar handbills at the same shop for his man and arranged to have the bundles switched when Sullivan's Irish lads came down to collect them for distribution. The Sullivan messengers got back to the clubhouse at the end of the day with the few circulars that remained. Rosie picked one up when he strolled in a few days later. He almost fainted.

One year, Stitch decided to run his bartender, Julius Levy, for alderman and Elias Dulberger, one of his pinboys, for assemblyman, on an independent ticket. He hired dress suits for them, filled their pockets with two-for-five campaign cigars, and sent them through "de Ate" on white horses, trailed by an orchestra of four hand organs. Neither of the candidates spoke English very well, but Stitch overcame that handicap by passing out free beer in their behalf.

In the midst of the campaign, Stitch had a sudden change of heart. What good would it do him if the city gained a Republican alderman and assemblyman if he lost a good bartender and an efficient pinboy? One night, while the candidates were speaking in Miner's Bowery Theatre, he sent sandwich men parading through the district with signs saying DON'T VOTE FOR LEVY AND DULBERGER. THEY ARE BUMS. When the candidates got back to the saloon, flushed with their dialectic campaign oratory, Stitch made them shuck the evening dress, and sent Levy back to drawing beer, and put the Assembly aspirant behind the pins again. Levy got one vote—his own— and the Democratic candidate got close to seven thousand. The pinboy was disqualified by the Board of Elections. He's a lawyer in Indianapolis now.

Thirty years ago, when locality mayors were not as common or numerous as they are today, Stitch became chief executive of Grand Street. In those days, the title, a purely honorary one, was gained by bailing out the neighborhood's chronic drunks and brawlers, by throwing pennies to the kids, fixing things with the magistrates in trifling court cases, and generally building up and sustaining a reputation for openhandedness. It's different today.

Ponderous Louie Zeltner, former East Side tipster for the local dailies, took over the mayor racket some eighteen years ago. He appointed mayors by the dozen, thought up gag lines for them to speak at elaborate dinners, and guided their destinies like a Mussolini. A few of the old-time mayors, such as Stitch, made some pretense of keeping up their neighborhood philanthropies, but most of them had only the title and the gold badge that went with it.

One of Stitch's early philanthropies as he struggled for the title of mayor almost got him a fractured skull. He was distributing Passover matzoth to the poor in an empty store on Grand Street, before a large sign advertising his generosity, when one of the matzoth applicants who could read a bit of English deciphered the Irish name on the poster.

"He's a *goy*," screamed the scholar. "He's a Stitch Mc-Carthy!"

Somebody heaved a brick through the store window. The matzoth line broke up into aggrieved groups, wrathful because they thought they had almost been duped into the sacrilege of accepting Passover food from a Gentile. Stitch climbed onto the counter, did some swift explaining in his Rumanian-Mulberry Bend dialect, and there was a scramble back into line.

A seven-foot safe in the back room of the bail-bond office on Centre Street held three enormous scrapbooks filled with news clippings accumulated by Stitch in his long years as a man in the public eye. He considered publicity—any kind—the yardstick of success and subscribed to several clipping bureaus.

The marriage of the Mayor of Grand Street to Lilly Marks, described in several stories as "the belle of Willett Street," got a total of forty columns in the local dailies. None of the reporters missed Stitch's classic admonition to his friends, just before the wedding, that "Any guy wot don't wear a dress suit to this affair gets chucked out on his ear." They listed the gems with which he adorned the bride. They were many and chosen with a special eye to size. Miss Marks was interviewed.

"He isn't what you'd call handsome," she said discreetly, in describing Stitch, "but he's good as gold."

Jerome, the Sullivans, Port Commissioner Murray, Sarsaparilla Reilly, Judge Otto Rosalsky, and Theodore Roosevelt sent congratulatory telegrams to be read at the wedding feast. Some years later, the Rothberg family moved, somewhat apologetically, to West 110th Street. In mitigation of this bit of snobbery, he pleaded that he had to do it for the children. He had two sons and a daughter, and hired a maid and a cook to ease the domestic burden from the broad shoulders of Mrs. Rothberg. Stitch, to whom pronunciation of the name "Columbia" came rather hard, referred to it as "that jernt uptown" and let it go at that.

Before prohibition forced him to close the Apollo, Stitch invested twenty-five thousand dollars in a factory for making balls out of wood pulp, cement, and potash. Visions of great wealth from the venture were ended when the supply of ingredients from Germany was cut off by World War I. Stitch sold all the machinery in the plant for fifteen hundred dollars, shrugged his shoulders, and took the loss calmly.

He saw the interesting possibilities of the bail-bond business in 1923. Up to that time, as saloonkeeper and locality mayor, he had bailed out his patrons and the neighbors' children as a friendly gesture. Then one day, when he was in the post office and saw the hordes of Volstead violators, he hurried to a sign painter for a bail-bond shingle. He was successful from the start. He got three per cent as a premium from each client, whether the bail fixed by the court was five hundred or a hundred and fifty thousand dollars. At least that was the amount fixed by law, and no bondsman ever took less.

Jack ("Legs") Diamond and his Greene County expeditionary force provided a steady and reliable source of income for Stitch until they were scattered or jailed.

Stitch liked Jack Diamond. When the Coll gunners were searching for "Legs" during his trial in Federal Court, Stitch took him in as house guest in the Rothberg suite on 110th Street. He never did that for any of his other clients.

Highway robbers and holdup guys did not attract Stitch as good business risks, because of the Baumes Law. Afraid of a life sentence, they are very apt to take a long walk and forget to show up for trial, with the result that the bond is forfeited. In the bail-bond business, such customers are known as "lammisters." They were Stitch's pet hate. Rats, he called them.

Volsteads, Stitch said, were the safest. They came in bunches and stayed around, because sentences for liquor-law violations were light. Stitch handled thousands without losing one.

Some cases dawdle along two or three years. In such instances, Stitch sent out regular quarterly notices reminding the clients that they were still his property. He found too many of them were apt to forget to keep their dates in court. Lots of tough muggs with public reputations for fearlessness often had to be handled like babies. Stitch kept their courage up by telling them there wasn't a chance of their being convicted, or that the worst they could expect was a suspended sentence.

Stitch lived a simple life. Pinochle and movies were his chief weaknesses. He liked almost any kind of film except gangster pictures. Thought they were "all hooey." Gunmen and racketeers to Stitch were only bums, and a bum in the films, having no bond-fee appeal, was a total loss as far as he was concerned.

Cigars—fifteen-centers—were to Stitch what the clerical collar was to Belasco. He wouldn't think of posing for the photographers without one. He used to carry ten or fifteen in his vest pockets, but court clerks and police lieutenants preyed on them until it became too expensive a habit. Stitch learned, during business hours, to wear only the one in his lips.

As Mayor of Grand Street—the title stayed with him, though he moved miles away from the place where he earned it—Stitch felt it necessary to spend a lot on his wardrobe, but his clothes never fitted neatly. He wore a large fraternal pin in his lapel. It was crusted with dia-mond chips. And when he was in the mood, he wore a diamond ring, parking-lamp size.

Stitch subscribed to the "tip-my-hat-to-no-man" school of philosophy. He would tell you very earnestly that he was no better than a poor guy; but that, on the other hand, no politician, even if he was a big shot, was better'n him. On the other hand, he acknowledged all introductions, whether to men or women, by tipping his hat.

Mr. Otto

WHEREVER there were important weddings around New York you were likely to run into Richard Henry Otto. He tied ascots for the bridegroom and for the ushers. It was his career for twenty-eight years.

Mr. Otto never seemed to get over the wonder of his great gift, his way with ties. His round face would flush and his pale-blue eyes would grow moist when he told how he tied ascots for Astors, Rockefellers, Morgans, and Roosevelts.

Mr. Otto's hair was white. An executive of Brooks Brothers on Madison Avenue, he was firmly loyal to the shop's 122 years of stern tradition. He tied ascots at weddings up to the last, wouldn't dream of giving it up.

"I love to tie ascots," he would say eagerly. "One time I went out eleven times in June. I tied one hundred and five ascots in one month."

Mr. Otto tied ascots in the deep South and in New England. He tied them in Newport, in Wilmington, in Philadelphia, and in Washington.

Sometimes he tied waterfalls. These are somewhat like ascots, but not quite. In a waterfall, Mr. Otto would explain, you use four-in-hand technique, except you do not slip the tie through the knot.

Mr. Otto's eyes would come out a little when he recalled how kind the customers had always been.

"They treat me lovely," he would say earnestly, "absolutely lovely. They wouldn't let me sit down until I had a drink and meet the family. It was really a picnic."

Mr. Otto put up boxes for bridegrooms and ushers. When he explained this his soft, white hands would go through the motions of putting things in a box.

"You put the tie in here," he'd say happily. "You set the gloves there. You put the spats here. That's how you do it. And you put the names on in gold."

Emotion brought water to Mr. Otto's eyes when he recalled the J. C. Brady wedding in Hyannis. Sunken gardens, colored water from the fountains. It was one of the nicest weddings Mr. Otto ever saw.

"Sixteen ushers," he'd murmur. "Sixteen bridesmaids. I tied all the ties. Just as they went up the garden the sun came out." At this point Mr. Otto would find it hard to maintain control. "What a picture!" he'd say.

Mr. Otto was not good at remembering names. His blue eyes would seek remote space when he forgot, but this was a gentle fraud. He could not, for example, remember essential details of his first ascot-tieing job. He did recall, though, that Mr. Wadsworth Russell Lewis took him from the store on what was his first automobile ride. Who was married that day, or where, was hidden in time's mist. Mr. Otto, however, would pounce eagerly on one important detail.

"I remember this," he'd say brightly. "I remember I tied twelve ascots that day. Yes, it *was* twelve."

Mr. Otto was always interested in tying ties. When ascots came in he was the only man in the shop who really got the hang of them. He learned it from one of Brooks' foreign representatives.

Sometimes Mr. Otto would find a bridegroom so excited that he could not stand still while his ascot was being tied. In these cases, Mr. Otto would take the bridegroom by the shoulder and steady him. It always worked. He remembered one bridegroom, of excellent family, who made things difficult for him.

"He stood there in his silk hat and shorts and kept jumping back and forth over the back of a chair," Mr. Otto would say, still bewildered by memory of it. He finally got the fellow dressed, all right, and saw him safely down the aisle. He'd shake his head whenever he thought of it. "Gosh," he'd say, "that one had me worried."

When Mr. Otto spoke of his assignments he'd say: "I tied Mr. Zulch," or "I took care of Mr. Mulch." He tied Elliott Roosevelt, James Roosevelt, and John Roosevelt. He tied one of the Wanamakers, once.

"Gosh, they were awfully nice to me. Senator Fletcher was a peach at that wedding. He took me all around the house and showed me all the presents."

Mr. Otto made it a point to find out the exact time set for a wedding, and how long it would take for the bridegroom to get to the altar. He timed his ascots accordingly.

Mr. Otto always wore double-breasted blue serge when he went tying, because serge fit in almost anywhere. He tried dark gray once, but was unhappy.

The dewy look would settle in Mr. Otto's eyes again when he thought how he has seen boy customers grow from Eton collars to ascots at weddings.

Men grown gray would call him for information on what to wear at inaugurations, weddings, dinners, special functions.   He delighted in knowing all of the answers.

Mr. Otto acquired this knowledge through study.   He was born in Brooklyn, lived there all his life, and had a Brooklyn accent.   He never finished grade school.   Went right into Brooks'.

He used to tell Mrs. Otto about all the weddings and whom he had tied, and how.   But not in the last years. Mrs. Otto, he thought, and it seemed to puzzle him, sort of lost interest.

Cartographer

EDWARD A. E. P. SAMSON is different from most cartographers. When he puts Sakhalin or Shikoku on a new map, when he inserts Kilwa or Kivinge, Tobago or Bucaramanga, he can shut his pale eyes and see these places. He has been to them. The average mapmaker, however, is apt to be a sedentary fellow, one who has nibbled timidly at *Bratwurst* in Hoboken or has tasted chowder in Egg Harbor City but does not know Antoine's in N'Orleans or shish-kabeb in its native habitat.

Mr. Samson confessed he does not get around much himself any more. *Blitzkriegs* and international penny-ante with sad little nations as chips are driving cartographers loony.

Mr. Samson, a Devonshireman, chief mapmaker for C. S. Hammond & Co., is a conservative man, a word clipper, not the kind to throw his weight about. He speaks modestly of his travels. To illustrate how unsettled things are in the map trade he displayed a printed blue slip sent out with current atlases. It says, "No boundaries will change officially until after the conclusion of the war and when peace treaties have been signed."

Mr. Samson and most other cartographers call on consuls almost every week to find how things are getting on. They want to put the most recent changes on the map. Consuls are only one source of new map information. Cartographers keep in constant touch with governments all over the world, with geographic societies, expeditions into wild and unknown country. They maintain contacts with builders of canals, tunnels, bridges, railroads, steamship lines. They read newspapers and other periodicals with microscopic eye, check and recheck at every possible source before they go to the drawing board.

Wars, Mr. Samson said, have been the greatest single factor in the growth and development of maps. Military men mark every hill and every tiny valley before they move their armies. Navies carefully chart the waters.

"Europe is the best mapped quarter of the world," Mr. Samson said, "because so many wars have been fought on it."

Mr. Samson said thousands of miles of United States territory remain unmapped except in crude fashion. This is true, too, of Asia, South America, and Africa.

Place names on a map, he explained, may mean merely that a traveler or explorer or military leader has given those names to something he can identify—a stunted tree, a colored rock—something to guide him back.

Cartographers take orders, incidentally, for queer kinds of maps. Mr. Samson once made a thirty-six-inch globe for the American Tobacco Company. It showed where the company gets its tobacco in different parts of the world.

Authors of travel books, explorers, and geologists come in with special orders. They submit notes or surveyors' data and leave the cartographer to interpret them.

One of the queer maps in Mr. Samson's twenty years' experience was a "Map of the Myth-Lands of Mesopotamia, Israel, Egypt, and Greece." It was an interesting thing. It made spots before the eyes. It showed Atlantis, the land of the Amazons, Eden, the Apsu of the Babylonians, the Sea of Atalontas (the original Atlantic Ocean), and violent blue and magenta lands that would make a philatelist's eyes water. Mr. Samson did this map for the late Professor Fessenden.

"It took a lot out of me," he said.

Mapmakers patiently keep answering questions by mail and telephone. People want to know, for example, what is an analemma? What's the altitude of this hamlet where I intend to spend my vacation? One woman in Belmore, N. H., wanted to know could the map people tell her the name of the witch doctor on Cocos Island who sold her nine dollars' worth of medicine for five dollars eleven years ago when she had the misery? She had lost the address.

An earnest fellow in Rhode Island can't understand why Massachusetts will not cede Cape Cod to Rhode Island. He thinks that right now Rhode Island is not big enough to take up a governor's working day. He inked in his proposed change.

Routine questions are apt to go to Mr. Samson. He knows, for example, that an analemma is a graduated scale of sun declination and time equation. You see it on globular atlases. Looks like a twist of wool.

Cartographers earn anywhere from $50 to $250 a week. Most of them have engineering background, art-school background, or both. They put in a lot of overtime during war periods. Sometimes this all goes to waste. When Germany anschlussed Austria, the company had to throw away 30,000 brand-new maps. A recent South American map raised a fuss because it did not please both sides in the perpetual boundary war between Colombia and Ecuador.

"Had to make separate maps for each country before customs men down there would let them pass," Mr. Samson said.

He spoke modestly of far places he had visited in his youth—Burma, Siberia, South America, Trinidad; how he seemed to have a knack for finding his way in and out of all kinds of wilderness.

"But take Brooklyn and the Bronx," Mr. Samson said. "There's a remarkable thing. My sense of direction fails me in the city. My wife has to lead me about or I get hopelessly lost."

Steve Is King

YOU WOULD not take Steve for a king. You would look at his three hundred pounds, at his soiled heavy-silk shirt and his thick fingers, and you would say he was the town butcher on a day off. But Steve is a king. He is King of the Red Dress Gypsies, a tribe out of Russia. Steve thinks altogether there must be 10,500 of them in the United States, Canada, and Mexico.

In Miss Morris' evening class in University Settlement, King Steve told how he made up his mind that his tribesmen must go to school.

He said, "Our women we do not send yet. We must have a trial. We must sit down and we must talk this thing over about our women. Most of the men they will say no. They will say 'What the hell?' "

Swart gypsy men slouched into the classroom, one by one. They wore pink shirts and shirts that once had been white. They had no ties. They were bare-throated. Their dark jackets were sleek with the drip of many dinners. Under Steve's grim, heavy-lidded stare each gypsy called awkward greeting to the teacher.

"Good evening, Miss Morris," they said.

"Good evening, gentlemen."

This seemed to please the King. His eyelids closed

down on his embedded eyes in a slow gesture of intense satisfaction. Hoarsely he whispered, "I get them dam-good education, by jee."

Spring breathed gently at the classroom windows, lifted the soiled white curtains in voluptuous billows. The class noisily pawed over notebooks, studied the words on the blackboard.

Miss Morris had trouble trying to teach them the difference between "sit" and "seat." To them the variation was subtle. Finally, Miss Morris thought they caught on.

She said, "Now, who can tell me the difference between 'sit' and 'seat'?"

A broad-shouldered man, built like Firpo, lumbered out of his seat with one hand eagerly waving. This was John, a Prince of the Red Dress. He beamed with self-confidence.

"Miss Teacher," he bellowed triumphantly. " 'Sit' an' 'seat' is a difference like this: 'sit' an' 'seat' is two diff'rence chairs."

A new pupil came in, a little belated. He was a short, paunchy man with a walrus mustache. A fat, black cigar stuck out from the fronds. It gave off a violent smoke. Miss Morris waggled a finger in coy reprimand.

She said, "Mr. Petro, it is not nice to smoke cigars in the classroom. You must put it out."

The fat man seemed dumfounded. A storm cloud shadowed his features. He stared at the teacher. The King spoke sharply. His nose made a noise like a trumpet. Mr. Petro sullenly ground out the light and stuck the butt in his jacket.

Miss Morris confided she lets the class choose its own reading. One gypsy, built like John Steinbeck's Lennie, triumphantly read from a newspaper clipping. It was an

ad for Mickey Rooney in the motion picture, *Young Tom Edison*. Lennie sat down all hot with his effort.

Hoarsely he called to a friend, "Dam fine stoff what I read."

"Sit" and "seat" were revived. Miss Morris wanted a sentence with both these words in it. The King's bull-necked son was sure he could do it. He got up in his place. His glance showed contempt for his uncultured fellows.

"Miss Teacher," he said with perfect assurance, "I set on a chair. I set down on that chair. I sit in a seat."

Miss Morris beamed. She said, "That's just fine. I think that is splendid."

Bull-neck seemed bursting with pride.

Before he sat down he added with gusto, "I want to sit comfortable. That's how I do."

Miss Morris ignored this.

The King hoarsely told how helpless his people are. No horses to swap, no copper to work on, no tinker jobs to be had. Profanely he put the blame on aluminum. He said that aluminum ware ruined all gypsy smiths. The King said that for 600 years his people have never gone to school. Once, in Russia, a perverted tribesman learned how to read and to write. He was shunned as a madman, the King assured me. Now things are different. Gypsies must learn how to read and to write, though they hate it. There seems no other way. The King, when he made this decision, wrote to the White House, and Mrs. Roosevelt—"She's one fine woman"—suggested WPA schooling.

Miss Morris tried to explain to the class what she meant by "republic." One of the gypsies thought that he got it. He said, "A republic, that is a president. All Republicans they must be president."

His head went down in his shoulders and his arms came up, with palms outward, when Miss Morris said he didn't quite have the idea. She said a republic is a country that has no king. The fat, cigar-smoking scholar shot up his hand.

"Missus," he said, "we got a king. Steve is our King."

Steve bowed modestly. The blandest of smiles slid over his features.

"Steve," he said contentedly, "is King."

The Capuchins

THE HEAVY oak doors closed. They shut out street cries, the shrill voices of East Side children, the discolored and untidy rookeries of Pitt and Stanton Streets. At once you stood in another world, in another age. Dim halls, religious statues faintly touched by late-afternoon light, the sound of sandals on black and white marble squares. This was the Monastery of the Capuchin Friars.

When it was built, seventy-two years ago, the lower East Side was *Kleines Deutschland*. Everything has changed. The East Side *Saengerhalle* are gone. Gone, too, are the *Studentenhalle* and Becker's Hall.

A tall friar came down the shadowed corridor. His sandals slapped gently on the marble. He wore the Capuchins' brown habit and the pyramidal hood of this austere order. His cassock was caught up at the waist with thick white cord. Sun, diffused by the mellow stained-glass window, softly gilded the tall monk's grave features. It struck a tiny glitter from his silver spectacles, made faint halos in his hair and in his beard. When he spoke his voice was rich in timber. He said, "I am Father Edwin."

Father Edwin spoke of the great change in the parish, how it flourished threescore and ten years ago and how it waned as the neighborhood changed. Now it has some 600 families.

The monk said: "But the old ones return. They come in August to the *Gemeindefest,* the Yard Festival. They come at Christmas. They do not forget the old parish."

The hooded friars still move through the streets on brief errands. They visit the sick or go out at night on emergency calls. On longer journeys they put aside the habit.

"It is more convenient so," Father Edwin said, "but in the old country Capuchins never put aside the habit."

Ten Capuchins tend the spiritual needs of the parish of Our Lady of Sorrows. Seven are friars. Three are lay brothers. All are bearded, as St. Francis was. Father Benedict is their superior. Father Edwin opened a great oaken door. He said, "We enter the enclosure here."

The way was down another marble corridor. The sandals started whispering echoes. An ancient hall clock gave the hour in tuneful melancholy that sounded like bass notes on the harp. They padded at the old oak walls, sighed into sad silence. Father Edwin opened another door. He said, "We go into the church."

The church was hushed. In the dome the light of waning day lay on seven warmly painted panels—"The Seven Dolors." Here and there, the paint seemed to be flaking away.

"It is peeled," Father Edwin said. "The old Penzarozi, the painter who touched up these panels when we had our golden jubilee, he comes here. He stands here and he weeps, this Penzarozi."

In this church the monks chant their offices in Latin.

Father Edwin said, "We are up at dawn, at five o'clock, and at our divine offices. Seven times a day."

He looked about him, a shadowy figure in the shadowy edifice. The altar was gray in twilight. In the brass sanctuary lamp steady flame burned in the ruby bowl. The refectory had the look of some medieval hall. Brother Accursius, the porter, gray-bearded and rosy-cheeked, thumped the thick oak table and the thick oaken benches.

"In your house," he said, "you do not have such a table, hey?"

He brought out the wooden plates on which the monks have their meat. These are pale with age and much washing. Many are cracked but it is difficult to replace them.

Father Edwin said: "It is so with sandals, too. We had a brother cobbler, but he died. We had a parishioner who was a cobbler, but he is gone, too."

In the old kitchen, Brother Louis fussed with meats and vegetables for dinner. He barely looked up. Brother Accursius set out the beer flagons.

The step from the Hall of the Capuchins to the old stone stoop outdoors was a step from a distant yesterday. The shrill voices of East Side children, after the monastic calm and stillness, seemed curiously vitreous.

You felt, somehow, that you had achieved, awake, a spanning of vast time, something that ordinarily happens only in a dream.

West Side

That Was West Forty-seventh

SUBURBAN peace and quiet lay over the West Forties at daybreak on New Year's Day, 1862, when the district's police answered the first roll call in the new station house, proudly described in journals of that time as "a superior, airy structure." Wearing warm jerkins under their navy-blue greatcoats, and therefore looking curiously lumpy, the bearded patrol dispersed to windy posts in a landscape broken by a patchwork of frame houses, rambling shacks, and, down by the North River, faded red factories and abattoirs. Captain Johannes C. Slott wrote his signature in the virgin blotter with heavy-handed but ornate script, turned the desk over to Sergeant Potter, and headed down-street with his coattails billowing and slapping behind him. The Sergeant took up the station-house pen, frowned in ponderous thought, and finally got an idea. He wrote, "Captain Slott left the station house."

The building that Captain Slott walked out of that first day still stands on the north side of West Forty-seventh Street, a few hundred feet east of Ninth Avenue. It is as ugly and plain as it must have been on the day it was built. Several years ago about $50,000 was spent on repairs. Metal ceilings, new floors, and some new plumbing were put in, the ancient woodwork was varnished for perhaps the hundredth time, and the iron treads on the spiral staircase that leads to the upper floors were renewed once more.   But nothing could disguise the fact that West Forty-seventh, as it is called, was doomed.   It was condemned by the city a few years ago and present activities transferred to a new station house in West Fifty-fourth Street.   The blotter, which has always been the soul of any police station, has been preserved, however; it is stored today in the basement record room of the old station house, a cumbersome stack of fat, leather-bound volumes.   You can read there the story of West Forty-seventh, from its first day on to the time when it got to be known as the busiest police station in the world.

On that first day, it is reasonable to suppose, Sergeant Potter stood by the window and watched white-sailed schooners and barks, heavy-laden, beating upriver three blocks to the west.   Every now and then he walked to the pot-bellied stove and warmed his hands.   There was, of course, no telephone, and even the magnetic telegraph, a fresh wonder of the period, had not been installed, though there had been talk of it.   Four hours passed quietly but for the howl of the wind before the first official customer came in.   "Lost girl brought in by a citizen who found her in Eighth Avenue," the Sergeant wrote in the blotter. He did not record her name.   An hour later he added a footnote to the entry, "Returned to her parents."   No further entries were made by Sergeant Potter that day.

At five o'clock, Sergeant O'Connor took over.   The calligraphic urge was on him, too, and for want of something more official he wrote, "Weather clear and beautiful." There were to be many such entries when the moon or the languor of spring raised emotional tides in the Celtic souls of West Forty-seventh's desk men.   Just before six o'clock, Officer Pinckney came in with the precinct's first prisoner. "Delia Maher," wrote the Sergeant. "Thirty years, Irish, servant, single, drunk and disorderly, reads and writes." The early blotters are always specific about a prisoner's literacy. Delia Maher spent the night in a station-house cell and a notation on the blotter tells the disposition of her case: "Taken before Justice Kelly, Jefferson Market Court, and committed for five days."

Officer Pinckney, who had taken up Delia, was to become the precinct's most zealous cop. He cluttered the station house with stray hogs, wandering cows, was forever staggering in with lost properties, and was a fanatic at reporting out-of-order street lamps. Broadway in the Forties used gas. The lights would go out in a high wind, or sometimes the larrikins, up from the river shanties, snuffed them out with bricks. It wasn't Pinckney who got the prize entry the opening day, however, but Officer Armstrong, who drove up to the station-house door at ten o'clock that night with a two-seater Rockaway "waggon" and reported that he had found it, abandoned, at Forty-second Street and Ninth Avenue. The horse was put up for the night in Skiff's Livery Stable, next door to the station house. On the following day, at noon, Tom Welch, a truck farmer, claimed the horse and the rig. Some hooligans had driven it off while Welch was clearing the dust from his throat with a noggin of rum in a Forty-second Street tavern.

The second day was duller than the first. A screaming nor'wester had howled in overnight and boats were snapped from their moorings. Ice cakes crunched in the river. The streets were deserted. Officer Pinckney had one entry: "3:15 A.M. Found door to carpet factory, corner Fifty-eighth Street and Eighth Avenue, open. Secured it." At 7:30 A.M. Officer Haire stuck his frozen beard in the station-house door and bellowed to Sergeant Aldis that he had caught a stray black horse. The Sergeant looked at Haire's prize and wrote in the blotter, "Found, a large black horse, switch tail and star on forehead, with curb harness on." Later he wrote, "Returned to Peter Farley, claimant, corner Sixty-third Street and Eighth Avenue." This horse became a nuisance. Subsequent entries show he was forever turning up on Haire's post, Broadway in the low Fifties.

West Forty-seventh's first mass arrest came on the third morning. At 1 A.M., Officers Jacquin and Bennett, from a downtown precinct, had arrested a man in Beekman Street as he rattled over the cobblestones in a light rig filled with boxing paraphernalia—belts, shoes, sponges, drawers, surgical plaster, and water bottles. The prisoner had confessed that this was to be used in a fight to the finish between the bare-knuckle men, Winkle and Elliott, for a purse of $300, somewhere on the Jersey shore near Weehawken. A police rider galloped from the downtown precinct to West Forty-seventh to warn Captain Slott.

Slott sent Sergeant Aldis and a platoon to the Weehawken Ferry House at Forty-second Street and told them to wait there, concealed, until the sporting gentlemen showed up. At 6:15 A.M. a buggy caravan came jolting over the rutted, hard-frozen road, led by one George Glancy, who kept an inn on upper Broadway. When a crowd of a hundred and fifty had assembled, Aldis and his men tucked their beards in their coats and engaged the "fancy"—the term for sports in the sixties—in hot encounter. When it was over, Aldis had fifteen prisoners, all more or less damaged. His blotter entry is a model of simplicity: "Second Platoon sent to Forty-second Street Ferry in charge of Sergeant Aldis to apprehend some prize fighters that had just arrived in carriages." He added the names of the prisoners and the notation, "The above were all arrested on a charge of going to attend a prize fight." The final entry shows that the sports were discharged next day in Jefferson Market Court. Their lawyer represented that they were going on a moonlight excursion, not to the Elliott-Winkle set-to. The fight, incidentally, finally was held in Weehawken in July of that year. It lasted through ninety-five rounds of what Mr. Greeley's *Tribune* called "extreme brutality and fierceness." Winkle fell and Elliott tried to choke him to death. Winkle's adherents thereupon kicked out Elliott's teeth. The official verdict was "No decision."

After the prisoners had been booked, the station house had a slow day except for a bit of excitement recorded in the blotter by Captain Slott at "eight o'clock plus fifteen minutes" that morning: "Captain Slott was the First Platoon returned from the fire in Forty-eighth Street and reported that the fire originated in a smokehouse belonging to Jacob Lang, 275 West Forty-eighth Street. Damage about Fifty Dollars. Fully insured by the Hamilton Insurance Company." The only other entry before the blotter closed for the night was "A citizen reports the Croton water running in No. 69 West Forty-first Street, on the first floor." The Croton water system was still a novelty to householders and leaks rated a line or two in the annals of West Forty-seventh.

At ten-thirty the next night, just after the desk sergeant had penned, "Cold, snowing fast," Officer George Taylor kicked open the front door of the station house and proceeded to undo a thick bundle beside the pot-bellied stove. In due time the sergeant took a quill in hand again and with handsome flourishes composed a fitting entry: "George Warner, 227 West Fiftieth Street, discovered a male child six months old, at the basement door of his residence. Officer Taylor brought it to the station house. On examination we found a slip of paper with the following: 'This is Alick Warner's son (Young Johnny). I hope you will take good care of it as I can't afford to do it,' pinned to the dress." The sergeant used the ʃ-shaped s throughout. Apparently this form was optional, because some of the desk men always wrote the letter that way, while others used the modern version. What became of Young Johnny the blotter does not tell. He'd be seventy-seven now if he were still around.

During West Forty-seventh's earlier history, criminals in the precinct were of a simple, understandable type and crime had a bucolic touch. The first larceny recorded in the blotter, for example, is: "Jan. 7, 1862: 8:45 P.M. Frances Coyle, 16, Reads and Writes, Stealing geese value $2, has 11 cents. Complainant, Thomas McKeon, 11 West Fiftieth Street. Taken before Justice Cossitt. Held in default of $300 bail."

Traffic accidents were not sensational in the sixties. The first of these recorded occurred during a snowstorm seven days after the station house opened. "Three P.M. Fire Engine 36, proceeding down Eighth Avenue to an alarm of fire, when crossing Forty-seventh Street one of its runners maimed Francois Mulhern, 22 years, born in Ireland. He accidentally fell, the engine passing over him, injuring him. He was conveyed to Bellevue Hospital." The first speeder recorded in the precinct was Charlie Fent, nineteen, a butcher's apprentice, who was arrested on September 24, 1862, for "fast and furious" driving in West Forty-fifth Street in his master's cart. The complaint was lodged by Catherine Heischer, a Forty-fifth Street housewife, who was almost run down by the mad butcher boy.

Assault and battery was the favorite diversion of the hot-blooded Irish who lived in the precinct. They relied almost entirely on their knuckles and rarely used guns. Even the cops walked their beats without firearms except on special occasions—during riots, for example, which were infrequent. The station-house blotters are replete with brief entries of heroic brawls and tell of lusty skull thumping, eye gouging, and shin booting. Fatalities were scarce. Wife beating was fairly common, and sometimes the bachelors were a bit hard on their lady companions in the beer saloons. One blunt report relates that "at five minutes past seven o'clock, Jan. 1, 1863, Elizabeth Penton, aged 37, was kicked in the face by some man at Ninth Avenue and Fifty-third Street. Taken to Bellevue Hospital with a broken jaw." Another tells how August Wegler, 448 West Fifty-third Street, was arrested for "disturbing the peace by beating Sadie Roher on the head with a stave from a hay bale." Once in a while someone might draw a dirk in the heat of argument, but not often. Officer Haire, who seems to have had a gift for getting in on knifings when he wasn't rounding up stray mares, began to tire of blade play. He reduced his reports, after a while, to a mere line or two. For example, "8:50 P.M. Fracas in back room of porter house, 47th and Eighth Avenue. John Gaffney stabbed twice in breast by Thomas Walsh."

During the sixties, construction gained and the West Forties began to lose their pastoral look, but Captain Slott's men still knew most of the neighbors by sight, especially the steady tipplers. James Brown, a blacksmith, was a frequent Saturday-night guest in one of the back cells. They would dump him through the station-house door from a wheelbarrow that came conveniently up to the level of the threshold, book him as "D. and D.," the abbreviation for "Drunk and Disorderly," and on Sunday morning Judge Kelly would discharge him in time for him to get to church service. Another of the neighbors who could not contain their week-end beer without winding up in one of the stone cells was an illiterate wench ("cannot read or write"), only twenty-two years old, named Cinderella Adams. Poor Cinderella would take her three days for "gross intoxication" and be back again within a fortnight.

In mid-January of 1862 the station house had got its telegraph line and the sergeants were making the most of it. At noon each day the Central Office would flash signal "10," the official notification that noon had arrived, and any eccentricities of the station-house clock would be recorded in the blotter: "Feb. 13, Clock one minute slow by C.O. signal 10," or "Monday, Jan. 20, Clock two minutes fast by signal from Central Office." The telegraph also gave official sunset time, which was duly entered in the book: "Jan. 12, 1862, Five o'clock P.M. Sunset by telegraph. Very foggy and drisling rain—Sergeant Gross." Sergeant Gross was the worst speller in West Forty-seventh. He always wrote "stabb" instead of "stab" and "excuze" for "excuse."

Although many of the homes in the lower part of Manhattan had gas fixtures, the West Forties seemed to adopt the new service with reluctance. Lamp accidents are recorded in the blotters in great numbers. One on January 12, 1862, is typical: "10:30 P.M. Hannah Shea, employed as servant in the family of Mrs. G., 263 West 43rd Street, while passing downstairs carrying a fluid lamp, the lamp exploded scattering the fluid all over her, setting her clothes afire and burning her severly about the neck, face and hands. Officer Pinckney was early in attendance and rendered all possible assistance." It seems only fair that Pinckney's bustling eagerness to serve was eventually rewarded. This is disclosed by a blotter entry of October 10, 1862: "Officer Pinckney promoted to Roundsman. Transferred to Thirty-first Precinct. Captain Bogart."

Despite the first building boom in the uptown precinct, all manner of livestock roamed the streets. Cows lowed and bellowed in what is now Columbus Circle, and pigs snuffled for dainties in the gutters of upper Broadway and in the river streets. On January 29, 1863, at 8:15 P.M., "Officer Connell reported that about 7:30 P.M. a cow knocked down Mr. John Aiken at the corner of Fiftieth Street and Eighth Avenue. Mr. A. taken to residence, Fifty-fourth Street between Eight and Broadway. Cow at last secured at Forty-seventh and Broadway and given to the owner, Mr. Fox." At dusk on October 9, "Officer Lamson found a live hog in the street corner, Tenth Avenue and Forty-third, which he drove down to the slaughter house of Messrs. Lippincott and Martin, 511 Tenth Avenue. Hog weighs about 250 or 300 pounds."

Lovers who ventured into what the blotter repeatedly refers to as "the Central Park" were always getting into difficulties. Footpads overtook them and horse thieves sometimes stole their rigs. An entry at 1 A.M., February 5, tells about "a lady and a gentleman" (the cops were somewhat more respectful toward citizens in the sixties than now) who had come to the station house to report the theft of a bay mare and a sleigh in one of the more remote parts of the Park. It is recorded that the young man carried in his arms "a warm sleigh robe." He asked the desk sergeant to notify Pelton's Stables, at Twenty-seventh Street and Broadway, if the rig turned up.

The first holdup reported at West Forty-seventh was at 3 A.M., February 5, 1862, when Patrick Matthews and a girl who said she was Alice Grey of Greene Street (it turned out later she was Kate Smith of Spring Street) were set upon in Broadway on their way home by sleigh after a night of it in Straukmann's Beer Garden at Striker's Bay, over on the North River at Ninety-sixth Street. Both were knifed and, by the testimony of the blotter, "were brought to this station in very feeble condition." Matthews died and John Reynolds, an Irish potboy in a West Side drammery, was sent to prison for the crime. On Washington's birthday the same year, the station house got its first burglar: "Thomas Moran, 21, on complaint of William Lewis, 164 West Forty-ninth Street. Taken with 12 cents, two lead pipes, a key-knife, silk kerchief and two candlesticks. Committed by Justice Q'bush." All the sergeants used "Q'bush" for this jurist, whose name was Quackenbush.

When spring came to the West Side the blotter reflected the vernal urge. Epidemics of wanderlust resulted in lost children, and the number of stray cows, pigs, and horses went up amazingly. In midsummer, swimming and fishing parties swarmed the rocky beaches along the river and a great number of drownings were reported. Life was more leisurely then and sometimes the cops of West Forty-seventh were late entering these fatalities in the record. One river tragedy that occurred on Friday, August 8, for example, did not get into the book until Sunday. "Friday evening last," says the belated note, "a party of six ladies and gentlemen crossed the river to Weehawken. On their return, when near the foot of Forty-seventh Street, the tide was so strong as to dash their boat against the pier, upsetting and drowning one of the party. He was Dr. Ingraham, who lived at 3 Striker's Cottages [Fifty-second Street]. Body not recovered."

Through these years soldiers thronged the lower part of Manhattan. Deserters heading for open country beyond Bloomingdale had to pass through West Forty-seventh's bailiwick and Captain Slott's men caught a lot of them. On the Fourth of July, Sergeant Aldis, in a spasm of patriotism, decorated the blotter with red ink, making fancy scrolls and curlicues along the margins. Nine days later, Captain Slott and his command were going without sleep, doing their part to put down the fierce Draft Riots. These started on July 13, 1863, and the men of West Forty-seventh were shifted to more congested points downtown to help the military and the lower-city police. Scattered notes in the blotter show the progress of the riots in the home precinct: "July 15: Mary Ann Carmody, aged 12, residing in Forty-second Street below Eleventh Avenue, was shot dead during the attack on the military by the Rioters at Forty-second Street and Eleventh Avenue, at 8 o'c, P.M." "4:30 P.M. John Sheehey, aged 35, residing at Sixty-fifth Street and Tenth Avenue, was found lying inside the garden gate in Forty-eight Street between Ninth and Tenth Avenues with a pistol shot wound in the back." "Sent Roundsman Roberts and six policemen to special duty with the military at the bullet factory at the foot of Fifty-second Street and N. River." "Captain Slott and the First Platoon dispersed a mob at Forty-second Street and Tenth Avenue." "Sergeant Aldis broke up an assemblage of rioters at Forty-seventh Street and Seventh Avenue" and turned back a gang of drunken water-front hoodlums who were about to burn the Ward and Camp-bell houses at Forty-second Street and Tenth Avenue. The rioters burned the Weehawken ferry house and the gasworks just beside it. For a fortnight the Captain and his men went around recovering loot taken by the mobs, and the station house was filled with it. Each item is listed in the blotter.

The last riot booking was an arrest at noon on July 30 by Officer Files: "Fergus Brennan, 35, Irish, Reads and Writes, charged with being a leader of the Rioters by Mr. Gardner T. White, 82 West Forty-third Street. Held in $2,000 bail by Justice Kelly." Until this disorder, the newspapers of the city had paid virtually no attention to West Forty-seventh because it was too far from the urban district. They had not given a line to the opening of the station house and there had been no crimes big enough to make it worth a reporter's while to come so far uptown. After the riots, though, all the newspapers had pieces about the part that Captain Slott and his men had played in putting down the hooligans. Their exploits even got into the first comprehensive history of the New York Police Department, Augustine G. Costello's *Our Protectors,* which came out in 1885. "The Twenty-second (this was then West Forty-seventh's official precinct designation) closed its riot service brilliantly," wrote Mr. Costello.

Meanwhile, within the precinct boundaries, little changes forecast the great changes that were to come to what would eventually be Times Square and the theater belt. These changes the blotter of West Forty-seventh quietly absorbed, and you can find them now, including records of the district's first beggar, its first swindler, and its first cutpurse. The riots, unfortunately, quite overshadowed another great historic event that went into the blotter on the night of July 11, 1863: "Officer Connell reported that at about 10:45 this day a woman named Catherine Norman, living at 98 West Forty-ninth Street, was shot by her husband (Charles Norman) who had unexpectedly returned from New Orleans. The ball passed up her right nostril. She fell insensible and died at 3:15." Viewed in the light of twentieth-century journalism, this was a red-letter day. The love-nest murder had come to West Forty-seventh.

The West Forty-seventh Street police station, having wasted its youth and middle life in semibucolic languor, was compelled at the advanced age of seventy-seven years to accommodate its tired frame to a feverish pace. In the beginning, when only a few transients plodded the dusty side streets and cobbled highways of the West Forties, it warmed itself in the sun and took things easy. As city life in the booming area became more complex, it came upon an unhappy dotage. Until the precinct activities were transferred to West Fifty-fourth Street, several years ago, it served the restless millions who swarmed through the theater and night-club district, and a dozen men worked hard to document its annual business of 15,000 arrests, 30,000 summonses, 8000 ambulance calls, and 3000 accident cases.

Forty or so captains commanded West Forty-seventh. Most of them were colorless personalities who managed to keep a semblance of peace and quiet on the belligerent West Side. The first captains got around $2000 a year. Today a captain's pay is $5000. West Forty-seventh's outstanding captain was Tom Killilea, a Galway man born just a century ago, who commanded the precinct from 1870 to 1892. He was a giant, with a walrus mustache and fists like sacks of sand, who disliked subtlety and lace-edged legalistic fumbling. He preferred to administer the law with his hands and his thick-soled brogues. The sight of uncallused palms brought a cold light to his blue eyes. Street loafers knew this and fled before his ponderous tread. Tales had gone around of his trick of taking four men at a time and squeezing them with his strong arms until their bones ached. But down by the river, when, so legend has it, even the kitten mewed in deep register, the brawnier larrikins scoffed at such stories. Three days after the Captain took over, five of them sent a boy to West Forty-seventh with a challenge. They offered to take the Captain on, one at a time, with clubs or without, all holds unrestricted. Killilea sent back word he would meet all five at once with bare knuckles.

Men left their work next day to be on hand for the fray, and women came too, with the suds still warm on their arms. The Captain brushed them aside like a harvester moving through wheat and entered the ring, which was a twenty-foot space closed off by idle carts and drays in Forty-ninth Street just west of Eleventh Avenue. The thuds and thumps of bodies hitting the turf and a prodigious heaving and grunting went on for twelve minutes. Then the crowd fell back in awed silence and the Captain walked out, rips and tears in his clothes and on his knuckles. The water-front micks were all on the ground, with lumps like yams on their heads and their faces. From that time on, Killilea was master.

The Captain's widow, until her death a few years ago, lived alone in the Hotel Flanders on West Forty-seventh Street, two blocks east of the station house, and the walls of her suite were covered with pictures of her doughty husband. For all his great strength, she used to recall, he was a meek and gentle Christian. "He would never have me look upon him," she would relate to her friends, "when he was splashed, so he worked out this plan: he would send one of his men before him to the Killilea house at Eight Avenue and Fifty-second Street. 'Give my fondest to Mrs. K.,' he would tell him, 'and have her run a hot bath. She's not to come down till I call.'" Mrs. Killilea said this arrangement always worked out all right.

When he was not putting down the bellicose river men, the Captain warred against vice. The late Frank Farrell, who was to become owner of the New York Yankees, lived across the way from the station house and joined with other noisy urchins in hooting at ladies-of-the-town who were brought up from the river shanties and from Astor's Flats on Broadway after periodic raids. The Captain was stern with loose women, and the blotters reflect his crusading activity. Within a week after he took command, which was on June 6, 1870, one of his desk men made an entry: "A lost young woman restored. A stray young German woman, Frances Augusta Steinbock, aged 16, who had been eight months in this city and has been living at the Institution of the Good Shepherd, was induced to leave there by a woman who took her to house of prostitution. She was taken back to the Institution by Officer Schroeder."

The precinct had a sensational murder on April 28, 1871. This was the first crime in West Forty-seventh's jurisdiction that made front-page news and earned the distinction of a journalistic label. It was called the "Hook Killing." The blotter tells the story rather modestly. It says, "10 P.M. Avery D. Putnam, 40, residing in 3 Cottage Place, on stage No. 48 of the Broadway Line, in company with some ladies, got into altercation with a man on the

front platform and in getting off the stage at the corner
of Forty-sixth Street and Seventh Avenue was struck on
the head with some heavy instrument, fracturing his skull.
Attended by Surgeon Raborg and by his orders sent to
St. Luke's Hospital in ambulance. The driver of the
stage, Patrick Cunningham, under arrest as an accomplice.
Witnesses: Conductor, Fred. E. Goldthwaite; M. A. Duval,
702 Broadway; George B. Parkson."

Avery Putnam was a quiet and highly respected provision merchant. When he died in the hospital, three
days after the assault, it developed that he was a martyr
to his sense of chivalry. He had fought to defend the
honor of Mabel Duval, daughter of the witness M. A. Duval, who was a French dressmaker. William Foster, a
former conductor on the Broadway Line, had leered at
Miss Duval's pretty ankles through the door of the stage
and Mr. Putnam had shut the door in his face. Thereupon Foster hit the provision merchant with a car hook,
a device used for lifting the whiffletree. Mr. Greeley's
paper fanned public wrath, and his and other journals
were filled with red-hot letters about "Broadway Beasts"
and "Fiends who ride the stages in human form." Cunningham was freed, but Foster was eventually hanged in
the yard of the Tombs. At his special request, Captain
Killilea, who had saved him from a lynching mob during
his trial, walked to the gallows with him. Mrs. Killilea
often cited this as an example of the Captain's warmness
of heart.

Aside from routine assault-and-battery cases, the precinct was comparatively quiet for a long time after the
"Hook Killing." The water-front gangs and the shanty
muggs near Central Park, where goats and occasional cows
still browsed, sometimes stirred in rebellion, but always

regretted it. The neighborhood was beginning to change, too. Ramshackle lean-tos and sagging huts gave way to flat houses, and something like a faint veneer of culture spread over the northern end of the precinct. Captain Killilea rode herd on his men in stern efforts to keep them perfectly disciplined. A blotter entry on Decoration Day, 1871, typical of a great many scattered through the carefully written pages, shows just how stern he was. "Violation of Rules," it says. "Officer Hicinbotham was standing in conversation with a citizen on corner Forty-third Street and Eleventh Avenue from 4:05 till 4:15 P.M. Sunday, May 29, Witness, Sergeant Roberts." An entry on July 13 says, "Captain Killilea charges Patrolman John Lynch being in conversation with a woman on Ninth Avenue, between Fifty-third and Fifty-fourth Streets from 11:05 to 11:20 P.M. while on patrol duty—Witness, Captain Killilea and Sergeant Miller."

The Captain despised firearms and would have none of them himself. He suspended one of his patrolmen who used a pistol to bring down an escaping thug instead of getting him with his bare hands. Sometimes this prejudice made things rather hard for the men, as indicated by a blotter entry on June 12, 1870: "About 11 P.M. Officer Fay arrested a man on the corner of Eight Avenue and Forty-third Street for Disorderly Conduct when the prisoner's friends attacked the officer, beating him on the head and rescuing the prisoner. They made their escape. The officer's injuries are severe." Captain Killilea was not swayed by such incidents. He subbornly stuck to his orders against gunplay.

Lowing steers and bleating sheep, bound for river-front cattle pens in the precinct, remained a traffic problem through the seventies and eighties. On June 16, 1870.

the blotter tells how, at 7:30 A.M., "Horace Day, age 5, was knocked down and seriously injured by some runaway cattle, corner Forty-second Street and Ninth Avenue," and, on another day, how "Daniel Buckley, 724 Eleventh Avenue, reports he has a stray red-and-white cow which he found in Fifty-third Street near Eleventh Avenue." On the same day "Officer Casey reports a sorrel horse, white hind foot, astray at Sixth Avenue and Forty-fifth Street," and "S. A. Braddock, 175 West Forty-fifth Street, complains that a sick cow has been turned into his vacant lot at Forty-fifth Street near Broadway." Beef steers and lambs were forever stampeding on the water front and making a break for what was to become the Great White Way.

Runaway horses caused a lot of excitement on Broadway, and the blotters, every few weeks through the seventies, eighties, and nineties, had long accounts of them. An entry dated June 18, 1870, reads, "At 9½ o'c P.M. Charles E. Jenkins of 49 East Forty-first Street left his team and wagon, containing his lady, in front of the Central Market, corner of Forty-ninth Street and Broadway. While he entered to make a purchase the horses became frightened and ran away, up Broadway, at a furious rate. The lady had the presence of mind to jump out and escaped injury. The horses continued to run up Broadway and shortly after the wagon was broken to pieces. The horses were caught at Fifty-third Street and Broadway by Officers Monahan and Curran."

Here and there, throughout the Killilea dynasty, the blotters can be found to speak of quaint odds and ends of mishap and property loss that give the flavor of the period: "June 22, 1870: Officer Connell reports having in charge a row boat named Maud Muller, found adrift off Forty-second Street by a man named John Harrigan, 631 West Forty-second Street." "July 3: Reckless Firing. Between Five and Six this P.M. some unknown parties discharged a gun or pistol, the ball from which entered the window, passing through the partition into the dining room of the German Sisters of Charity on Forty-ninth Street, between Ninth and Tenth Avenues." On this day and the next the blotter was filled with Fourth-of-July casualties.

Smiths still worked their bellows throughout the West Forties, but sometimes were not quite so even-tempered as Longfellow's hero. On July 15, 1872, at 11 A.M., "John Curtin and George Gaillard, both horse shoers, had a dispute in the blacksmith shop at 209 West Fifty-seventh Street. Gaillard took a red-hot iron out of the forge and assaulted Curtin, injuring him severely about the face and breast. He is still at large."

Ten years passed between the "Hook Killing" and the next big event in West Forty-seventh. At nine o'clock in the morning of May 24, 1881, as the blotter tells it, "Hattie J. Hull, aged 25 years, residing at 1558 Broadway, attempted suicide by throwing herself in front of a train at the elevated railroad station at Sixth Avenue and West Fiftieth Street and sustained a fracture of the hip and other internal injuries. Cause unknown. Reported by Roundsman John Dunn." It was the first reported suicide attempt of its kind in the district, and when it turned out that Miss Hull had been betrayed by a customs official who was married, the newspapers erupted against him. He ought to get, they agreed, "his just deserts." For some reason, the papers never told whether he did or not.

In 1892 Captain Killilea was transferred to Harlem, where he subdued the Frog Hollow gang with much the same methods he had used on the West Side river gangs.

Ten years later he retired and tried to live in quiet in Forest Hills, but he was always homesick for Manhattan. He died in 1906 in the Hotel Theresa, on upper Seventh Avenue. He had long outlived his achievements as keeper of the peace in West Forty-seventh and newspapers gave only a few lines to his obituary, which Mrs. Killilea resented to her death, thirty-two years later. "There's been no captain like him to this day," she would say bitterly. "He *was* West Forty-seventh."

Captain Killilea died just as West Forty-seventh began to groan under increasing precinct chores. The south wall of the Tattersall Horse Market at the north end of Times Square only a year before had burst into brilliance with the Trimble Whiskey electric sign, first of the large white-light displays that were to alter the whole character of the district. Traffic was beginning to pile up and horse-drawn hacks had found noxious competition in the new-fangled motor taxicabs. The subway was in operation, too. West Forty-seventh, however, still used pot-bellied stoves for heat and sickly yellow gaslight for illumination. From about this time on, the blotter no longer speaks in the leisurely, tolerant language of earlier decades. The notations are curt and abbreviated. Desk lieutenants had no time to woo the muse before they made their entries. Mellow comments on the weather vanished.

Murder, once rare in the precinct, occurred more frequently as gamblers, cutpurses, touts, and painted women swarmed toward the white lights; and it was a new kind of murder, foul and ill-flavored compared with a few earthy homicides of West Forty-seventh's youth. On June 18, 1909, the blotter made written note of the most shocking of these crimes: "At 4:45 P.M. an unknown woman, white, about 33 years, 5 feet, 130 pounds, dark complexion and hair, partly dressed with white cotton underwear, otherwise nude, was found dead in the room occupied by Leon Ling, in a trunk on fourth floor, rear hall room at 728 Eight Avenue, with a sash cord tied about the neck. Body in badly decomposed condition. Patrolman John A. Reardon in charge. Discovered by Fitzgerald and Reardon. Trunk tied with cords and opened by the above officers in presence of Samuel and Isaac Friedlander, locksmiths, 349 West Fortieth Street, who took lock from the door; also witness Kim Yee, 216 Broadway." Subsequent entries established that the woman in the trunk was Elsie Sigel, granddaughter of General Franz Sigel, the Civil War hero whose statue on Riverside Drive at 106th Street faces the Jersey shore. Miss Sigel, a graduate of Wadleigh High School, had been a zealous missionary in Chinatown, and the blotter lists the religious tracts, Testament, and thirty-five of her love letters that were found in the death chamber. All the letters, couched in terms of feverish endearment, were addressed to Leon Ling, a waiter in a chop-suey restaurant, who had been her favorite pupil. At the station house, Paul Sigel, Elsie's stern father, looked at the body and his jaws stiffened. "I do not know her," he said. An aunt was equally firm in her refusal to identify Elsie. "My niece," she told the desk man stiffly, "was a faithful member of the Audubon Society and would not wear a bird on her hat as this poor creature did," but in the end she broke down and got the sad business done. The police never caught up with Leon Ling. The trunk in which the body had been found served for a long time as a seat for patrolmen on reserve in West Forty-seventh when they played penny ante in the station-house basement. Finally it was removed to the office of the Property Clerk, where, according to legend, it still gathers dust, awaiting the vague possibility that someday the murderer may be brought to book.

Another murder was entered upon the blotter at West Forty-seventh early on the thick, muggy morning of July 16, 1912. It was recorded in the bored, unimpassioned style of the latter-day desk men: "Sudden death. 2:40 A.M. At 104 West Forty-fifth Street. Herman Rosenthal, age 38, white, U. S. Gambler, married. Reported by Officer Brady.

"At about 2 this A.M. while standing in front of the Hotel Metropole, Forty-third Street east of Broadway, was shot and killed by four [the "four" was crossed out later with red ink and "one" was substituted] unknown men about 24 years, white, 5 feet five or six, smooth-faced, dark complexion and hair, dark clothes, soft dark hat, who, after shooting Rosenthal, jumped into a waiting automobile, No. 13131 NY or No. 14131 NY (slate-colored touring car) which contained four other young men, smooth faces. The touring car proceeded East on Forty-third Street to Madison Avenue and North on Madison Avenue to Fifty-eighth Street when all trace of the same was lost by Lieut. Frye who had pursued said touring car in a taxicab No. 26256 NY owned by John Horan. Body was searched by Patrolman Mooney in the presence of Patrolmen Brady, Taylor and Hughes and the following property delivered at the desk: Cash, $82 in bills and $3.87 in silver; 2 Yale keys, one pair glasses in case; 2 yellow cuff buttons, 2 yellow collar buttons, 3 handkerchiefs. Property at Coroner's office."

At 3:20 the same morning, an entry says, "District Attorney Charles S. Whitman visited this station and held investigation." The prosecutor went into the reserve room, where the body of Herman Rosenthal lay on the rough board floor under a gaslight that burned steady in dead, humid air. He got down on his hands and knees and searched the pockets, looking for a gun. Rosenthal had been in the District Attorney's office only twelve hours before the shooting to inform against policemen who were taking graft from his gambling houses, and had predicted, "You'll find me dead one of these days and you'll find they've planted a gun on me." There was no gun.

Another entry for that morning says, "Police Commissioner Rhinelander Waldo visited this station at 4 A.M.," but this is crossed out and in the margin beside it, written in red ink, is the word "Error." The next entry says, "4:25 A.M. Lieutenant Charles Becker of C.O. [Central Office] visited this station." Lieutenant Becker was the man Rosenthal had named in his talk with the District Attorney as the chief grafter. By 6 A.M. the significance of the murder had become evident, and the blotter says, "Patrolman Fick left for the office of the Police Commissioner to deliver Unusual Occurrence Report." The rest of the case was recorded at Police Headquarters. Two years later, the four gunmen died in the electric chair for the Rosenthal murder. By that time the District Attorney who had crawled on the dusty reserve-room floor searching the body was on his way to the governorship for obtaining their conviction. Becker was executed after Whitman had taken office. This was West Forty-seventh's greatest case.

Another five years brought war and prohibition, a mad combination that left West Forty-seventh frenzied and breathless. Theaters and night clubs, subways, ever-increasing motor traffic, homicidal bootleggers and drug addicts, beggars and peddlers, overran the precinct. Night encroached on day with the glare of millions of electric

lights. West Forty-seventh was never out of the public
prints. Men and women read about it in far-off countries
and came to stare at its wretched bulk. After the war the
pace grew dizzier and dizzier. Offenders against the law,
piddling fellows and arrogant gang leaders, bootblacks
and men like "Legs" Diamond and Dutch Schultz, crossed
its worn threshold in ceaseless parade.

Just after midnight on October 2, 1928, the big desk
room was cluttered with fifty-five actresses and mincing
male players from the cast of *Pleasure Man,* being booked
for "participating in an indecent performance at the Biltmore Theatre, 259–263 West Forty-seventh Street," when
the door swung to admit a large, self-assertive woman,
generously curved and making the most of it. When she
identified herself to the desk lieutenant, he took up his
pen again, in cramped fingers, and wrote in the blotter,
"Arrest 15,929, Mae West, Hotel Harding, West Fifty-
fourth Street, White, Single, U. S., authoress," and booked
her on the same charge. A footnote shows she was "bailed
by S. Silverman, $500 on Home and Lot, value $23,000,
708 Quincy Street, Brooklyn."

Another gambler, sixteen years after Herman Rosenthal, gave West Forty-seventh's blotter a major anecdote
for its long autobiography. By this time the volume of
station-house bookkeeping had grown so tremendous that
no single blotter could contain it all, and a complicated
system had been set up to document everything that went
on. There were separate books for arrests and summonses,
separate blotters for roll calls and traffic accidents, and
little pink cards to record injuries and deaths. A card
made out at 10:45 P.M. on November 4, 1928, says, "Arnold
Rothstein, Male, 46 years, 912 Fifth Avenue, gunshot
wound in abdomen, found in employee's entrance, Park

Central Hotel, 200 West Fifty-sixth Street. Attended by Dr. McGovern, of City Hospital. Removed to Polyclinic Hospital. Reported by Patrolman William M. Davis, Shield 2943, Ninth Precinct." Two days later the word "fatal," in parentheses, was written in after the word "abdomen," and a second report, with more detail, was added: "Rothstein apparently had been engaged in card game with others in Room 349 on third floor of Park Central Hotel when an unknown man shot him and threw revolver out of window to street. Body found by Lawrence Fallon of 3164 Thirty-fourth Street, Astoria, employed as house detective for the hotel."

After repeal there was a let-down in major crime, but the daily grist of routine police business in Manhattan's midtown even so remained enormous. Every night the main room of West Forty-seventh was filled with a clutter of bootblack kits and the paraphernalia of pitchmen who worked the sidewalks without permits. Outside, under the weak green electric lamps, were droves of pushcarts left by peddlers rounded up on the side streets off Broadway and taken to Night Court. The street was noisy with the whimpering of many babies, and slatternly women and unshaved men hung over blackened window sills and watched the comings and goings of the nightly haul of criminal small fry. Men, a couple of years ago, though, came and lifted out the old blotters and took them to the new station house on West Fifty-fourth Street. West Forty-seventh was ready for the wreckers.

Freddy

FREDDY GILMAN usually shuffles slowly into Jefferson Market Court around ten o'clock in the morning, but this one day he was late. While I waited, Johnny McElkenny talked about him.

"Freddy," he said, "is the oldest guy in Greenwich Village. He will take one of the back benches when he comes. He will listen for a while, but he does not hear the cases. If it's a homicide or just a summons for spitting on the sidewalk, it's all the same to Freddy. He will try to catch some of it, but he will not hear. He will fall asleep. He does not want to sleep, but when you are ninety-one years old, like Freddy, you can fall asleep any time. He has been doing this the past forty years."

I stood by the magistrate's bench, facing the solemn old wall clock in the dark-paneled court chamber.

"That is the last of the twelve clocks that Boss Tweed passed off on the city at $1200 apiece," Johnny said. "It keeps good time." He suggested we climb the court's old bell tower. "Freddy will be here when we get down," he whispered.

We left the courtroom and went into Tenth Street. The custodian opened a stout oak door in the Tenth Street side of the red-brick courthouse wall and a damp, stale wind washed into our faces.

"You take it slow going up," the custodian warned. "There's one hundred and seventy-five steps and two ladders. I'll watch for Freddy."

The ancient stone staircase rose in brief spirals through semidarkness. At the little landings a pale-yellow and green glow lighted Johnny's face. It was the sun coming through the small stained-glass windows. At the top step, I looked down, as through a cannon's bore.

"It's like London Tower," Johnny said. "God help the wrecker who takes the contract, someday, for tearing down this place."

He lifted the wooden skylight and I climbed onto the ten-by-ten roof, more than two hundred feet above Greenwich Village.

"Here's where the old firemen used to watch for fires," Johnny said. "Freddy told me."

The old fire bell, not heard these forty years, is bronze. It is six feet high and about eight feet wide at the mouth. It is weathered and corroded a pleasant sea green, suggesting complacent old age. Down near the bottom, in an ornamental band, we could barely trace the maker's name: "Jones and Company, Founders, Troy, N. Y." The great clapper, built like a sledge hammer, lay on the roof, red with rust. Johnny flicked the bell with his forefinger and it gave off a ghostly "ping!" We looked out through the cupola—east and west and north and south—on the rivers, and on endless rooftops. The wind blew in our faces.

As I stepped into the street again, I almost stumbled against an old man. He was seated on an upended milk crate by the tower door. He looked up through childish, watery blue eyes. His round face was covered with white stubble, and the skin, where it showed, was mottled. His blue-serge coat, a trifle tight, was spotted with food stains.

So was his old gray vest. His gray hatband was dark with sweat.

"This is Freddy," Johnny said. "He is the only one allowed to sit here, by the tower door. Freddy guards the bell tower. Is that right, Freddy?"

The childish face creased in an eager smile.

"That's right," Freddy said.

I squatted beside the old man. He asked if I had seen the bell.

"Jimmy Walker's father used to ring the bell," he told me. "He was the first one, when he was Alderman." He lifted a mottled, brown hand and his narrow coat sleeve tightened as he pointed across the street to the gate that gives into Patchin Place. "I lived in there forty-five years," said Freddy. "The milkman would come by in the morning and he would ring a hand bell. They don't do that no more." He was silent a moment. "I was born down in Corlears Hook," he suddenly remembered. "That was on New Year's Day, ninety-one years ago." He put his hands on his knees and rocked. "You don't see many that's ninety-one years, now, do you?"

I said, "No," and Freddy seemed pleased. He grinned like a mischievous child. He spoke of many things, most of them vague and unrelated. It was like a man glimpsing pictures in a swiftly riffled book.

"I worked under Grover Cleveland," he suddenly recalled, "down in the old sugar house in Laight Street. I was a laboring man, taking out packages." He seemed inordinately proud of this. "I heard all the old fire-house bells when I was a boy," he said. "I heard the bell down in Houston Street. There was one in Essex Market and one was the Mechanics' Bell, down in Lewis Street." Out of a semidoze Freddy remembered the old Harlem River boats. "There was the *Silver Dell* and the *Silver Stream,*" he murmured sleepily. "They run up the river to the old wooden bridge. They had music."

He fell silent again and dozed briefly in the sun. When he awoke he spoke of other things. Of a sister who died at eighty-seven, though he did not say when or where; of his remote childhood in another century. Freddy, Johnny told me, never married. The old man came out of his little naps somewhat like Alice's dormouse.

"I used to swim off Ninth Street dock," he said, "and I used to go barefoot-ey when I was a boy. I used to catch striped bass off Ninth Street dock, by Roche's Foundry." He remembered the rich people of old Patchin Place, the Trainors, mostly. "They had horses and good rigs," said Freddy, talking as out of a dream. "They would drive up Fifth Avenue and the horses had big bloomers on their head."

I prodded him a bit on this and it turned out that Freddy meant plumes, not bloomers, though he kept calling them bloomers. He bent down with difficulty and fingered the toes of his stubby black shoes.

"We used to have copper toes," he fetched out of his memory. "We used to slide on a sliding pond, here in Tent' Street."

In Sixth Avenue traffic navigated noisily around a WPA sewer job. Freddy pointed to the avenue.

"I seen that elevated go up," he said proudly, as if the structure still loomed before his watery stare, "and I seen it tore down." The blue eyes lighted and he caught my arm. "I seen Miss Jones in *Seven Charmed Bullets* at the old Bow'ry."

He got this off hurriedly, as if he might forget. After a while he stood up. We waited for an opening in Tenth

Street traffic and slowly walked among the shadows in Patchin Place.

"I don't see so good," Freddy said. "I get a pension. The City Chamberlain's got a hundred and twenty-five dollars to bury me. I got it out of the bank in Sevent' Street." A light wind rustled the dead leaves on the concrete walk in the old lane. "I got to go to court, now," said Freddy.

In the court corridor he feebly shook off my supporting arm and shambled toward a seat. A minute later Freddy was asleep. He was smiling. Johnny McElkenny looked down at him.

"Freddy's a great old guy," he said.

Sometimes He Was Pale

YEARS of newspaper work are apt to develop case hardening in a man. But if you can keep your capacity for astonishment fairly fresh and green, no city runs out of news material. Odd personalities and odd situations, you find, are self-seeding, and Gab-mad-on-Subway yields fresh crops the year round, with a minimum of cultivation.

Sometimes stories are so startling, so incredible, that they never get into type. Despite what some knowing fellows say about journalistic sensationalism, newspapers frequently kill out of their columns a certain amount of stuff that might make readers gulp their breakfast grapefruit, rind and all.

One night, for example, a bulletin came in over the City News ticker with the innocent tip that an ambulance was on its way to an address on York Avenue in the lower Eighties. Ambulances are forever pushing motorists to the curb in a city of seven millions, but this was a dull day. The desk said, "Look into it."

At the address on York Avenue the sidewalk swarmed with murmuring men, women, and children. They kept looking up at a second-floor window in the blackened old tenement. The butcher was there, a fat fellow with unpleasant stains on his soiled apron, and the vegetable man.

"I knew her," the fat butcher was telling the neighbors earnestly. "She is a chicken pincher. She will pinch a chicken to see how much fat it's got. Then she will go to the meat market two blocks up and she will pinch chickens there. Always looking to save a penny. A miser, she is. Crazy like a fox."

On the second landing a gray-haired policeman leaned on the banister and stared gloomily down the stairwell at faded mustard-brown oilcloth patterns on the floor below. He straightened when I gained the landing and nodded toward a frosted-glass door panel.

He said, "I am twenty-seven years in the job and I never have one like this before."

"One like what?"

"What's behind that door."

New York cops are seldom subtle or mysterious. The behavior of this one was puzzling. He put his elbows back on the banister rail, to ease the excess weight off his feet, and resumed his brown study down the stairwell.

"All right to go in?" I asked him.

He did not lift his head.

"If it was me," he said darkly, "I would keep the hell out of there. That's what I'm doing. I'm keeping out of there."

I said I would go in.

"Go ahead," he muttered bitterly. "Poke your snoot in, if you want. I'm only tellin' you."

The door was unlocked. I pushed it in gently. It opened on a typical two-room tenement apartment. To the right was a kitchen flooded with late-afternoon sunlight. Its green walls were festooned with brown-paper shopping bags. Someone had nailed them up so they hung like enormous bats. They moved in the light breeze that came through the kitchen window. In the old iron sink stood an earthenware bow. Tomatoes were soaking in it, ripe, red beefsteak tomatoes. The table was neatly covered with a red-and-white checkered tablecloth, the kind you see in Italian spaghetti places. It was laid for two. Plates were set out, with flatware beside them. There was bread on a tray.

Two new kitchen chairs were pulled up at the table, one on either side, where the dishes were. The chairs were unpainted pine. Someone had cut the legs off them, so the seats were only four or five inches off the floor. I remember wondering why this was done, how anyone could eat in that position. The table was of normal height.

I turned, still on the threshold, to the left, and suddenly, I knew what the old policeman had tried to tell me.

Just over the threshold, to the left, was a small bedroom. It was only eight feet square. Light dribbled into it from a hole cut in the kitchen wall. The bed was painted white enamel, but the enamel had peeled. The side nearest the far wall—the bed was flush against that wall—was covered with an immaculate white sheet, doubled the long way. This covered the far half of the bed. On the near side of the bed, within arm's reach of the door, a skeleton stared up at the ceiling. Decay was something less than complete. Even strips of fuzzy flannel underwear had resisted it. You could tell it had been a man, an old man. I closed the door.

I backed into the hall and stood beside the old policeman. He still stared down the well, like a man hypnotized. He talked from that position and the words had a melancholy hollowness.

"You seen everything?"

"Yes," I said.

"You got a good idea of that bedroom layout?"

"Yes," I said.

"An old couple lived in the apartment," the policeman said. "The old man was some kind of Czech, around eighty-five. His wife was eight or ten years younger. The old man drew old-age pension. The rent was only eight dollars a month."

One night in October, 1936, the old pensioner died. Natural causes, the medical examiner found. He issued a death certificate. He assumed the old lady would scrape together the price of burial. Neighbors did not know the old man had died. Death had come suddenly and quietly. Whenever neighbors passed the landing at night, they would see the old lady's silhouette between the kitchen lamplight and the frosted door panel. Her voice would be shrill, her arms would wave. The neighbors would grin. The old lady always quarreled with the old man. Come to think of it, a withered upstairs tenant recalled, the old man did not answer these later tirades. No one tried to figure out why.

The old Czech's wife was scrupulously neat. Every night she carefully climbed over her motionless spouse and spread a freshly washed sheet on the far side of the bed. Every night for eleven months and some twenty days. In the vegetable store, and in the meat market where she pinched chickens, the old lady would discuss her husband's poor condition.

"He is too weak to get out of bed," she told the neighbors and the merchants. "I got to cook broth for him all the time, soft things to eat, but he can't get up from bed."

Pension Bureau workers came to the frosted-panel door at regular intervals.

"You can't come in," the old lady would quaver. "My

husband is asleep." Sometimes she would say, "He has gone on a visit to his sister in Scranton."

She spoke through the door but never opened it. Finally, someone at the Pension Bureau told the worker for the district she would have to get in.

"Get a cop, if you have to," the superior said.

She got the melancholy old cop who had the York Avenue beat, but the old lady would not open the door.

"The old lady is a little crazy," the butcher told the policeman. "If you could think of something smart she would open the door."

The policeman climbed the stairs again with the girl from the Pension Bureau. He rapped on the frosted panel.

"Who's there?" the old lady called.

"This is the Police Department. They tell me you have a dog in there without a dog's license."

The policeman and the Pension Bureau girl stood in the hall in deep silence for a moment. Suddenly the door was flung open. The old lady peered out, her face creased in a grin. There was laughter in her staring, watery eyes.

"It is a lie," she said triumphantly. "I do not have a dog. You can search."

The policeman and the girl from the Pension Bureau saw what lay on the bed. The girl screamed.

Doctors questioned the old lady when the ambulance brought her to the Psychopathic Ward in Bellevue Hospital. "Didn't you know he was dead?" they asked. "Couldn't you tell?"

The old lady's trembling fingers fumbled at her shrunken mouth. She looked up at the doctors and her eyes grew more moist.

"Sometimes," she said thoughtfully, "he was very pale. Sometimes he would not take his broth."

Wedding Rings and Poison

MR. HARRIS said the most unusual wedding-ring order in the store's history was one his father got, twoscore years ago, from a romantic couple who were in the cast of a play at the Maxine Elliott Theatre on Thirty-ninth Street.

"Anyway," Mr. Harris said, "this couple came in one night and wanted to know if there was some way they could seal their commingled blood in a wedding ring. Dad thought it over, and finally figured out a way."

Harris *père* chose a bloodstone, because the girl had been born in March. It was a thick stone. He split it, grooved the lower half, and sealed the stuff in with diamond cement.

"I remember the names of those two customers," Mr. Harris said, "but it's a rule of the house not to tell. You know how people are about wedding rings."

Another time, Mr. Harris said dreamily, two young musicians came in, a girl and her instructor. They stood by the counter and said what most young couples say when they come to decide on a wedding band.

"We want something unusual," they firmly insisted.

Mr. Harris drew out the story of their romance. He had a special knack for that sort of thing. Finally he asked the girl if she remembered the first full piece she had played for her instructor. She said it was a Bach suite for the cello.

"Write out the first three measures," Mr. Harris suggested. The girl did this. "Now," said Mr. Harris, "how would you like this—the notes in rose diamonds, the staff in white against black enamel?"

The couple expressed delight. Mr. Harris couldn't remember, though, whether their married life went along like a song.

"Never saw them again," he told me sadly.

Mr. Harris reached behind the counter and took out a special case of assorted ancient rings. These were not for sale. He just collects them as a hobby. Sometimes, for special customers, he would adapt the old designs for modern wedding rings or for modern betrothal bands.

He showed a very old carnelian, the color of rare cider in the sun. It was set in heavy silver and the face was engraved in ancient Arabic. Mr. Harris said it was about six centuries old. The inscription was deciphered for Mr. Harris by a man on the faculty at the University of Minnesota.

"Yea, Ali," it says, "With Thy Divine Favor, Naught Matters but Thy Grace, God's Benevolence and Eternity. . . . Thy Slave."

Mr. Harris showed another, a Saracen seal set in silver. The inscription was two hundred years old. "Allah be watchful over Thee," it said. The Minnesota professor thought this was a gift from some girl to a dignitary or to a soldier.

I was fascinated by a heavy gold ring. It had a large pale emerald, flanked by two fiery rubies. Harris *père* got it when he ran his shop in London, fifty years ago.

"It was brought in by an Italian count," Mr. Harris said. "It had belonged to the Medici family."

He pointed out that the ring part was hollow gold, one eighth of an inch wide, one fourth of an inch deep. Into this hollow, through a trap hidden under the right ruby (he lifted the stone to show this), the Borgias poured vegetable poison. Mr. Harris touched a golden flower near the second ruby and a trigger shot up. As he moved the trigger a tiny gold point emerged from the bottom of the ring. A happy light shone in the jeweler's eyes.

"Get it?" he asked eagerly. "The Borgia would shake the victim's hand. The gold point would pierce the skin, an imperceptible prick. At the same time the venom would flow. Very little was needed to do the trick." Mr. Harris fondled the poison ring. "My *pièce de résistance,*" he said. "Not for sale."

There was a Mississippi gambler's ring, a device of heavy gold set with an enormous scarab. Mr. Harris flicked an almost-invisible lever and the scarab slowly lifted. Under it was a polished mirror. When the gambler dealt he could see every card he passed out.

A Norwegian wedding ring in the collection seemed to belie the general belief that the Norsemen are a cold, phlegmatic lot. This ring had two tiny gold hands, one clasping the other. Each of the hands was hinged at the wrist, and lifted separately, exposing under each palm a tiny golden heart. Each of the hearts was inscribed with initials.

"Very odd," said Mr. Harris, "and extremely sentimental, but I have adapted these for a few customers."

A homicidal band that seemed to deserve a place with the Borgia poison ring was a Mexican creation. With his fingernail Mr. Harris flicked up from the center of the band a tiny curved knife blade almost an inch long and extremely sharp.

"Mexican murder ring," Mr. Harris said proudly. "Quite rare."

Mothers who have lived happily with their husbands often come into the shop to ask Mr. Harris to split their wedding bands to make two. The mother keeps hers and gives the other half to an engaged daughter. On one occasion twin sisters shared a family heirloom—their grandmother's wedding band—the same way.

The Harrises have made rings for magicians. The jeweler showed me a hooked ring with which the great Kellar did his "levitation" act. A tiny hook in the bottom of the ring would fit into a tiny ring in a table and the audience—even the committee on stage—would think the table was rising by Kellar's magic.

Mr. Harris talked a lot about wedding-ring superstitions. Syrians, for example, believe that a beryl will prevent childbearing. One Manhattan rug merchant, sire of eight healthy sons and daughters, came in one day and asked that his wife's old wedding band be changed for one with a beryl. Mr. Harris filled the order.

"It didn't work, of course?" I asked.

Mr. Harris closed the box of ancient rings. He shrugged.

"Anyway," he said, "the woman had no more children. The rug man died four months after we delivered the ring."

Monk and Peasant

A FAT, glum-faced man opened the Fortieth Street door of the Metropolitan Opera House. He said, "O.K., supers," and the queue of talkative men along the opera-house wall pushed in from the street. They handed their postcard bids to a grumpy little man at a scarred flat-top desk and he gave them soiled-blue tickets good for one dollar on the way out.

Some of the supers, judging from the talk, had been in *Boris Goduno* before. A red-nosed vagrant who needed a shave told a threadbare companion to grab for a long red soldier outfit when they got downstairs.

"You get one of them, Skull," he said, "and you don't have to take off your pants and you get away quicker when the show breaks."

Skull said suppose they didn't want him to be a soldier; how about that? Red-nose assured him everything would work out all right.

"You're tall, see?" he said. "And the tall ones get to be soldiers. They're the Tsar's bodyguard."

Skull shrugged and took a red soldier outfit.

Down two flights of stairs to a low, whitewashed-brick chamber of somewhat medieval aspect. Wire-guarded lights in the ceiling glared harshly on sixteenth-century

Russian costumes, all highly colored but grimy to sight and to touch. A Mr. Romano, who has been wardrobe man at the Met for thirty years, quickly sized up each super before he decided to make him a soldier, a friar, a monk, or a peasant.

The supers retired to wall benches to change, and the room grew uncomfortably warm. It filled with smoke and stale human odors, with a babel of accents and small metallic sounds. I stuffed my suit in a bilious green locker and stood before Mr. Romano. He gave me boots of green, mottled with gold, and draped me in the habit of a medieval Russian monk, complete with cowl.

I sat on a bench and listened to the other supers. They ranged in age from eighteen to sixty. Some were high-school students; some were clerks of one kind of another; some were hapless actors without other assignment. Two red-eyed supers getting into peasant costumes discussed with extraordinary violence a Bowery restaurant that served inferior beef stew.

"I took mine back to the counter," one of them said, "and I told the guy I'd stick his puss in it."

Some of the supers were fussy. They came to the blackened wall mirrors to adjust their shiny steel soldier helmets. One dark-haired stripling sat on the edge of a large wicker costume basket and sneered at his image in the glass. Before 7:30 P.M. the place was packed with soldiers in scarlet, soldiers in white, peasants in every shade of pastel.

A bald-headed super in scarlet said: "I had part of my picture in *The Times* last year. This was in *Aida*." He said it was almost a full-view picture except that you couldn't see the top of his face. A courtier in false ermine over a dirty-soft-collared shirt said he almost got

in a picture, too, but some unmentionable pushed him out
when the flash went off.

Mr. Romano, making his way from one super to another, stopped at my bench. He told me to watch for the
wig man and to get a monk's beard before starting upstairs. After a while a little man came by with an armful
of beards and I timidly asked for one.

The little man said, "Oh, my heavens," and walked
away.

Men, all shapes and sizes, stood on benches and on the
concrete floor, struggling into costumes. These were the
late-comers. Ballet boys daubed themselves with lipstick
and grease paint and made black-pencil mustaches and
eyebrows on their faces. They used a lot of eye shadow.
Two melancholy, middle-aged men in ermine and white
Cossack caps started upstairs.

One of them said, "You got your own pants on, Heckie?
They will lose the crease."

Heckie said, "These are my old pants. They ain't got
no crease."

I gathered my robe from the floor and followed them.
Backstage was a fantastic cavern, something out of a nightmare. The eighty-foot ceilings were lost in shadow. Gigantic stage properties crouched like monsters in the
brooding dark. Women supers—peasant women with
kerchiefs, girls as nuns in black, one as a witch—kept cutting across our path. Mr. Barone, one of the assistant
stage directors, pushed out of the wings.

"Hey, monk," he said, "you carry this in the procession."

He thrust out a crude cross made of twigs. What procession? Mr. Barone vanished in the dark before I could
ask.

Another monk—he is an attorney, he told me later—
came up. He said: "You stay with me."
I hovered close, afraid to lose him. My glasses were in
the locker and the scene was a meaningless blur of darkness,
webby lights, and faces that seemed to lack detail. Out
front the principals sang. The strings came backstage
thinly; strains of sadness. Peasant women, boyars, and
soldiers were grouped in the wing. Someone caught up
a blue banner and the procession marched onto the stage.
I hoisted the cross of twigs and stumbled out.

Dimly aware of the orchestra leader's white shirt front
and of a semicircle row of orange lights, like a long glow-
worm, that marks the diamond horseshoe, I got across the
set. I tripped once, on the lower hem of my habit, but
recovered. Beyond the wings the second monk shook his
head.

"Your technique," he said, "if you don't mind construc-
tive criticism, was quite bad. You held the cross too
high."

Jostling soldiers and peasant girls flooded past. A few
stepped on our hems. Humbly, I thanked the lawyer
monk. Then I went downstairs to get my peasant outfit
for the Forest of Krony scene in Act IV.

Mr. Romano told me where to drop the monk's habit.
From the table he took a very grimy Russian blouse and
a pair of blue and gold pants. I murmured about the
blouse.

"It is very dirty, Signor Romano," I said.

The wardrobe master froze.

"Pay-zants," he said coldly, "are ver' dir-tee people."

Everyone sat around in the stuffy dressing chamber and
smoked. Ballet boys dashed in and out, making swift

changes. One of them had a rest period. He told another how he had dislocated a knee dancing in Cleveland.

"And, really," he said, prissily, "I think my dancing's improved."

A kindly faced man with gray hair, wearing a uniform of the Imperial Guard, talked about the time he played Farmer McCarthy in *Our Town*.

"I got forty-two weeks out of it," he said.

A Mr. Meyerowitz quoted some poetry he had written for a veterans' magazine. He got copies of the magazine from the locker and showed them around.

Finally the call came again. Everybody went upstairs. The poet, in a suit of mail, gently pushed me from behind. I was on the stage, behind the boyar Khrutchov. A woman knocked off my muzhik cap. When I stooped to pick it up someone almost dumped me. Painted peasant women rushed excitedly past, gesturing and making Russian noises. A little persimmon-faced chap in peasant garb was at my side. I asked him what to do.

"I am first time here," he said helplessly.

The cries and confusion mounted. I stood on a property rock and tried to look out into the audience, but vision stopped where light ended, at the orchestra pit. I came down off the rock when someone yanked at my blouse. It was the poet.

"You hafta kneel," he told me hoarsely.

I kneeled. From the flies snow fell. It covered everyone. Little squares of white paper. I looked up and got some in my eye. The poet grabbed my arm as a white horse clumped onto the set.

"It is Dmitri," he whispered. "We must cheer."

I let out a yowl and a peasant woman stared at me.

That was the end. Pretty soon I was back in my own clothes and out in the street. At the corner one of the Bowery supers passed. He tipped his cap and grinned.

"You was swell tonight, Pinza," he said. "You done noble."

Old Floors Make Violins

MR. STOCHEK's violin shop was small. It was crowded with cellos. Eight of them rested against the shop walls and on the floor and a ninth was cradled on the workbench. One more cello, you felt, and Mr. Stochek would be out on the landing. In the hall a saxaphone moaned. Mr. Stochek apologized.

"In this building you hear strange sounds," he said. "Ignore them. We shall talk only of violins."

He wiped his fingers on a soiled white apron. He had seen a story from Rome in the morning papers that said violins do not get their tone from special varnish, a belief long held even by experts, but he took the news calmly.

"To some it may be news that a Stradivari does not get its tone from the varnish," he said. "To me it is not news. For years, now, I have known this."

For a long time the talk was of varnishes. Spirit varnish dries quickly because it contains wood alcohol, Mr. Stochek said, but it gives a brittle tone. He gestured with thin shoulders to indicate he does not like brittle tone.

"Stochek," he said, "does not use spirit varnish on new violins. It would be desecration. He uses oil varnish. Stradivari used oil varnish."

Mr. Stochek uncorked a jug of oil varnish. It was

amber-colored, more kindly to the nostrils than the other. The gentler odor, the violinmaker explained, comes from pure alcohol.

"So pure," he said, "you could drink it and you would be happy. You would sing. It makes a box mellow. It gives it soft tone. It is not brittle. It does to the fiddle what good whisky does to a man. It makes him mellow."

Oil finish, however, takes from three to six months to dry. Men who turn out violins in large quantities will not use it because from three to six months is too long when your aim is quantity.

"For me," said Mr. Stochek, "it is not too long. If I do five or six instruments in one year that is enough."

Mr. Stochek was stubborn on this point. He would take no rush orders, he insisted. The work must be perfect. As a young man he was a violinist and he learned patience. A bare part of an inch in a back or a top and the tone is gone.

"So did Stradivari work," said Mr. Stochek. "So I work. I go to the library and I study. I am a purist."

Mr. Stochek thought a violin would have truer tone if it had no varnish, but there is a drawback to an unvarnished instrument. Without the protective coat the wood would weather. In ten years, perhaps, a good violin would lose its voice. And it would soil. It would not look so good. A cunning look lighted Mr. Stochek's dark eyes.

"The wood for my violins," he said. "Where does Stochek get his wood?"

Stochek prowls around old buildings. When an old house comes down, you will find Stochek there. He will kneel in a deserted dwelling and he will examine the floor boards. He will appraise supporting beams with his sharp eyes. He took down a rough board from a shelf.

It looked like any other piece of lumber. Stochek gloated over it. He touched it gently.

He said: "This is a hundred fifty, two hundred years old. This is rare curly maple. I found it in New Jersey. It was a floor board in a shabby lean-to."

Mr. Stochek carefully pulled out another board, marked for a violin back. You could see the outline, drawn in soft pencil. This prize came from an old house in Elizabeth Street, near Canal. Mr. Stochek paid the watchman fifteen cents for it. He stroked it.

"Fifteen cents I paid. It is one hundred years old if it is a day."

The violinmaker produced a brown old quartered log. He called attention to its rich, warm color.

"Age," he said. "This piece has age."

He found the log in a yard back of an old house near where the old race track stood in Sheepshead Bay. It was extremely light. Spruce, Mr. Stochek said; excellent for sound posts and base bars. He pulled out another board. Once, the violin man said, it was part of the Shelburne Hotel at Coney Island. He found it when the hotel came down, about twelve years ago. Mr. Stochek lifted a violin from the rack. He called attention to the rich patina, a warm, friendly shade of brown.

"Oil varnish," he murmured.

He nestled a hollow cheek into the rest. His head cocked to the left and his dark eyes sought the ceiling. The bow moved across the strings and the instrument sighed. Mr. Stochek's words barely topped the whispering strains.

"Wood from an old house in Elizabeth Street," he said. "Wood from a lean-to in New Brunswick. A floor board from a house in Pennsylvania. A wall board from a house in Maine. People have lived with this wood. People have died with this wood. They have sat by the fires and they have loved and they have quarreled. All the stories are here in Stochek's fiddles. Someone will play and the wood will tell these stories. Aaahhh——"

The music stopped as a child suddenly stops its sobbing under a mother's touch.

"So," said Stochek. "I have talked enough."

He went back to the workbench and bent over the cradled cello.

Broadway Blackout

THE CROSSROADS of the World were cold and windswept. The subway gratings breathed mustily and strongly when trains came by. Each sudden exhalation scattered cellophane wrappers, cigar bands, and grimy papers on the sidewalk in front of the United Cigar store.

The dark-faced man at the corner newsstand jammed his hands into his overcoat pockets and toyed with his change. He seemed sullen and aloof. Men who live on Broadway in the bleak predawn are not friendly with strangers.

At two A.M. the Spearmint sign blacked out and plunged Times Square in sudden darkness. Blue exhaust chuffed steadily from heated cabs that lined the curb. Drivers were huddled shapes behind the wheels. Pedestrian and motor traffic thinned and the din slowly faded.

Strange creatures came by: a man with a screwed-up face staring bleakly ahead in blind despair, his neck pulled down in a grimy tan raincoat; an old man with a matted beard. He stooped to pick up cigarette ends. These he thrust into a soiled shopping bag. His eyes never lifted.

For a time the street seemed very quiet. A red trolley rumbled over the Forty-second Street crossing. The newsstand man became more sympathetic. He talked about the parade that passed.

"Same guys every morning," he said. "They look like they ought to croak but they never do."

One by one the neons died: the Cadillac, the bars and grills in the deeper Forties. Store windows darkened and theater lights drained off. The Square huddled in ever-deepening shadow. Taxis deserted the line. They U-turned with violent protest of tires and tore away with a rush.

Two greasy baskets fell from a lumbering green garbage truck and rolled to a stop between the trolley tracks. The uniformed barker in front of the Rialto was wearying. His repeated call, "Still time for the last show," was reduced to a flat "Hee-ya, lasho," and none to hear.

A crowd of newspaper vendors had assembled on the corner. One was a tall, thin youth. His front teeth showed through a lip widely severed by an old surgical cut. Meech, the dark-eyed man at the corner stand, spoke up.

"Give him an interview," he said. "He's The Killer. Give the guy an interview, Killer."

Killer stared at me out of hollow eyes. He sucked in his thin, unshaved cheeks.

"I don't want no notoriety," he said. He muttered about the papers he was stuck with and moved off toward Eighth Avenue. Meech apologized for The Killer.

"He's a wack," Meech said. "You know. He's shell-shocked from eatin' peanuts. How we call him The Killer: he won a dance contest in Brooklyn and he knocked them dead, and that's how we give him the rib and call him The Killer."

A bent old woman, tightly wrapped in a shapeless gray coat, with a kettle-shaped old black felt covering her neck and forehead, came slowly by. She held out a small box of chewing gum, an automatic gesture. The sidewalk was bare of pedestrians where she stood. She stopped at the haberdashery and you wondered what there was about overgay shirts and gaudy ties in the window that could so hold her attention. She stared at the display for five minutes before she resumed her southward trudge.

One of the men came out of the cigar store with a flashlight. He held it close to the grating. It threw a pale light on countless bits of paper and cellophane, but at the last north gate, in front of the Rialto, he saw something.

"There's a quarter down there," he said, "in the corner."

Meech said the fishers would be along any minute. It was three o'clock. In the cigar shop a strange little woman leaned against the mirrored wall. She seemed out of a drawing, like a bad job in soft clay. Her imitation brown fur coat looked like something left in a wet corner. She was reading a playbill.

"That's Broadway Rose," Meech said.

He said that Broadway Rose came to the store every morning around three o'clock. Every morning she leans on the mirrored wall and reads a playbill or a pamphlet, something picked out of the street.

"Three hundred sixty-five days she comes and does the same thing," Meech said. "Around four o'clock she buys a pack of butts, always a different kind, and she goes out and takes the Eighth Avenue subway."

The man with the light defended Broadway Rose.

"She's a religious woman," he said, righteously. "She's got education."

A shabby man came out of the cigar store. He told Meech that a crippled man, "a good-dressed fella," had put a dime on Rose's arm because he thought she was penniless.

"So she shakes this dime off on the floor," the shabby man related. "She says it ain't her dime."

"Broadway Rose has got plenty of jack," the man with the light said. "Plenty."

Broadway Rose folded the playbill. She bought her cigarettes and put them in her lumpy, knitted bag. She made awkward feminine gestures at the fan of dead hair lumped under her shapeless velvet hat and headed up-street, toward Eighth Avenue.

The Square, north of the Crossroads, was a black pit now. It was almost four o'clock. Only one or two neon signs glowed redly through the dark.

"The fishers won't come no more," Meech said.

I looked around at the garbage trucks, loading at the restaurants. The Rialto lights were out. It was blowing colder.

Haunted House

AT THE crest of the 158th Street hill, where you look westward toward the Viaduct on Riverside Drive, the four little boys stopped their snow fight.

A tow-haired lad with silver-rimmed spectacles took the proffered newspaper clipping in wet blue mittens. It told of a $1,200,000 apartment house that was to go up on 158th Street, beside the Viaduct. It said, "An old dwelling on the property, said to be more than a century old and now tenanted by a recluse, will be demolished."

"That must be the haunted house, Mister," the boy said. "You can't see it from here. You gotta go all the way down the hill. It's the last house on the right. It's set back from the street. It's all broken and old."

I came upon the place just east of the Viaduct. It was set on a small rise about forty feet from an old iron railing. Soiled snow lay in deep drifts on the lawn. Rising out of the drifts was a pale marble statue of a little girl of long ago, daintily lifting her skirts as if to avoid splashing. An iron deer's head poked through the drifts. Ancient trees and bushes rose from the snow. On the largest tree a sign said, KEEP OUT, BEWARE OF DOGS. Two heavy stone gateposts showed the way up the rise to the house. On one was crudely painted the single word ENTRANCE. Beside it, a black hand pointed the direction.

The roadway was muddy. Melted snow coursed down the ruts in brown rivulets. Flights of swallows, all atwitter, swooped from the mansard roof. Ornamental iron urns, red with rust, leaned at crazy angles in the neglected gardens. One bore the stern warning KEEP OFF!

The building was scaly white brick, fronted with bronze and marble. The porches sagged, showed wide breaks. Wisteria vines, thick as your wrist, twisted crazily over the whole structure, vanished after they climbed the roof.

The windows were shuttered and the shutters had lost their dark paint. The shades were yellow and green. They hung in loose folds. The double front doors were ebony black, three inches thick, weathered and mildewed. A yellow card tacked to one of the doors said: OLD-FASHIONED BELL ON INSIDE DOOR. RING HARD.

I pushed the doors. They creaked and whined. I felt the resistance of some hidden counterweight as it clumped in its wooden housing. Now a vestibule, high, wide, and dark. The floor was marble, large alternate black and white squares. These were cracked.

The bell was a turn bell. I twisted it and the sound echoed dimly beyond the opaque glass panels of the second doors. I heard the sound of feet. The footfalls were remote, and slow. The door swung back. Dampness pushed out as if it had body and substance, and with it came the heavy scent of decay. The air was cold, too.

A young man peered at me from the dark. He was a cheerful fellow, which seemed astonishing. He grinned and adjusted the bright yellow scarf at his throat.

"Hello," he said. "Come on in."

He shut the door and I stood in deep gloom. Light filtered in. It turned a melancholy crimson where it touched the red velvet of a round old settee. Dark old furniture was huddled in the shadows. I could make out the heavy walnut staircase, a gigantic old clock with carved figures, some old chests. The young man took my arm, opened a great door, and led me into a library. He knew about the clipping. He knew about the two surveyors who had fled from the grounds the previous Wednesday.

"These surveyors," I explained, "came back with a story that a wild-eyed hermit crept up behind them and tried to hack off their heads with a great sword. They said his hair was 'way down his back."

The cheerful young man allowed his grin to widen.

"That was Emil," he said. "Emil is a deaf-mute. He has worked here for twenty-five years for Mr. Jermon."

The young man went out. I studied the room. All the furniture was massive ebony, rich with extraordinary carvings. The woodwork was carved ebony, too. Where the sun filtered in thick bars through the broken shutters, it turned to molten gold. It splashed on faded green velvet carpet. It was alive with dust. The gold-framed pictures were faded: old prints, old canvasses, old lithographs. The room was filled with marble and ebony statuary.

The door opened and the young man came back. With him came an elderly man, thin-faced, with long gray hair. The elderly man wore a gray felt hat pulled down around his ears. He was swaddled in a long, thick brown coat. A soiled gray scarf hid his warped throat. In his mouth he clenched a carved pipe and from the bowl a broken cigar end jutted.

The young man said: "This is Mr. Jermon—John Jermon. He has rented this place the past thirty-four years. He can tell you the history of this place. It has nineteen rooms."

The elderly man nodded. He sucked at the pipe before he spoke.

"I was one of the nation's leading theatrical producers long ago," he said. His voice was rich and gentle. "One of a syndicate that ran forty theaters from New York to Omaha. We built the Mayfair here in New York, The Casino in Philadelphia. My wife was Lillie Tyson. She was in musical comedy."

We went through the dark center hall into another gigantic room. There was a picture of Lillie Tyson, a lovely young woman, pink-cheeked and blonde. Her smiling head rested on chubby arms. The picture was set in a gilded easel.

"Dead," the elderly man said. "She's a long time dead." He spoke about the rich carving in this chamber. "Satinwood, all real satinwood." More statues. More grotesque carvings. I looked through the dusty windows at the far-off Palisades while Mr. Jermon talked. "This was the home of Mr. Wheelock, head of the Erie Railroad. He lived here one hundred years ago. All farms here, then. We had a crystal chandelier, all silver. This chandelier is rich majolica. Boys came into the yard at night and broke the windows with stones. James Audubon roamed these fields. This was the country one hundred years ago. Could see for miles. Woods. Small game. The gardens are still rich. When the wisteria is in bloom the windows and porch are hidden. It would be lovely on summer nights."

I asked about Emil and the sword. He only meant to frighten the surveyors, Mr. Jermon said. Emil is intelligent. Emil would harm no one. Mr. Jermon smiled and all the lines in his furrowed face seemed to merge.

"My wife got Emil," he said. "I swear, I don't know

where. Some institution, maybe. Harmless fellow, though."

We went through other dark and musty rooms, each with a fireplace, each filled with faded pictures, carved woodwork, each darker than the one before. The ceilings were broken, showing lath ribs. Wherever we sat our prints showed in dust.

When it was time to go Mr. Jermon and the cheerful young man took me to the door. The melting snow tinkled into little pools, a steady drip from the porch eaves. Mr. Jermon said he didn't know where he'd go if the place does come down.

"I don't know where I'll find a place for my old things," he said. "I have so many of them."

Cut a Diamond

THE LARGEST diamond plant in the United States was fourteen floors above Forty-seventh Street east of Sixth Avenue. The little man at the narrow grille examined my credentials with extraordinary caution. He pressed a button and a door opened on the left. Beyond there was another door, and then a third. Each closed as I passed.

A slender middle-aged man with the tight squint of the nearsighted peered at me through his spectacles before he offered his hand. He was the owner. He introduced a bright-faced young man, his son. He pointed to an oil portrait of a slim foreign-looking gentleman not unlike himself. He said: "That was my father. We are three generations in diamonds."

We all sat down. The nearsighted man said his shop was silent because diamond workers were out in the first strike in the trade's history in this country. Diamond workers, he said, earn around seventy to seventy-five dollars for a thirty-five-hour week. Most of them are Flemish or Dutch artisans, members of one of the proudest guilds in America.

"There is a joke about diamond men on strike," he said. "They do not throw stones, not precious stones."

No one laughed. A gnomelike man with gray hair and

astonishingly bright eyes came in and was introduced as the boss cutter. A box of rough stones was put on the table. The gnomish man lifted out a small parcel and poured from a paper a rough diamond about the size of a robin's egg. It had no luster. It might have been so much rock salt. It was divided by an irregular line drawn with India ink, and on it was marked, in tiny letters, the word "Full."

"This means 'full cut,' " the gnomish man said. "If I wanted it emerald cut I would mark it with 'E.' "

He explained that a diamond man studied a rough for a long time to figure how to get the most from it. If the rough has imperfections, the stone must be cleft or sawed so that the imperfections are left out.

He said: "It is like a spoiled apple. You save as much of the apple as you can."

In diamonds, the boss cutter said, you pay according to size. The bigger the stone, the more you get per karat. He balanced the rough in his palm.

"Here," he said, "is twenty-eight karats. If we get fifty per cent yield in one stone, or better, we are satisfied. From the rest we get smaller stones."

In reducing a rough, the diamond cutter explained, you work according to grain, cleave with the grain, saw against the grain.

"You got to think of one thing all the time," he said. His bright eyes watched to see whether I caught on. "You got to bring life to the stone."

He led the way into a great loft. Screened workbenches lined all the walls. On each table stood a silent grinding wheel, set flat. They were black with accumulated diamond dust and olive oil, the stone-polishing compound. The boss diamond man brought out an envelope filled with roughs somewhat darker than the first we had seen. These were commercial stones, called "borts" in the trade. They average around $1.25 a carat, against $40 and more for gem roughs. Borts provide the working dust.

"Diamond cut diamond," the gnomish man said. "You've heard that before." He started a wheel. "It spins at 2800 revolutions a minute," he explained. "The paste of borts and olive oil cuts the facets when the stone in work is held against the wheel."

Greasy playing cards lay at each table. These, the boss said, are slipped under the wooden working arm that holds the stone against the wheel. They are used when a shade more angle is required for a facet.

Diamond workers, the gnomish man said, prefer natural light. Diffused sun through a north window is ideal. On very bright days the men draw white muslin across the panes to shut out glare. Open windows are strictly barred. There is too much danger of stones in work shooting from the wheel.

"Sometimes," the boss said, "windows are open an inch or two at the top, but diamonds are tricky. They manage to find those little openings."

He walked to a rear window and pointed down into a series of disorderly back yards, two hundred feet below. One had a rock garden in which a red chow roamed nervously.

"One of our workmen," he said, "lost a twelve-karat emerald stone off his wheel. We searched the whole shop, turned it upside down, and no stone. The window was open two inches at the top."

Then, without much hope, the workmen went down into the rock garden. There lay the stone, kicking fire back at the sun.

A tall, simple-faced fellow stood within earshot. He was Herman, who resurfaced grinding wheels, cleaned and swept the shop.

"I am a story, too," Herman said.

Simply, but with some excitement, he told about the time a six-karat job got down the elevator shaft that gives into the shop. He found the stone on one of the cushion springs in the elevator pit.

"If the elevator hits that spring once," Herman said, "crush goes the diamond. Six karats."

Another time Herman was scouring a wheel and a diamond shot forty feet across the workroom into a back pocket of his overalls.

"All the time," Herman said, "the men eat inside. I find a diamond in the coffeepot when they have searched every other place."

He would have told more, but the gnomish man seemed impatient. Herman resumed his sweeping. The talk turned to other things: how diamond men get so accustomed to handling stones hot off the wheel that sometimes they stick their fingers into the Bunsen burner, where they heat solder to fix diamonds in work, and do not feel it; how a veteran diamond man can identify the maker of a stone by the workmanship; how a good stonecutter senses, rather than sees, grain.

We went into the safe room. There, at two desks, each wired for alarm, the diamond men brought out box after box of finished stones. One, carefully wrapped in cotton, was one and three-eighth inches long and three fourths of an inch wide; emerald cut. For no good reason it set you thinking of the bevels on bar mirrors.

They spread out 1840 diamonds cut from nine carats. These, they explained, were done abroad. American manufacturers do not bother with tiny sizes. They require the same care and the same number of facets as large diamonds. For contrast the boss diamond cutter brought out the model of a stone that weighed 609½ carats in the rough. It was as big as a fair-sized lump of coal.

"Big fella," the gnomish man said. "No?"

Throughout the examination of all this wealth in crystal, I had been making an unconscious effort to keep my fingers off the table. When I reached the street I found my hands hurt slightly. I looked at them curiously as I relaxed my fingers. Nothing dropped out.

Al Capone Snubs de Lawd

WHEN they bore de Lawd's coffin through the echoing halls of the Cathedral of St. John the Divine, I stood under the cathedral's soaring arches in chill March twilight. I thought of the time de Lawd met Public Enemy Number One.

It was in the gloomy Federal Court chamber in Chicago where Al Capone was on trial. There was a lull in the proceedings and Capone, flanked by his bodyguards (they carried guns even in the court chamber), plowed through the crowd for a quick smoke outside.

An importunate little man, a press agent, suddenly blocked Capone's rush. He said, "Al—looka, Al. I want you to meet de Lawd." The little man was leading a gentle-faced Negro, a benign old man, by one sleeve. "Al," he said, "this is de Lawd. He'd like to have you pose with him for a picture."

You could tell it was the little man's idea. De Lawd seemed unhappy about the situation. He fumbled with his soft felt hat. His kindly features crinkled in a benevolent smile. His lips parted and his voice broke into a rich baritone.

"Pleasure, sir," he mumbled.

He put out a brown old hand. Capone's face went dark. Rudely he brushed de Lawd aside.

"Get the hell o' my way," he snarled.

Bodyguards elbowed de Lawd against the wall as they pressed by, running interference for Public Enemy Number One. I stood with de Lawd as bulky Capone and his men-at-arms bustled down the hall. The old man's eyes were moist with pain and humiliation. His hands gripped his old hat tightly. He stared after the receding gunman.

"He didn't have to go for to do that," he said.

Three years later, I stood under the cathedral arches. It was de Lawd's burial day. Richard Berry Harrison was going to meet the real Lord.

Tremulous organ music, rich-timbred Negro spirituals, the faint scent of many floral wreaths, and the mystic light of breeze-blown tapers awed more than 7000 mourners. Bishop William T. Manning probably never before had looked down from his pulpit on so mixed a throng as listened in deep silence to his solemn eulogy of the venerable Negro who for five years had played the role of "de Lawd" in *The Green Pastures*.

Every foot of space, even the area around the communion rail before the great white altar where candles flickered against a background of scarlet drapery, was filled with sorrowing Negroes and white admirers of the old actor. They flowed into the chapels and even into the street. Negro ushers, grave and dignified in frock coats, mingled with the customary laymen who act as ushers in the cathedral. Aristocratic white men and white women, richly attired, most of them well advanced in years, sat beside shabby Negroes from Harlem.

Throughout the service the quavery pitch of emotional Negro women rose above the warmly blended notes of the choir from *The Green Pastures*. Here and there one could see a gray-haired woman swaying to the chanting of the choristers and clenching withered fingers to suppress spiritual ecstasy. As the throngs filed silently into the pews beneath the towering arches the organ poured a continuous flow of soft music. The thousands who had come down from Harlem sat staring at the deep shadows and the rich fittings high over their heads.

The organ music died away. A hush settled on the multitude. The procession moved past the coffin between the rows of gleaming candles; the crucifer, the black-gowned choir, the clergy in white vestments tipped with purple and scarlet and black; then the honorary pall-bearers, Paul Lawrence Harrison, the son of "de Lawd," and the cast of *The Green Pastures*.

They walked to their appointed place in the stalls at either side of the chancel, half the choir on one side, half on the other. Dean Milo H. Gates pronounced the sentences that opened the service and the chanting of the choir lifted in the simple hymn, "The Strife Is O'er, the Battle Done." A moment of silence as the echoes died away, then the chorus rose again in swelling, somber volume, in the burial chant: "I heard the voice of Jesus say, come unto Me and rest."

Below the pulpit, on a small camp chair, an old Negro woman in a threadbare plush coat joined in the singing with a cracked voice filled with religious fervor. She held a hymnbook in her work-worn hands, but it was upside down. She knew the words by heart.

The sun, which had struggled through the huge windows, hid behind a passing cloud and something like a chill closed down on the mourners. The candles flanking the coffin with the great blanket of carnations and red roses guttered softly with every breeze. Then the black-clad verger, with snowy head bowed, led the way to the pulpit, followed by the Bishop's chaplain holding aloft the golden pastoral staff. Bishop Manning ascended the pulpit.

"We are gathered here in this cathedral," he began, "to commit to its rest the body of Richard B. Harrison and to commend his soul to the care and the loving-kindness of the God and Father of us all. And as we remember him before God and lift up our prayers for him, we give thanks for his good example and for his service here."

The gray old Negro woman with the shabby plush coat turned her face toward the soaring arches. A tear slipped down the high lights on her cheek and splashed on her prayer book.

"His life and example reflect honor upon his own race. May he have blessing, and peace, and fullness of reward in those Green Pastures where he is now with Christ, the Good Shepherd, forever."

The Reverend Shelton Hale Bishop's eulogy was a tribute to the simple old man who had been "de Lawd."

"This service," he said, "is the simple Christian tribute of an adoring populace to a man who walked upon the earth and touched men like himself in a mystic way that made them feel that they had been with God."

No outside sounds filtered into the vast cathedral. The assault of the strong March wind was stilled by the great walls. Only an occasional sob from some woman broke the quiet.

Charles Winter Wood, the gray-haired successor to the role of "Lawd" in the play, went up into the pulpit. In accents short and simple, he told of Harrison's death in the dressing room of the theater.

"Terrified, I saw him stricken," Wood said. "He looked up. 'Charlie, old man,' he said, 'hold me, Charlie old

man. Don't let me down. The world needs this play.' "
The simple recital evoked fresh sobbing. The speaker
turned his face toward light streaming from the upper
windows.

"We thank Thee, O God, for the victories and the tri-
umphs of Richard B. Harrison."

Hall Johnson, tall and impressive in a sweeping black
gown, lifted his arms as he stood facing the white altar with
his back to the candles and the coffin, and the choir from
The Green Pastures flooded the cathedral with spirituals:

> *Oh, de blin' man stood on de road*
> *An' cried,*
> *Oh, de blin' man stood on de road*
> *An' cried,*
> *Cryin' "O Lordy," save me!*

All over the cathedral, men and women took up the familiar, slow-rolling chant and the old woman with the
cracked voice sang triumphantly high above them. It was
then that the mourners began to sway.

> *Lord, I don' feel noways tired,*
> *I'm seekin' for a city, Hallelujah.*
> *For a city to the kingdom, Hallelujah,*
> *For a city to the kingdom, Hallelujah.*

Bishop Manning lifted his right hand and intoned the
benediction. The last hymn was sung:

> *In heavenly love abiding,*
> *No change my heart shall fear.*

Then the recessional, the silent departure of the Bishop
and the white surpliced priests, the lifting of the dark

coffin with its cover of 1657 blossoms (the words *Green Pastures* done in white carnations, on a bed of deep-red roses, one blossom for each performance of the play), and the throngs filed out into Amsterdam Avenue.

Policemen kept the crowds moving, but thousands stood fast on the cathedral steps, holding their hats against the high wind. Traffic stood still in the sunlight and the black-robed choir assembled around the hearse.

The pallbearers came slowly down the steps with the coffin on their shoulders—Frank Wilson, who was Moses in the show; Oscar Polk, who was Gabriel; Ivan Sharpe, the Prophet; Reginald Fenderson, candidate magician; Daniel Haynes, who played Adam; Morris McKenney, who played Noah, and Do Do Green, understudy to Gabriel. A lane opened before the pallbearers on the long stone flight and the cleavage of the human tide recalled Marc Connelly's most powerful line:

"Gangway! Gangway for de Lawd God Jehovah!"

Broadway Chiseler

BROADWAY supports more low forms of life today than a primordial swamp; it swarms with types beside which the old-school gold-brick peddler, the cutpurse, and the square-rigged streetwalker seem like dimpled cherubim. But the chiselers are not like any of these. They are artists, living for and by chiseling with no thought of profit, to hear them tell it, and all the others are sordid mercenaries. While the others prey on small and helpless game, chiefly gullible peasants from Oneonta and Painted Post, the chiselers practice their skulduggery on fair-sized victims—the Telephone Company, subway interests, the Automats, big hotels, and the owners and backers of slot and vending machines. These corporations have spent and are still spending tens of thousands of dollars and no end of corporate wrath in futile attempts to eliminate them, but the chiselers carry on. Private detectives and new automatic safeguarding gadgets only quicken their ingenuity.

Fluctuations in currency and all the balderdash about gold and silver standards amuse the chiselers. They explain that you can live in New York, and live pretty well, without money. You use slugs instead.

Slug manufacturing is an organized industry now, em-

ploying agents to peddle the disks from the Battery to 181st Street. The best markets are in midtown Manhattan along Sixth, Seventh, and Eighth Avenues, and, of course, Broadway. The chiselers pay ten cents for fifteen nickel-size slugs, and slightly more for the dime and quarter sizes. Sometimes the agents get into a trade war and the chiselers get bargain rates.

The Telephone Company is more heavily beslugged than any of the other corporations, because the chiselers spend the equivalent of hundreds of dollars a week on out-of-town telephone calls. No profit in it, but most chiselers are not native New Yorkers and it is a cheap way to keep in touch with the folks back home. It isn't sentiment so much; they do it just for the fun of the thing. This winter one of the Telephone Company operatives caught a chiseler in an Eighth Avenue telephone booth passing the time of day with some of his pals in Sacramento, and it got into the newspapers. They found five pounds of assorted slugs on him. Once in a while the chiselers make local calls with a cent dipped in damp salt. The salt, it seems, makes the coin as thick as a nickel and, being a good conductor, establishes the necessary electrical contact. The chiseling guild claims credit for that discovery.

Marty Franklin might be called a typical chiseler. Franklin is not his real name, but neither are any of the half-dozen different ones he uses from time to time. He changes his name frequently, sometimes to escape from an embarrassing set of circumstances, and sometimes out of sheer whimsy. He has used Marty Franklin on several occasions. He is about thirty-seven years old. He isn't married, because he thinks matrimony tends to make a chump of a man (all nonchiselers are chumps). He has met one or two women he really liked—chorus girls, they were—but didn't follow them up because he thought it would interfere with his career. Most of the time he lives alone, in a furnished room, or perhaps even a furnished two-room apartment.

A child of the machine age, he regards all automatic devices as science's greatest boon to mankind. He gets his coffee and cake at the Automat with slugs, and provides himself with handkerchiefs, chewing gum, candy, shaving cream, razor blades, and even automatic shoeshines in the same way. Occasionally he'll invest a load of slugs in a large supply of vending-machine merchandise and sell the stuff for real money when he finds he needs some.

Marty Franklin doesn't say much about his youth except on rare occasions when he feels homesick for Providence. He was born there, and shirked school until he went into the army in 1917. His first bit of amateur chiseling after adolescence was the sale of some army supplies to finance an A.W.O.L. tour of France. It seems he was detailed to drive a lorry full of stuff to the front lines, but found the blankets, canned rations, and other goods were marketable and decided on the vacation instead. After the war he came to New York, looking for a job as bellboy, but found the citizenry here so gullible that he went in for chiseling instead. It isn't an easy life, he says; you have to keep thinking up new angles all the time, but it's fun even if you do live in cheap rooms or small apartments and don't carry much ready cash.

If he wants congenial company, he knows where to find it. Southern chiselers, for example, gravitate toward Forty-ninth Street and Seventh Avenue; the New England brothers, who are in the majority, meet in the vicinity of Broadway and Forty-sixth Street. Even the chiselers don't know why they favor these particular corners. But then, nobody knows exactly why acrobats congregate at Eighth Avenue and Forty-seventh or why carnival workers stick to the doorways of the Paramount Theater on Forty-third Street off Times Square.

Marty is proud of his knavery. He is eager, when he has what he considers a sympathetic listener, to describe his angles—every new twist is either an angle or depart- ment—for solving the problem of living. He shudders at the thought of existing on a slot-machine diet; he prefers the table-service restaurants, where he can pit his wits against men instead of against automatic food dispensers. He works the restaurants during the rush hours. It is easier then, he explains, because crowds help to scatter the employees' attention. He'll wait until he sees a group of men—three is the best number, he finds—entering a place. He tags along, confident and breezy, sits at the same table with them, and cuts in on their conversation. He's a master at that, and before the second course he's a blood brother. He finishes his meal just as they finish theirs and walks to the counter with them, keeping the conversa- tion going. "You do that," he has explained, "to create the impression with the cashier and the man at the door that you've known them all your life and that they're handling your check. You walk right on out, but not too fast." The cashier won't follow you into the street, it seems, be- cause of the danger of grabbing the wrong man in the crowd. Such mistakes have resulted in costly lawsuits in the past and the restaurant people are more apt to take the loss than risk being dragged into court.

Another bit of jugglery is reserved for cafeterias where a machine that dispenses blank meal checks stands just in- side the entrance door. These machines are equipped with gongs that are supposed to ring each time a check is taken, but the chiseler can flick two checks out so fast that the gong rings only once. This trick requires constant practice and natural skill and Marty advises amateurs not to try it. He goes to the counter, orders a full meal, and has the full amount punched on one of the checks. Then when he has finished eating he goes to the washroom and disposes of the punched check. On the spare check he orders some coffee or coffee and cake—that means five cents, or ten cents—for which he pays in conventional coin. You tear up the first check, he explains, so that they can't find it on you if they happen to be suspicious and start to search. "No corpus delicti, if you get what I mean," he says.

"Events Tonight," a daily feature in the *Sun*, usually gives Marty a wide choice of places for dinner. He prefers a chummy fraternal-lodge banquet at the Astor, Commodore, or Waldorf, though sometimes he tries a college reunion or civic-betterment spread. Testimonial dinners he usually avoids. "Food's good," he says, "but the courses are served too fast because of all the oratory to come." Long experience has taught him what organizations serve the best meals, the best cigars, and the best brands of Scotch. He can tell after a quick glance at the *Sun* column what group will serve a tasty *filet mignon* or breast of chicken, what crowd is partial to sautéed filet of beef, and at what niggardly banquet will be served inferior cuts of meat disguised by heavy sauces and French names. Marty gets into the hotel dining halls as a representative of the press. Once in a while some fuss-budget on the dinner committee may try to block him, but he boasts that he can outbluff any committee member he ever met. As a matter of fact, he seems to enjoy these tilts. "Kind of sharpens your wits," he says. "Gives you a chance to prove to yourself that New Yorkers, who think they're about the smartest people on earth, have more sap than a sugar maple." Real reporters always count one or two chiselers at the press table, but don't do anything about it. They know that the free-loaders—chiselers' term for dinner grafters—will tend to their quail-on-toast and peach Melba, be reasonable about the liquor, and try to be more dignified than the *Times* man. Once, though, at a dinner of the Daughters of Louisiana in the Brevoort, where the guests were met for the sole purpose of lambasting Huey Long, Marty Franklin misjudged his liquor capacity, wabbled to his feet, and launched into a glowing defense of the King-fish. The Daughters fluttered and clucked their tongues, the waiters came, and Marty was forward-passed into Fifth Avenue.

None of the good shows get by Marty Franklin, though he doesn't care a rap about the opera or concerts. He walks into the theaters during the first intermission on sell-out nights when there are lots of standees. "You go in with the crowds that have been out for a smoke," he says. "The guy at the door can't keep track of return checks and doesn't try to. But leave your hat home when you try it." He never sees the first part of a show, but he takes that philosophically. Sometimes he has read a review of the drama and knows fairly well what happens in the first act. But if he hasn't, he finds he can pick up the plot very quickly. "Nothing much ever happens in the first act anyway," he says.

Getting into the Paramount, where the ushers stand shoulder to shoulder, is, he thinks, one of his best bits. He spent a lot of time thinking it out, but the finished plot is simplicity in the raw. You get in through one of the Forty-third Street doors by explaining to the usher that you want to speak, for just a second, to a friend in the lobby right where he can see you. In the lobby you stop a stranger (any stranger), borrow a match, and start a conversation. Then wave good-by to the usher and stride through the lobby to the front door, which is on the Seventh Avenue side, stopping only long enough to get a return check from the man at the door. You come back later the same day to see the show. In the salad days of his chiseling career, Marty would go to the Eastman Kodak shops, pretend he was shopping for home movie films, and run off a few, at his leisure, in one of the booths set aside for the purpose; but he considers that freshman stuff now.

The hotel men's association has done more to discourage chiselers than all the other benefactors on the list; it has convicted and jailed more members of the chiseler group than Marty Franklin likes to recall. But it was easy, in the old days, he'll tell you, to get a double room with bath and meals on nothing more than an imposing front and a handbag loaded with telephone books or Central Park gravel. He had to lose the bag each time he did this, but pawnshop bags cost only a quarter or so. Incidentally, he reveals that it isn't the clerk or the house detective who judges the paying capacity of transients, it's the bellboy. The bellboy can tell fairly accurately by the heft and by shaking it whether the contents of a bag are legitimate or merely so much ballast. Sometimes a decent tip—a quarter or a half dollar—may persuade the bellboy that his unfavorable verdict was bad, Marty says, but you can't count on it. The best hotels are too well policed, nowadays, for safe crashing, but there are still some fairly good ones where you can get by on front and the loaded bag. They're dwindling steadily in number, though, and Marty doesn't work them too hard; he reserves them for winter nights when his room rent is overdue and the landlady won't listen to reason. If he does get by, he may let one or two of the chiseling brothers share the place—heeling in, they call it in the trade. Sometimes in emergencies he uses private drinking rooms, reserved in hotels by convention delegates or banquet guests, but repeal has crocked that, to some extent. During prohibition, he could walk into one of the private rooms almost any night as a press representative (he's never just a plain reporter), keep the drinkers roaring with the latest and smuttiest, and, after they'd all gone home, turn in for the night. Usually he would manage to get out before the maid came, but even if he overslept, he could always explain he had a bit too much at the private swigging bout the night before. That used to be infallible, he says.

The I.R.T. and the B.M.T. tried to save their shareholders some anguish by hiring detectives to frustrate men like Marty Franklin, but, when they saw they were making no headway with the gumshoe men, spent a fortune installing the illuminated magnifying glasses on turnstiles to spotlight the buffaloes and Indian heads. Chiselers have a deep contempt for subway detectives who keep an eye on the turnstiles at busy stations, but they are cautious, too, because every now and then a chiseler falls in the detectives' hands through sheer carelessness, and several have been sent to jail. Besides, the slugs are still good in the Eighth Avenue subway. The city uses what chiselers call "blind boxes," and the walk across town to the Independent system is a reasonably short one. There is no risk in using slugs on the Independent, Marty says, unless you work a spot too hard and too often.

Marty Franklin loves parties, but hardly ever is invited to them in advance or even knows what party he is going to when he starts out in the evening. He finds them by ear, chiefly down in Greenwich Village. Shrill ladies and noisy men act like buoys in the dark, only instead of sheering off when you hear the hubbub, you lay your course directly on it. You go up, ask for Ernie Klemfuss or Herbert Lindsey or somebody, and if the hosts are sober enough to know he isn't there, you back away looking wistful as hell, he explains. If it doesn't work at the first place it will at the next, and you can find a hundred parties in the Village almost any night, particularly on Saturdays. You meet interesting people in the Village, Marty finds. Nuts, most of them, but the sandwiches are good and the gin's not bad, he says. Farewell parties on outgoing ships are good fun.

There are times, even for him, when a need arises for quick money—funds with which to meet emergencies such as the need of a new blue-serge suit or new shoes. You can't do without a blue-serge suit in his line, he confides, because it makes the best front and won't offend even at the press tables of the most formal hotel parties. A blue-serge suit sets you apart from the ordinary overdressed Broadway lugs, he says.

Sometimes quick money comes easily. Marty may get a job as a movie extra representing a true New York type, or he may hire out as a genuine Zulu warrior for the sidewalk display of a motion-picture house featuring an African film. He always looks for jobs that cannot be anything but temporary.

Another angle, a bit worn but still in use, is the note game. Marty used to learn what stars were headlined at the *Follies*, the Palace, or at the variety shows and would dig back in his memory for someone who played on the same bill with them in better days (the midtown district is congested with vaudeville's has-beens), and sign the name of the back number to a sobby note asking for help. Willie Howard, the comedian, has been taken in on that a hundred times by different chiselers, and so have Eddie

Cantor, George Jessel, and Al Jolson. If Marty has any misgivings about this kind of chiseling, he doesn't show it.

He admits, with what seems to be some reluctance, that he occasionally uses the "crying gag" to collect capital. For this one, he explains, you borrow a violin case or a brief case to give the impression that you're a deserving musician or a professional man. You stand near a Hudson Tube station and exhibit a few pennies to likely-looking prospects. You explain, with a stammer and a bewildered look to indicate embarrassment, that you've left your wallet home and must be in Newark within a hour. With the proper front and half-decent dramatics, he says, a good man can make from seven to fourteen dollars a day. Lots of good people, he explains, shower down quarters and half dollars, give you their card, and go away happy. No self-respecting chiseler works the game, he hastens to add, unless it's a matter of life and death, or unless he's slipping. He can't explain precisely why he thinks there is something reprehensible about the crying gag.

One of the golden legends of the chiseling guild tells how Marty Franklin himself boasted one day that he could get along comfortably for twenty-four hours on one cent, slugs barred, and made good. He had breakfast at Childs, lunch at Dave's Blue Room, and in between meals used the salted cent to call an uptown agency for a demonstration of the latest in town cars. Posing as a member of the New York Athletic Club swimming team, he entered the clubhouse by the back door after lunch and had a dip and a shower. He doesn't use the front entrance, he explains, because the man on the front door is poison to chiselers. After his swim, he went to the Waldorf, where he read the free papers, got a free flower for his coat from one of the vases, and waited for the town car. At teatime a bellboy came through the lobby paging "Mr. Jordan Blackstone" (Marty had changed his name to this for the afternoon). The Waldorf, or any other hotel for that matter, will page guests or nonguests merely for the asking, and Marty knows it. Spinning up the Drive and through the Park with the automobile salesman, Marty discussed automatic clutch and streamline to show serious intent, and then had the salesman drop him off at the hotel again. Dinner that night was at the Astor—a merry shindig of the National Library Association, he remembers, with rather high-brow cigarettes and excellent Martinis. He dropped in on *Anything Goes!* and then found a night's rest in a private drinking room at the Biltmore. Up betimes and to a Walgreen store for a bicarbonate of soda. They're free there, and good after a night of hard drinking and that rich banquet food.

Death Avenue Cowboys

I WENT down to the West Side freight yards, just before the last Death Avenue cowboys were taken off.

The yardmaster's shack trembled as the freight string lumbered by. Red coals shivered in the rusty pot-bellied stove. Dispatchers' books jigged on the wall. When the string had gone by, the yardmaster stared through the window over the flow of converging tracks. He said the Death Avenue Cavalry was cut down now. Only three riders.

Pete O'Connor, a glum West Sider on the four P.M. to midnight ride, said: "It's the same every day. You make two or three trips a day."

A man in cap and dungarees came in from the yards. He slumped onto a bench, stared into the coals. He listened to the talk awhile. He was a rider once; worked up to brakeman now.

He said: "We had a horse once by the name of Tackhead. Tackhead wouldn't go past Seventeenth Street, heading south. You couldn't make St. John's Yard on Tackhead. Tackhead, he backed up three blocks on me once."

Pete O'Connor leaned against the shack boarding. He said: "We ain't got Tackhead no more. We got Cyclone and Tom and Midget."

The riders were men grown up near the West Side yards. The yardmaster said the riders always had been West Side boys. Pete O'Connor was West Side. So was George Hayde and Marty Ahern.

The brakeman said: "Hayde, didn't he meet his wife down here? Didn't he marry one of the neighborhood gals who kep' askin' him for a ride on the horse? The girls always wanted to ride on the horses."

No one answered. Far off you heard boxcars taking the frogs in a stream of clicks that came up through the ground. Viaducts now carry the freights above Tenth Avenue. This spelled finish for the riders.

"They've been a long time riding the avenue," the yardmaster said moodily. "Ever since 1850. That's almost a hundred years, when you think of it."

The first troop had thirty riders. They jogged ahead of chuffing locomotives to warn buggy drivers and teamsters out of the way.

"It was a city law," the yardmaster said. "The horses used to get scared and bolt."

On hot summer days, forty-fifty years ago, West Side urchins trailed barefoot behind the riders. They dreamed of growing up to be riders, as Huck Finn and Tom Sawyer dreamed of growing up to be Mississippi steamboat pilots. In those days Tenth Avenue of a summer day still held some of its rural atmosphere. Old Mike Ragg, the one-legged shepherd, would come by on his crutch herding a flock of sheep down the cobblestones. His collie would run, panting, on the flanks, keeping the sheep in huddle. By and by the New York Central stopped hiring boys. Riders had to be eighteen or more. Their number kept dropping off.

In the old days people called the riders "dummy boys"

because they rode ahead of a special light dummy engine. Some people called them Tenth Avenue cowboys. Officially they were "flag boys" because by day they waved red signal flags as they rode before a string. At night they waved a red lantern.

The melancholy brakeman seemed hypnotized by the glow in the grate.

He said: "The kids would run after you when I was riding. They would holler, 'Paul Revere! Here comes Paul Revere!'"

Thirty years ago most of the horses in the service were worn-out fire horses. Their legs would give out in two years on the cobbled street.

"Put rubber pads on the shoes," the yardmaster said, "and they were good for seven-eight years."

Worn-out mounts were sold at the Bull's Head Auction over on Third Avenue. In the last years mounts were hired.

O'Connor the rider stared out through the rain. He said: "They get full o' beans sometimes. They try to throw you."

Another line of freights darkened the shack window. It shivered the scarred tin flooring under the old stove.

I went from the yardmaster's shack at Thirty-third Street and Eleventh Avenue on slippery crossties to the riders' booth at Tenth Avenue and Thirtieth Street. No one spoke. In the scarred octagonal booth where the riders' got their calls the walls were covered with old pictures. One was "Miss America 1938," in color.

Pete O'Connor said: "I got to go down to Seventeenth Street."

He crossed a cobbled stretch to a small stable in the

street. He came out with a patient brown saddle horse. He vaulted lightly into the saddle.

Pretty soon all you could see was Pete O'Connor's head and the horse's back, rhythmically bobbing southward in lanes of shiny sedans and gigantic motor trucks.

Tunnels and Dominoes

THE TUNNEL Inspector tooled the Port of New York Authority car toward the toll booths at the mouth of Lincoln Tunnel. He stopped and pointed to upright wires sticking out of the concrete alongside each booth.

He said thousands of motorists drive over these and similar wires on highways, at tunnel and bridge entrances, day after day, and still think the wires are automatic counting devices. I had thought they were counting devices, too.

The inspector said, "They're no such thing. They simply ground each car as it comes by, draw off the static electricity before the toll is handed to the men in the booths. If we didn't have them the men would be shocked into paralysis."

The inspector said this was discovered when Holland Tunnel was first opened. The unfortunate toll collectors became coin shy within a few minutes. Every time they accepted toll payment they came six inches off the ground. For weeks thereafter, cars were grounded by a crude water system. A hose was trained on the concrete just ahead of each booth approach. This carried off the static electricity and it was safe, thereafter, for collectors to handle the coins.

The car slid into the tunnel. Eyes straight ahead, the inspector said motorists who use the Holland and Lincoln tubes, year in and year out, do not know that cars feed faster into a tunnel than they come out of one. Bridges, the inspector explained, are highest at their center. Tunnels, on the other hand, reach their lowest level at the center, under the river. Motorists, unaware they have reached an upgrade, lose headway. That's why you see policemen frantically waving motorists onward where the upgrade begins. Some people have a silly notion that policemen wave in a spirit of play, or because they are lonesome, or have poor circulation.

A few hundred feet from the mouth of Holland Tunnel, on the Jersey side, the inspector showed a powerful searchlight set on a foot-high concrete base. This is another device that seems to puzzle tunnel users.

The light is thrown at right angles to traffic lanes. It creates sharp shadows and highlights. It enables a practiced eye to detect low or sagging tires, rubber that is apt to poop out in mid-tunnel. Inspectors wave these weaklings off the tunnel lanes. Three quarters of what the inspector called "stoppages" in tunnel traffic are caused by weak or deflated tires. It takes from four to seven minutes to put on a spare.

There have been no serious tunnel fires. Brake band fires of short duration are the most common kind. Holland Tunnel averages about fifty of these each year. Firefighting equipment is within easy walking distance the full length of the tunnels. There are emergency exits in both tunnels but so far they have never been used.

I walked through the ventilation and control buildings of both tunnel systems on both the New York and New Jersey sides. They were high-ceilinged, stern-walled places with languid men staring at lighted electric panel boards.

The supervisor at the New Jersey end of the Lincoln Tunnel showed what happens when the carbon monoxide context in the tubes rises higher than two and one half points to every 10,000 points of air. A light flashed on and an alarm bell noisily called attention to it. The supervisor walked to the lighted panel and threw a switch. The warning light dimmed and the alarm died away.

"I just opened another blower," the supervisor explained. "Draw off the impure air that much faster."

Tunnel policemen work two hours on the tunnel catwalk and two hours in open air at the tunnel plazas. They have an eight-hour day. There are no health hazards in the job. It's the monotony that gets them. The constant stream of cars seems to have a dulling effect on a man if he's on the catwalk too long.

Sometimes a bewildered cat or dog gets into the tunnel. Occasionally a duck or a hen falls from a poulterer's truck. There are not enough of these exciting events to hold a policeman's interest. The inspector remembered when a steer dropped off a cattle truck in the tunnel.

"That was a red-letter day," he said.

A patrol wagon takes the policemen in and out on the two-hour shifts. The chart for this maneuver is extremely complicated. The inspector seemed rather proud of it.

"Figured it out, in a couple of nights, in my home on Staten Island," he said. "In my experiments I didn't use cops. Worked it out with dominoes."

Too Much Spice

SPICE odors came downwind two blocks from the spice mills in the weathered brick plant on Franklin Street. The closer you trod the sharper the odors seemed. The inner brick walls, once white, were a melancholy yellow and coated with fine spice dust, mostly brown and red, something like brick dust.

Mr. Weyer said, "That yellow you see is from volatile spice oils. It has settled on the walls through the years. It's on everything; all six floors."

The stranger's sense of smell became, in a manner of speaking, somewhat hysterical. It struggled frantically to identify individual pungent odors but made no headway. Mr. Weyer peered down the length of the gloomy loft as if he could *see* the odors. His nose wiggled like a rabbit's over a carrot.

"Can't say for sure," he said. "But I'd guess what we're getting right here is mostly caraway. Some kummel, maybe."

He felt his surefooted way between high mounds of en-shadowed bales and bags of spices. The place was ill-lighted and spice dust hung in the half-light like red fog. We clumped along rough wooden flooring, past silent gnomish men who toiled at fragrant bales. Their faces seemed inordinately grave, had the rust-and-yellow tint of the walls. Their work clothes were colored as in a Disney cartoon, only slightly subdued. At an open, narrow elevator shaft at the end of the floor Mr. Weyer leaned over an ancient wooden gate. He shouted down into the dark.

"John!" he hollered. "Ho, John!"

A wooden elevator, rusty with spice dust, creaked slowly into view. The operator was a solemn fellow, dusty-browed under a dusty stocking cap. He shut the wooden gate and we ascended at laggard pace into increasing colored fog. Mr. Weyer stepped into another cavernous loft, darker than the one below. Gyrators throbbed and pulsed in the shadows, grinding and sifting red pepper, cayenne, cloves, caraway, cardamon, mace. These ponderous devices, distorted in the weak dust-infiltrated light, ground the crude stuff and dropped it through fine silk mesh. Cloth bags at the bottom bulged and breathed as the spices blew through. Mr. Weyer explained the cats that kept staring at you all over the plant. They fixed golden-grape eyes on you from lofty bale mounds.

Mr. Weyer said, "They keep mice away. Mice thrive on spices. They're suckers for paprika."

At one end of the loft, at Mr. Weyer's demand, a thin-faced man moved through the shadows, slitting bag after bag to exhibit raw spices. He held up some dried brown sticks.

"Cinnamon," he said. Another handful. "Short-stick Batavia."

He brought out African ginger, Granada mace, allspice from Jamaica, red pepper from Japan, coriander from Morocco, curry from India, cloves from Madagascar, caramon from the Malay archipelago. My eyes smarted and I looked wistfully at the clean air beyond the dusty windows. I reflected there can be too much spice in a man's life.

On the mill floor, below, leather belting slapped at great iron wheels lost in deep upper gloom. Great galvanized pipes and middle-sized pipes ran through the flooring, carrying off milled nutmeg, milled cayenne. A dusty-red miller patiently scooped crushed nutmeg from a mound on the floor and fed it into a hopper. He said, no, he didn't mind the strong odor, not after twenty-five years of it.

In a deep Hibernian brogue he said, "There's some that can't stand it. Get drunk as a hoptoad on it. It's only the chilis that get me, the peppers. Chilis'll grab at your throat."

In the slow-motion lift Mr. Weyer said millers are hard to get. You've got to break them in as apprentices. Most spice millers are Irish, but he didn't know why. Spice workers, generally, hold onto their jobs. I met six who had been with the company twenty years, or better. The United States, Mr. Weyer told me, uses about 100,000,000 pounds of spices a year. Pepper, nutmeg, and cinnamon are used the most. Per capita consumption, Mr. Weyer figured, is something like 1.35 pounds.

The mill workers and office workers dislike muggy days.

"You get in the subway," Mr. Weyer explained, "and the people around you start sniffing. They can't figure you out. You look all right, but you smell like the hold of an Indiaman."

Tugs

THE TUG dispatchers' windows on the twenty-fifth floor of the Whitehall Building gave you an airplane pilot's view of Lower Bay and the Hudson's mouth. There was only clean, cold wind between the pane and the distant horizon. The Highlands lay blue behind Brooklyn. Washed clean in the pre-Easter sunlight were Buttermilk Channel, Governors Island, the Statue of Liberty, Red Hook Flats, all New York Harbor. White-plumed tugs and wide-bodied ferries crosshatched the metal-blue waters with curling wake.

In the office the radiotelephone made throaty noises. The wind quivered the aerial outside the window and the glass insulators sparkled. Gusts whimpered and sobbed at the sill. Captain Miller looked at the ticker.

He said, "It's blowing thirty-two miles out of the West. Nice breeze o' wind."

Captain Anglim and Captain Miller spoke with tug captains by telephone and by radiotelephone. Sometimes they opened the window and held out the blue-and-white Moran Towing Company flag. Captain Anglim pointed downbay. He said, "Here comes Eugene Moran. I'll shake out the flag and he'll put in at the Battery and call us for orders."

He held out the flag and it snapped in the gale. At

night, Captain Anglim explained, the dispatchers signal
with lights. One red, for example, is a call to the *Alice
Moran* to call in; two red, for the *Elizabeth Moran;* one
white, the *Eugene.* The company runs twenty-seven boats
in its fleet.

The telephone rang. Captain Anglim listened a moment. Then he spoke into it.

"Come on up here for the *Challenger,*" he said. "We're
taking her out of Pier 84 in North River. It's a three-
boat job." He listened a while. "Yeah, it's the *Peter,*
the *Richard,* and you," he said. "Step on it, Johnny.
You'll have to come fast. . . . What the Hell . . ." He
put up the receiver. Cut off. The phone rang again.
". . . Come right on up, Johnny. You're taking the
Challenger over to Brooklyn, south side of Pier 16. . . .
If we get the *Alice* we'll hail you."

He put up the phone. Now the bay was slate gray.
Night walked the sky and his boots were great clouds.
Their shadow lay like blue wash on South Brooklyn. The
radio gave off a strong rush of sound. Hoarsely it said,
"One ship in sight. . . . Can't make out who she is. . . .
One ship in sight to the south. . . . Don't know who she
is. . . . Will not port before five o'clock."

Captain Miller tuned the voice down. He said, "That's
one of the harbor pilots. They hang around off Ambrose
waiting for ships to come in."

Boatmen came in, weathered chaps with a leaning toward rather strong pipes. You picked up some of their
gab. A cook, you gathered, is a "belly robber." When
you eat you "grub up." When you take on water for
boilers you "Croton 'em." Captain Anglim wanted to
know why writers always describe tugs as "dirty little tugs"
or "squat little craft."

"They ought to let some of those guys polish the brass on *Alice,* hey Joe?" he said.   The other dispatcher nodded. The radio sounded like frying eggs.

"This is the *George Keogh* calling the *Carrie Messek.* . . . This is the *George Keogh* calling the *Carrie Messek.*" Then it died away into silence.

By radio and by land phone the dispatchers moved their tugs across bay and upriver.   They assigned one tug to pick up the wreck of the *Rosie McNeil* at the foot of Noble Street in Brooklyn.

A white-shirted man came from the outer office.   He said, "It looks like we'll have to send the *William* and *Sheila* to Baltimore tonight.   That's what it looks like."

A pilot's voice roared in on the radio.

"Passing the *Asiatic.* . . .   Don't know what to tell you. . . .   It may be a job. . . .   The way things look I can't tell. . . .   Not before midnight. . . .   You can figure accordingly."

Now the harbor lay dark.   Captain Anglim stood by the window and stared up the river.

"No sign of the *Challenger,* Joe," he said.   "No sign of the *Arkansas.*"

Next morning I went down to board a tug.   Down the blue pasture of the sky a fresh cool wind herded white clouds like woolly lambs over the bay.   Questing sun, sharp-angled by city dust, thrust broad red beams in the massed canyons' dark.   On the stringpiece where Rector Street leaps into North River the breeze snapped at your topcoat, tried for your hat.   A morose, heavy-paunched watchman sucked at his pipe and regarded the water.

He said: "The *Dalzellea* comes soon.   Seven o'clock

she's coming. She takes the *Talamanca* from here to Pier 9."

Twenty of seven, now. A Luckenbach freighter slid downriver, headed toward sea. A battered tramp briskly moved upstream. Gulls dived in her foam. The tide patted the pier, smacked its lips, gurgled and sucked like a child. Near Jersey shore a great ship valved steam from its side, a giant gasping as if his lungs might burst. The *Dalzellea* nosed in. Reflected tide wriggled and blazed in her pilothouse panes. We went aboard and she moved into the dock, nuzzled the *Talamanca*'s hull. Captain Alan Howell thrust his head from the *Dalzellea*'s pilothouse, peered up the *Talamanca*'s towering flank in the ardent sun.

"Good morning, Mister Mate," he called. The hail was answered from the lofty rail. Captain Howell bawled a series of orders. "All right, boys, drop us your towline. . . . Take a turn, now. . . . Slack away—easy. . . . One man for'ard to take my headline. . . . Make that fast on the forrid bitt, sailor."

Tug men moved lively. Bells clanged. Sunbeams bit at the *Dalzellea*'s burnished brass pilothouse wheel. Two other Dalzell tugs took lines from the *Talamanca*: the *Dalzellace* on the stern, the *Dalzellance* at the bow. A short, red-eyed man with his coat collar up came in and took over the wheel. Mr. Finn. The captain left for the *Talamanca*'s deck, to give orders from the bridge. Mr. Finn moved restlessly from one pilothouse window to the other, studying leverage.

"You part a line and it can cost you a million," he said.

Captain Howell blew whistle blasts from the bridge and we moved. The stern hawser grew taut. Water sudded under the *Dalzellace*'s strain. The tow, hoarsely blasting the stillness, moved out toward midstream.

Mr. Finn leaned far out of the window. He hollered, "Take up the slack on your stern line, there!"

Slowly the white *Talamanca* emerged from the shadow in the dock. The *Dallzelace* hauled and the two others pushed. The towed ship faced north. The *Dalzellea*'s radiotelephone beeped and talked like a parrot. Mostly tug orders. Gently we nosed into Pier 9. Captain Howell's whistled signals were matched in the *Dalzellea*'s pilothouse by the clang of engine-room bells, were acknowledged by blasts from the tug.

By eight A.M. the *Talamanca* was snug in her berth—hardly a bump or a jar. The captains of the other Dalzell tugs bade profane good-bys and chestily chuffed down North River. Mr. Finn put the *Dalzellea*'s buffalo head to Pier 9 and took Captain Howell aboard. We backed off and moved on sun-dappled water past Governors Island, past Liberty. Just below Bedloes we picked up an Englishman, docked him in Brooklyn.

Spring breezes played sibilant tag through the pilothouse windows. Captain Alan, forty years on the tugs, talked of their history. They're good for fifty years, rightly handled, he said. Tugs come high, anywhere from $100,000 to almost a quarter million, or more. Boilers alone at $20,000 or better. Captain Howell said: "You take our engines. They'll kick up 800 horse and there are times when you need all the horses." He recalled some of his distinguished passengers. "I had Teddy, once, the real Teddy Roosevelt. I took him off when he got back from the River of Doubt. Him and Mrs. Roosevelt and Quentin. Docked them in Oyster Bay."

The radiotelephone hissed, burst into sudden uproar.

Some tug dispatcher was frantic. He was saying: "Oh my God, Jasper, you got the wrong tow. We're not getting paid for that job. Who gave you those orders, Jasper?" There was a momentary pause. We could not hear the answer. "Oh, my God Almighty," the dispatcher finally said, anguished. "Hang that barge up, Jasper. Hang it up somewhere. Beat it back to the Gulf boat. Step on it, Jasper."

Sidewalk Fisherman

SAM SCHULTZ has always been hydrophobic. Even as a kid, in a Central Park rowboat he would go white with fear of the water. When he grew up and friends invited him on fishing parties he'd always refuse, saying he had a tendency to seasickness. It took a vast economic disturbance, the depression, to throw him into grate fishing when all his natural instincts were against it, but today he is probably the world's champion grate fisherman, the man who can haul up coins from subway gratings with more efficiency than anybody else in the business. Grate fishing was a primitive art when Sam became identified with it after losing his job as a truckman's helper seven years ago. It was just something that bums worked at for beer money. Sam has made it an exact science, and he earns a living by it.

Sam works with a few feet of light twine and a plummet of his own design—a piece of steel five inches long, an eighth of an inch thick, and about an inch and three quarters wide, just right to lower through the grate slot. He lets it down endways until it gets to the bottom, and then lets it fall broadside on the coin. Sam will point out that his five-inch plummet thus covers a potential working area of almost ten inches. The flat side of the plummet is

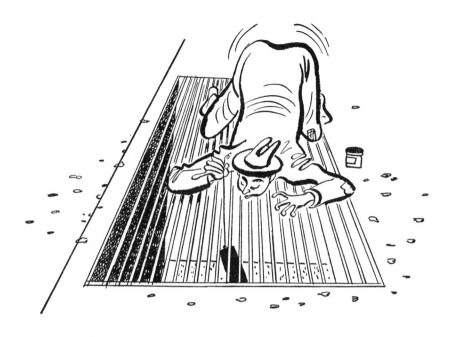

greased so that the coin sticks to it; all Sam has to do then is to haul away and he's got the money. The bums of the grate-fishing industry use tiny weights for plummets and have to maneuver their lines a long time before they hit. "My way," Sam will tell you, "is pure headwoik."

Sam's second and equally important contribution toward uplift of the industry was an all-weather stickum to take the place of the chewing gum or taxicab-wheel grease which the bums use on their casting plummets. Chewing gum was all right in summer but it hardened at the first frost. Taxi grease worked into your pores, got under your fingernails, and made your hands untidy. It took months of experiment before Sam found the right thing—

white petroleum jelly, or vaseline. A thin coat of this on the plummet will pull pennies, dimes, nickels, and even big money out of any subway grate, come frost or heat wave.

Sam buys the vaseline in the Liggett's drugstore on Times Square. The clerks there know him now and they plop the jar on the counter the minute he walks in. A single jar will last a month in winter and about three weeks in summer, if you husband it and don't oversmear, which is the general fault of amateurs. Runoff, because of heat, accounts for the extra summer waste, and so far Sam hasn't found a way around that. When you're after big money (quarters and halves), it is better to thicken the vaseline coating on your plummet, but not too much. Sam figures, for example, that proper bait for a silver dollar would be around a sixteenth of an inch. That's pure theory, because cartwheels are practically extinct in New York and he has never had a chance to work on one.

Sam may not look it now, but he was a machine gunner in the World War. Hunching over grates has rounded his shoulders and has taken something from his five feet, seven inches. He keeps his hat brim far down over his face, which is red from exposure. He got into that habit when he first took up grate fishing. He was ashamed of his work and always afraid he might be recognized by the Brooklyn crowd who used to invite him around to pinochle and poker games when he was a truckman's helper. Incidentally, he thinks that stuff about Times Square being the crossroads of the world is just a myth. He's fished the Square almost every night for seven years and hasn't seen one of his old acquaintances.

Sam's people were German-American. They died before he got through 6B in Public School 25 on First Avenue at Fifth Street. He wasn't much at school except in history and arithmetic, and most of that is gone now. He doesn't think, though, that he will ever forget the stuff about George Washington, Abraham Lincoln, and Captain John Smitz. The sturdy Captain sticks in his mind. "Captain Smitz," he will say, "was so tough a tommyhawk bounced off his neck and the Indians had to turn him loose."

Sam always liked horses, and when he got out of school in the middle of the sixth year he drove a wagon for a neighborhood fruit-and-vegetable man. That's how he came to get his first job as a truckman's helper when he lived in Harlem. He had to give that up when he was drafted into the Thirty-second Machine Gun Battalion and sent to Camp Meade. He liked machine gunning. He recalls that it made a man feel like somebody to have a Lewis gun kicking against his shoulder. Sadness overtakes him now when he remembers how Spanish flu swept the camp in October of 1918, forty-eight hours before his outfit was scheduled to go to France. The quarantine held until the war ended.

When he got back to New York from Camp Meade, Sam looked around for another helper's job and finally landed one over in Brooklyn. He started at twelve dollars a week and worked up to twenty-six. That had been cut to twenty-one dollars when the job was swept out from under him altogether by the depression. With that he lost all his Brooklyn interests, even his (up to then) unshaken faith in the Dodgers. He doesn't get to the ball games on Sundays as he used to, but if he could raise the price of a bleacher seat he supposes he might root for the Yanks. Sam thinks a man ought to be loyal to some team and he never liked the Giants anyway.

Grate angling prickles with fine points that you'd never dream of if you hadn't put your mind to it as Sam has. He knows all the midtown gratings by heart and can tell you, within a few cents, what his yield has been in each one. He watches waste cans for discarded newspapers, and scans the lists of goings-on in town to figure out the night's working schedule. If there is nothing happening at Madison Square Garden, for example, he will stick to Times Square, which is to the grate angler what the Grand Banks are to a Gloucesterman. Sometimes he'll just play a hunch and go over to the East Side, now that the King-fish has disappeared. The Kingfish was a giant Negro who would pound your ears right down to your ankles if you poached on his Lexington and Madison Avenue grates. No one seems to know what has happened to him, but he hasn't been around. Rival fishermen hope it's nothing slight; Sam, in any case, is uneasy every time he works on the East Side. He figures that the Kingfish, who used to spend all his haul for gin, may merely be doing a short bit on the Island for assault or something and may get back any day. Sam, by the way, isn't a drinking man at all, though he will take a glass of beer on hot days.

The Garden is the best spot in town on fight nights, or when there's wrestling or hockey. Patrons of those sports are A-1 droppers. If you're a fast worker, like Sam, you can fish from fifty or sixty cents all the way up to a dollar on the Garden side of Eighth Avenue, from Forty-seventh Street north, on any night when there's a good fight card. Sam keeps away, though, during the Horse Show or when there is a Communist rally. He has come to learn that the Horse Show crowd either use their own cars or, when they pay off a taxi, simply don't drop any change. Communists, he'll advise you bitterly, are the lousiest droppers in the world. You can't count much on special events, either. Sam figures from what he'd read in the newspapers, for example, that the American Legion Convention would bring a big week of fishing. He worked like hell all through the thing, and at the end, what had he? Less than if those apple-knocking wise guys with their electric shockers had stayed home on the farm. The whole thing still puzzles him. Sam hates to see his carefully worked-up theories go to pieces. Things like the flop of the American Legion Convention make him lose confidence in his judgment.

Newspaper stands set up on subway gratings are highly favored spots, for obvious reasons. When Sam first figured that out, he had wild ideas about canvassing the stand people all along Broadway and Seventh and Eighth Avenues to move their positions from building fronts to the curb. He toyed with the project for a while, but could never quite bring himself to making the proposition. Some of the paper sellers looked sour, and then, too, maybe it wouldn't have been honest. Sam is a stickler for honesty. He turned down an idea advanced by a Broadway chiseler who thought Sam might induce some kid to bump into people counting out change near the gratings. Sam just walked away from the fellow.

He has a working arrangement, however, with several of the busier newsstand owners. The man who operates the big stand on the northwest corner of Forty-second Street and Seventh Avenue drops on an average of $1.80 or $2 a month. Every time Sam comes by, the stand man indicates where coins have been dropped and Sam does his stuff. If the haul is small money he keeps all of it. On quarters, though, he gets only ten cents and on half dollars only thirty cents. He thinks that's fair enough, and even if he didn't what could he do? Let some other fisherman get the business? He had a trade argument one time with another stand owner, a woman, and before he knew it she had her own kid fishing for the drops.

Movie-house barkers will tip Sam off when people drop money, as they often do while fighting to buy tickets in a crowd. Some barkers, though, are apt to be snooty, especially the ones with fancy uniforms. Sometimes they snarl at Sam and tell him to scram. That always makes him curl up inside. Whenever it happens he tries to think of Camp Meade and the machine gun kicking away at his shoulder. One night a man dropped a twenty-dollar bill, wrapped around a half dollar, through the grating in front of the Rialto. Sam got the flash from the barker but a subway porter beat him to the money—lifted one of the grates and got two dollars' reward for the job. Whenever Sam thinks of the incident he grows wistful. Even without the reward it was a swell chance to set a world record for grate fishing.

Sam walks from ten to fifteen miles every night covering the grates, but never has foot trouble. The only time he ever had sore feet was a few years ago when he took a laborer's job up in Narrowsburg, New York, clearing out underbrush on the site of a Boy Scout camp. The ground was so soft and so alien to his feet that they slid all over the place and finally burst out in big blisters. He quit the sylvan quiet and was glad to get back to Times Square.

Sam usually works twelve hours a day, from five o'clock at night until daybreak. In addition to the general avenue runs he visits certain selected spots, in the manner of a trapper looking over his traps. After the early-evening rush the bus stop on the east side of the Times Building in the Square is nearly always good for twenty to thirty cents. The yield might be even better if some busybody hadn't wired boards under part of that grating. Sam doesn't know who's responsible, the *Times* people or the I. R. T. Another favored spot is the Lexington Avenue side of Grand Central Terminal in the morning and evening rush hours. Commuters use that entrance and they're very good droppers, especially on quarters; Sam can't say why. Loew's Lexington, between Fiftieth and Fifty-first, isn't bad either. At both places, of course, you've got to watch out for the Kingfish. The Waldorf is a continual disappointment—not nearly as good as Bickford's Restaurant at 582 Lexington Avenue or Foltis-Fischer's, next door to Bickford's. They're on the same side of the street as the Waldorf, one block farther north.

No part of the garment center is worth working, and that goes, generally, for everything below Forty-second Street except the Hotel New Yorker. At that, the best bit of fishing Sam ever did was in front of the Hotel York, on Seventh at Thirty-sixth, but it was just one of those freak things. He fished up a fountain pen with a lot of people watching and someone thought it might be a good idea to hold a sidewalk auction. The bid went to $1.10, the highest single sum Sam has ever earned at grate angling. He fished another pen—a two-minute job in front of the United Cigar Store at Forty-second and Seventh—but that was a flat-rate assignment from the owner and paid only fifty cents. The pen was a gift, with initials on it, and the fellow was very grateful; couldn't get over Sam's skill.

Sam tried Brooklyn once, on a sudden inspiration, but came back disgusted. He didn't so much as make carfare and bait money there, although he surveyed every grate in the neighborhood of the Fulton Street department stores.

The same goes for the Manhattan shopping district around
Macy's, Saks, and Gimbels. Women drop less than men
because their handbags are so big-jawed that change usually falls right back into them. He's never tried Queens,
but feels instinctively it would be no better than Brooklyn.

Sam figures his fishing nets him an average of a dollar
a day, or a little more. Some days, he says, you're lucky,
and you may get as much as $1.65 or even $1.85. Lots of
days, though, it's like going out for trout; you just don't
have any luck at all. Once Sam hauled out only six cents
in fourteen hours on the grates—a nickel in front of the
Rialto and one cent from the Times island bus stop. He
knew the recession was coming even before the papers
began to notice it. Almost overnight Times Square was
overrun with outsiders (any newcomer is an outsider to
Sam) working the grates with disgustingly primitive
equipment.

When the day's yield is a dollar or over, Sam feels justi-
fied in spending fifty cents for a room in the Seventh Avenue Mills Hotel. If it happens to be a little less, he puts
up at the Vigilant, on Eighth Avenue near Twenty-eighth,
where they charge only forty cents. He prefers the Mills
because the guests are more genteel—not so apt to get
boisterous. You don't get soap or towels with the rooms,
so Sam carries his own, neatly wrapped in newspapers.
He carries two suits of underwear, too; an extra pair of
socks, a Gillette, and a stick of shaving soap. He bathes
once a week in the Municipal Baths on Forty-first Street,
at Ninth, when it's cold, but will go two or three times
in hot weather. He feels a man loses his grip altogether
if he doesn't clean up at least once a week.

Sam has no fancy tastes in food, although his work in
the open air sharpens his appetite. When he finishes the

early-morning run of the grates he has breakfast at the Manhattan, on Seventh Avenue near Forty-first. It's pretty nearly always the same—wheatcakes and coffee, for a dime. On good days he tries to get down to Beefsteak John's, at Third Avenue and Twenty-first, where they serve a stew, coffee, and bread for fifteen cents. If the day's haul warrants it, Sam may have a cut of coconut pie, the only dessert that ever tempts him. Sometimes, but not unless he has room money reserved, there's a late snack at the Manhattan and, because Sam's imagination doesn't seem to work where food's concerned, it's very likely to be wheats and java again. He has a good stomach —always did have—and never gets sick.

It's a mistake, unless you're out to bait Sam, to bring up the subject of stinkers. You wouldn't know about them, but stinkers are the parasites of the grate-fishing industry. When they sense that Sam is having a lucky night, they run on ahead and cut in on his grates. There's nothing you can do about it, either. Gratings are more or less public domain and anybody can fish them. What stirs Sam's gall, though, is the utter lack of ethics (he says "ettics") in the business—something he's tried to correct, but without much luck. "By me," he's apt to tell you with astonishing violence, "a stinker is rat poison—in spades."

Most grate fishermen are antisocial. They don't so much as ask one another's names. Oh, once in a while one of them may look up from a grate and say, "Hya, fisherman!" but you can't count on it. On chatty occasions they may ask about your luck, but that's more or less perfunctory, too. No old-timer in the business will tell another fisherman how much he's made; certainly not *where* he made it. Sam does have a working arrangement with a young grate angler who has been in and around the Square the past four years. He's a shy, shabby fellow who has an expression of constant bewilderment. Cab drivers make him the butt of their unsubtle jokes (Shellshock is their name for him, because of that rabbity look), but he's rather handy with the plummet. Once a week he or Sam will ride down to Barclay Street on the H. M. T. and buy a dozen flashlight batteries at a cut-rate hardware store. All grate anglers use flashlights to show up what's at the grating bottoms. At the cut-rate stores the batteries are three cents apiece, against five cents for the same thing at Woolworth's, so Sam and Shellshock save a total of fourteen cents on the deal, even when you count in the carfare. There's always a chance, too, to fish carfare out of the downtown grates, but outside of William Street and maybe Church, financial-district fishing is lousy.

Three batteries make one fill for the flashlight and will last about three days. Sam always has three extra ones bulging his pockets, along with his portable toilet kit. Most grate anglers are rather sloppy—carry their plummets in their pockets, grease and all. Sam is a neat fellow and packs his equipment in a Prince Albert Tin. It took him quite a while to convince Shellshock that it wasn't nice to get his pockets all smeary, but he never has sold Shellshock the vaseline idea. Shellshock just wipes off his plummet after each performance and gets new grease from the wheels of the nearest cab.

People keep asking Sam if it's true that grating fishermen find valuable diamonds and things like that. He knows of but two cases. One time a traffic cop lost a diamond ring near Penn Station. This cop went home at the end of the day, rigged up a childish fishing outfit, and came back to fish. By that time, of course, the ring was gone. Sam doesn't know who got it. In the other case (Sam won't vouch for this, because it's only hearsay), the Kingfish was supposed to have done a job for a woman who lost a five-thousand-dollar bracelet on Lexington Avenue. The woman gave him a quarter, so the story goes, and the Kingfish would have busted her crumpet if she had been a man.

Sam is doing some research on a pocket-battery outfit—something on the automobile-lighter principle—that will melt thin ice at the bottom of the grating. If he perfects this invention, he feels he can practically control the industry. He hasn't thought the whole thing through yet, but he's the dogged type and will probably work it out all right.

PART FOUR

All Around

The Town

Pickup Man

OVER coffee and buns in an uptown Broadway cafeteria the lottery pickup man talked about his job. He covers his route every day except Sunday by automobile, taking up little slips holding lists of numbers collected by runners or storekeepers. He picks up the cash at the same time. The play—"action" he kept calling it, or "the work"—is in nickels, dimes, and quarters, but the runners convert this into banknotes for his convenience.

"Silver is hard on clothes," the pickup man explained. "It wears holes in your pockets and pulls your suits out of shape."

His clothes were rather shabby. His russet shoes were badly scuffed and his overcoat sleeves were stringy. He was about twenty-three years old and genially apologetic about his job.

"I'm on straight salary," he said. "I draw thirty-five dollars a week and commissions on any numbers I get on my own. I drove a truck for four years and never got out of the bag. I owed my life."

At 11:30 A.M. he said it was time to start. He got into a small sedan. The upholstery was soiled. He apologized for that, too, and started north toward East Harlem.

The pickup man slid the sedan to the curb in a side street off Broadway. He looked nervously around, got

229

out, and threaded his way through a group of screaming children of preschool age to a little tailor shop. His hands were deep in his overcoat pockets. The tailor barely looked up. From under the fur coat in his lap he drew his little stack of numbers and some green money. The pickup man stuffed these into his trousers pocket and hurried out.

He made three other stops in this street: one in a grocer's shop and two in tenements. He looked up and down the block before he came out of the hallway at the last place. Back in the sedan he folded the numbers slips into little bundles and dropped them into a secret flap under the hood. I wondered how he could dispose of the slips if the cops came.

"Some of the guys eat them," he said, "but I can't do it. Anyways, I carry too many. They'd kill me if I ate them."

The pickup man talked about runners. Any runner whose "action" is less than thirty or forty dollars a day, he explained, is "a stiff," looked down on by the others. A good runner brings in from forty to eighty dollars a day. He said New York rates low as a numbers town since Dutch Schultz was killed. Detroit, Philadelphia, Chicago, and St. Louis get much heavier action.

"No organization here any more," the pickup man explained. "All small bankers. The guy I work for started with only a couple hundred dollars. If he gets big play on a number he has to lay it off on some one bigger, and I ain't sayin' who."

The sedan shuddered to a sudden stop in another side street, opposite a shabby hotel. The pickup man bucked his way against the wind and disappeared into the lobby. He was out again in less than a minute. He grinned as he resumed the wheel.

"That's the way I like them," he said. "That guy never keeps me waiting. If he ain't around I pick up from his mailbox."

It was amusing to watch uniformed traffic cops gravely wave the sedan on. The pickup man said uniformed men never bother him, anyway. It's the division-office men and plain-clothes detectives from the borough squads who cause trouble. He cursed them as he turned into a block off Amsterdam Avenue.

"This place is hot," he muttered. "I don't like this part of it. They been hangin' around here since Satiday."

Reluctantly, or so it seemed, he slid from the car and walked into a soiled tenement. He was gone ten minutes. When he slipped back into the car he got off to a jerky start and mismanaged his gears in his nervousness and anxiety to leave the neighborhood. All this seemed unnecessary. The street looked deserted.

Down by the river we stopped at a factory and at a garage. This took about fifteen minutes. When the pickup man was back in the sedan he had a fistful of money and numbers. His confidence seemed restored. Besides, no one was in sight except an old Negro pushing a hot-dog cart against the river blow.

The pickup man said that people were goofy when they said that bankers manipulate the mutuals to make the figures come out to their liking. He said no current banker is big enough; not since the Dutchman was killed.

"These bankers got their headaches, too," the pickup man explained. "Suppose they get turned off, say. They got not only the cops but the state-income-tax guys and the Federal-income-tax guys on them."

Bankers, he said, often hold back the payoff and play money for two or three days. If they are "turned off" the

income-tax men take this money as a single day's earnings
and compute the annual tax on that basis.

"It ain't right," the pickup man said.

More hot coffee and buns in a tiny restaurant, farther
north, on the river. The proprietors were a white-haired
couple. The pickup man took a handful of slips and cash
from the old man; "Pop," he called him.

A garage mechanic in greasy tan work clothes was working the pin-ball machine. He stared gloomily at the
lights as his score came up. He plucked the woman by
the dress as she came by with the steaming coffee.

"Very poor, Mamma," he said. "I do not so good
today."

The old man came from behind the counter and gave
the pickup man ten cents; his own bet.

"Today," he said, "I play 567. That's my laundry number this week."

The pickup man grinned.

"That's a stiff, Pop," he said. "You're wasting your
dough."

Later stops included a filling station, a janitor's apartment in a dingy basement in the Eighties, and two more
stores: a butcher shop and a grocery store. The car
headed south again.

"One more," the pickup man said, "and I'm through."

He said his boss likes to have all numbers in by 2:30
P.M. before the track figures are ready. This gives him
time for layoffs, if he feels he needs them.

The pickup man saw his last runner leaning against a
tenement-house wall at a windy corner. The runner was
hatless and had no overcoat. He was a tall, blond youth.
His face was red with the wind.

"Get movin'," he said excitedly through the sedan window. "The bulls just went up the block in a Plymouth with a C license. I threw my numbers under that parked car there."

He indicated the car.

"I'll see you tonight," the pickup man said, and suddenly he seemed all thumbs.

The car jerked away, whisked through a light just gone red, and turned left. He said he would get the last runner's numbers at night; better than waiting around. He kept turning his head nervously to look for the C Plymouth as he scuttled out of the district.

Kitty Bundles

STERLING PLACE in Brooklyn is a sad sort of street on an overcast day, all but deserted when the kids are at school. Where the street slopes toward Sixth Avenue the brownstone tenement fronts are blackened and sullen, like weathered canyon walls under sunless sky.

Shutters still blocked the light in the six-room flat on the first floor, right, at No. 90, where Kate Powers had let herself starve to death though the rooms held bankbooks showing deposits of some $40,000, more or less, not including the dividend checks in the mail she had not opened in five years.

Mrs. Cullom, ground floor right at No. 88, stared into the quiet street.

"She's better off, poor thing," she said. "I said to my Mary the other night, I said, 'Mary, it's a pity about that Miss Powers. The poor thing is ailing.' I noticed she was just falling away."

Mr. Cullom stopped rocking. When he and Mrs. Cullom moved into the block just after they were married, thirty-two years ago, Katherine Powers a buxom, healthy woman in her early thirties.

"She had good color, you'll remember, Charlie," Mrs. Cullom said. "She had good education. She was a typist and she played the piano."

Mr. Powers, the father, died in his eighties. He was a
laborer in Prospect Park. The mother was a kindly
woman. There were two sisters and Lawrence Powers,
a brother. They were quiet, Mr. Cullom said, but they
would pass the time of day with a neighbor.

"This one would, too. Until she got queer. Then she got some fear she would be poisoned. Some people said she was just spiting someone. We didn't really know."

Mrs. Cullom stared into the street.

"Poor soul," she said. "Living alone in them six rooms. The poor thing."

"This is only surmising," Mr. Cullom said, "but I always thought what might have got her was the way her family died off. The way I remember, they all went in less than five years. Around that. The brother died eating supper, I believe, and one sister was found dead in bed."

Mrs. Cullom nodded. Mickey, her big Airedale, tried to force his head in her lap. She pushed him away gently.

"Josephine, that was the last sister, she died of pneumonia," Mrs. Cullom said. "After that, I'd say, was when this one broke up. She naturally had to break up, the poor soul. She and Josephine were always together. They went back and forth to church together."

The room was still. You heard the dog breathe. Mrs. Cullom told how Kate Powers took to carrying paper bundles wherever she went, to the store, to church, even to Sunday Mass. Queer bundles. Four or five at a time, tied together like beads on string. The neighbors talked about Kate Powers, but never to her face.

"She wore the same black plush coat, winter and summer, from the time Josephine died," Mrs. Cullom said. "You would see her on a summer night coming up the block, from church, and she would have that black plush coat tight at her neck with a safety pin."

The dress that had once been cream-colored, Kate Powers wore that twelve or fifteen years.

"She fell away to skin and bone," Mr. Cullom said.

"She was only a bit of a thing, here, toward the end. She stood only five feet, or so."

In the delicatessen store where she bought her Grade A milk, and bread, and cocoa, some of the customers shied from her.

"There goes Kitty Bundles," some of them would say, or, "There goes Mary Bundles."

Kate Powers' strange fear of poison puzzled the neighbors. Kate would fill her milk bottles in the one place she trusted: St. Augustine's Church, on the corner. She would fill the bottles with water in the sacristy and carry them home in paper bags. More bundles.

Kitty Bundles went to all the weddings and to all the funerals in St. Augustine's. She sat under the great soaring arches, her string of bundles beside her. Sometimes she stayed in the vast edifice alone, after all the others had gone. She stared at the votive candles dancing their endless dance behind the ruby glass down by the altar. When the sexton called her, at closing, she would gather her bundles and toil slowly up the aisle.

At home no visitor crossed her threshold. She had cousins, but she would not let them in. Sometimes, but not often, she would bang on the floor with her chair and Rosie Rosetti, the little girl downstairs, would come up. Rosie would go to the store for Grade A milk or bread and Kate Powers would reward her with a coin.

"She was no miser," Mrs. Rosetti said. "Not like people say."

Sometimes, on summer nights, the bundles would be too heavy. Kate Powers would undo the strings. She would carefully set one or two bundles in the street. She would carry the rest to the vestibule at No. 90. Then she would come back for the others.

Mrs. Cullom said: "One of the women tried to get a peek in one of the bundles, once, when it was laying in the vestibule, but Miss Powers got there and the woman had to go away from the bundles."

Mr. Cullom and his wife figured maybe the bundles had cleaning things in them; things for cleaning the church. But the cops found out what was in the bundles. Mrs. Rosetti was there when they opened them.

"It was nothing," she said. "In one bundle they find milk-bottle caps, cardboard caps. In another bundle they find cord, strings, all kinds of cord. They find soap wrappers and papers. That's all."

Mrs. Cullom said: "We won't see her no more. I think of her and that old-rose straw hat with the feather. And that plush coat. I knew it was coming. I said to my Mary. I said, 'Oh, there's a big change in poor Miss Powers. The poor thing can just about walk.' May the Lord have mercy on her soul."

Under the City

IN A city rich in paradox, it is not astonishing that subway trackwalkers, who seldom see the sun, are men from sunny Italy. More than ninety-five per cent of the men who work "in the hole," to use the trade term, are from Naples or near Naples. The rest are from Sicily.

The first trackwalkers in the city's subways were Neapolitans brought here in boatloads, about forty years ago, by the late John D. Crimmins, a contractor. These, in turn, sent for fellow townsmen. Now they monopolize the field.

You seldom hear or see this underground patrol. The supervisor of roadway for the Independent Subway dramatically referred to his walkers either as "the eyes of the system" or "silent policemen." The various subway systems together have close to 800 or 900 trackwalkers. The Independent Line has 244. These men work eight hours a day, six days a week, and get about thirty-six dollars a week.

Walkers are always finding things like men's hats, umbrellas, rings. Nervous women drop their purses between cars. Playful children dump stuff from windows. During the American Legion convention a walker came in with a woman's bag containing bankbooks showing deposits of $20,000. The bag was claimed.

Walkers put out subway fires. These usually start when train sparks ignite accumulated grease. The flame often spreads to paper scraps.

Flat feet and fallen arches are great hazards of the track-walkers' trade. In the main, though, they are a healthy lot. They average around thirty-five years of age and most of them are married.

The average walker covers a section of about eight miles of track. He moves at the rate of one mile an hour. His section may have only two tracks over a four-mile stretch, or four sets of tracks over two route miles.

He inspects the inner and outer side of each rail, throwing the beam of his carbide lamp alternately left and right. By strict regulation he always moves *against* traffic. The wall cavities into which he steps are called "manholes."

In addition to the lamp, he carries a three-foot track wrench to tighten nuts, bolts, tie plates, or to hammer loose spikes. He keeps a sharp eye for cracks, strains, all structural defects. If a defect seems dangerous the walker flags the first train. He waves his lamp from side to side with the back, or red lens, showing. He reports the defect by telephone. The telephones are 500 feet apart along the entire right of way. Walkers call on them every hour, to report to the Log Office under Forty-second Street.

To tell a train to resume movement, the walker lifts his lamp up and down, twice, showing the clear side. The engineer responds with two toots before he moves.

Under the Fourteenth Street station, Saverio Romolo, a quick, eager man, leaned against a steel upright to demonstrate what to do when two express trains come by, either side. If the walker leans against a support, conflicting wind currents are less likely to dislodge him. In the tunnels under the river the pressure is greater. There the men cling to handrails when trains go by.

Mr. Romolo discussed, with some reluctance, the superstitions of the trade. Wherever a walker dies underground fellow walkers mark the spot with a cross. This is to ward off further evil. Mr. Romolo crossed himself as he told of the practice. Sometimes, he confided, strange things happen underground. Cats and dogs get into the subway. They die on the third rail or under train wheels. Sometimes they go mad with fear. Then they are hard to catch. Several years ago, in Brooklyn, a walker was startled at a small ghostlike shape coming toward him. It was a goat. Sometimes, though not often, men or women get onto the tracks and wander in a daze. Once Mr. Romolo ran an indignant elderly gentleman, fellow with a long beard, off the tracks below Canal Street. He thought it was a mental case, but couldn't be sure.

"He swear like-a hell," Mr. Romolo said.

I stood a long time with Mr. Romolo, fascinated by the roar of rush-hour traffic. The trains came one every minute. Mr. Romolo assured me the constant roar did not affect the men's ears. Nor do they miss the sun. Mr. Romolo said he had heard of men who took ordinary jobs, on the street, after years of trackwalking, and became ill.

He led the way to the stairs, watched my ascent to the platform, and waved good-by with his lantern. I stared after him, a bobbing light going north in deepening dark.

Twilight Patrol

THE CUSTOMS Patrol left the Barge Office at four o'clock in the afternoon with orders to clear a British ship in the lower bay.

"Count and size her guns," the officer had said, "and check on her ammunition."

A few minutes later Patrol Boat 3 stood out from her slip and pointed for the setting sun. Spray snapped over her bow and streamed down the pilothouse windows in gelid patterns. Gusts whipped lesser spray through side windows. Watery furrows twisted away from the stern. Manhattan, receding, was a huddle of graying monuments against a sky of postcard blue. Governors Island, as the boat surged past, crouched in the dusk. Her windows were lighted with sun fire. On the bay's darkening rim smoke went up from enshadowed tugs and spread black velvet smudges on the deepening blue. The choppy surface of the bay was green, highlighted in gold.

A black ship stood between us and the sun, each structural angle sharp in silhouette against the orange glow. Two Customs men wiped the fogged panes and studied her. At last they knew her name, but she was not the ship they had to clear. Two gun snouts reached from her stern. High overhead, dark shapes stirred at the rail, men peering down at us. Patrol Boat 3 rocked violently with motors stopped. She drifted under the black ship's sable overhang. Then she resumed her vibrant purr and headed into deeper dusk. The four men in the pilothouse looked back.

"Limey, with guns," they said, "and loaded 'way down. Those guns are three-inchers."

The wheelsman looked ahead.

"Fat lot they could do against a Heinie man-o'-war," he said.

The patrol boat pushed eagerly onward and we came to a wide place in the bay where giant ships stood all around us. They put on their evening jewels, topaz anchor lamps and emerald and ruby navigation lights. Off to the left a rusted tanker pressed against a blackened merchant ship and wet-nursed her with oil. A creamy fishing boat, colored like lamplit parchment in the waning light, slid smoothly across our course. Ahead lay Staten Island, something done in India ink against the red-stained sky. Pete Webster, at the wheel, a grim-jawed man in dungarees, pointed toward Stapleton, to a slip where a great ship lay.

"*Ile de France*," he said.

He pointed out another Frenchman, her decks piled high with crated goods, riding at anchor in the bay. He cut the motors and we slid under the stern of the towering *John Mackay* of London. The patrol boat's siren blatted impatiently and the *Mackay* dropped a ladder. Johnson and Lampe held it, and Hanson and Sergeant Roncoli went aboard.

The patrol boat rocked, backed away to wait. One of the men pointed to a huge French ship that was breaking out her evening lights.

He said, "She's a good bet for the Heinies."

The patrol boat heaved in the swells. Faces showed at
the portholes of the *John Mackay*. Young English seamen
stared mutely at us in the growing dark.

"I guess those fellas don't hear a hell of a lot of what's
going on," a Customs man said. He tamped his glowing
pipe. "They're just a bunch of kids."

The men talked of their work, how they check on ships,
about the kids who get out on rafts and have to be picked
up.

"We got two in one night this summer, didn't we, Pete?"
a Customs man said, and Pete said, "Yup, two in one
night."

The sergeant called hoarsely from the lofty deck of the
John Mackay. The wind tore at his jacket and whipped it
back. The motors rumbled into action and the patrol
boat came up to the ladder to take the men off. Heavy
boots clumped on the patrol-boat deck as the men jumped
from the *Mackay*'s ladder. The patrol boat backed away.
The sergeant came into the pilothouse, wet with spray.

"She's a cable-layer," he said. "She's got three cable
tanks in her would knock your eyes out."

We got under way again for Stapleton. There one of
the men went ashore to ring the Barge Office for possible
new orders. The sergeant explained that there are Customs House telephones on every pier for this purpose, and
a boat's crew is expected to report every hour. While the
man was at the phone, the crew talked more about their
work. They search ships for narcotics and other contra-
band, keep watch for small boats that put out from shore
to make contact with foreign ships.

"They might just be bringing a visitor out to the boat,"
the sergeant explained, "but you got to watch them."

He said a lot of work, in times like these, was "watching

for sabo," foreign agents trying to commit sabotage on merchant ships of enemy countries. The man came back from the telephone.

"We got to go right up to Pier ———." He named the pier. "There's a Portugee from a hot port. They think it's dope."

Pete reversed the engines and the patrol boat turned about. The bay was darker, now, and rougher. Pete had to open a window to see. The men pointed out, behind us, the red light that marks Fort Hamilton. It was a clear jewel against the night. Behind Staten Island the sky was rich with afterglow. Bay Ridge and South Brooklyn wore bright spangles. The men fell silent awhile. We met a Staten Island ferryboat filled with passengers. It lighted the waters all around and passed astern. The world before us was suddenly empty.

"We're in the main ship channel," Pete said. His face was wet with spray.

I asked about the engines.

"How many horse, Pete?" the sergeant said, and Pete pulled in his head.

"Two hundred thirty-five horse," he said. "We can do twenty-four knots." He stuck his head out again. The windows were under a constant shower. Water pellets rattled against them and ran down, hurriedly. They seemed, somehow, like a mess of eels suddenly disturbed, all heading in one direction. We got a bit heady with the boat's up-and-down motion, deeply conscious of our conflict with the tide. For a time we watched the water slide by the boat's sides. It was close enough to touch. If you watched it steadily it was hypnotic, an endless procession of plunging dolphins with wet backs. Pete pulled his head in again.

"Dead ahead," he said, "is the prettiest sight you'll ever see."

It was Manhattan. A bank of lighted panes, luminous dominoes against the dark, stacked high against the sky. Lighted dominoes in step-down patterns, broken only here and there. Set in among them were colored beacon lights, bright red and lambent blue and green, gems on a peasant woman's bodice.

The patrol boat plowed up the North River. At Cortlandt Street it blatted at an emerging ferry, laden with passengers. We pitched in her wake and the helmsman swore. On the right the domino pattern stood broadside, reaching uptown. We passed a Holland Tunnel ventilation tower, a square structure deep in shadow. At Seventeenth Street the patrol boat nudged close to a tug. One of the men hauled me to its deck and led me across to the pier.

"Good night," he said. "We gotta go after that Portugee."

World of Tomorrow

SOMETIMES at night I lie awake in the dark and try to recapture the vision and the sound of The World of Tomorrow. I try to remember how the pastel lighting glowed on Mad Meadow in Flushing: soft greens, orange, yellow, and red; blue moonglow on the great Perisphere and on the ghostly soaring Trylon. I think with a sense of sweetened pain of nights when I sat by Flushing River and saw The World of Tomorrow reflected on its onyx surface, in full color, and upside down. I try to recall the sounds, the carillon from the Garden of the Netherlands, chimes from Belgium's Tower.

I know now that under the white carnation worn by Grover Whalen, Great White Father of The Fen, beat the heart of a major poet. I muse, sometimes, on the distant day when archeologists shall dig up the Time Capsule where the Westinghouse Building stood on the Fair Grounds. I wonder if they will be able to reconstruct the Great White Father's World as it really was, if they will be able to picture it swarming with pilgrims awed by his handiwork, if they will realize it was a place somewhat more astonishing than the world into which Alice stepped on the far side of the looking glass.

Few persons knew the strange situations that bedeviled

the Great White Father in his Never-Never Land. Many of these didn't get into the papers.

One Sunday morning, when the gates opened, for example, the pilgrims poured through the turnstiles by the thousands. It was spring and the air was heady. Gay tulips swayed in the long borders. Fresh green leaves caught the sunlight. They shimmered when the breeze passed. The Great White Father looked out from his wide windows and peace was in his great heart.

In the telephone room a languid operator answered an incoming call. A woman spoke, a sharp-voiced woman. She said, "I am a nurse. I have a woman patient who is about to become a mother."

The operator said, "That's nice, that's very nice."

The sharp-voiced nurse said, "I'm out in Jackson Heights. I'm coming out to Flushing. My patient insists she wants her child born in The World of Tomorrow."

The operator said, "I'm sorry, madam. We're not encouraging anything like that."

The nurse wouldn't accept this as final.

"Don't you have a Blessed Events Department?" she asked sternly.

The operator said, "No, not a Blessed Events Department, only a Special Events. Mr. Reilly is head of it."

"Give me Mr. Reilly," the nurse said.

Mr. Reilly was an efficient, but conservative executive. He confirmed the operator's statements.

"The World's Fair Corporation," he told the nurse firmly, "doesn't want children born on the grounds."

Strictly speaking, this wasn't true. Before the Fair opened, statisticians had figured that at least twelve children would be born in The World of Tomorrow. The actuaries based this prediction on the Chicago Fair birth rate, which was six in two years. Mr. Whalen had been assured his Fair would do twice as well, or better. Somehow or other, things didn't work out that way and Mr. Whalen grew discouraged, which was astonishing in itself. Nevertheless, the grim nurse said she wanted none of this nonsense.

"My patient," she told Mr. Reilly stonily, "is in no condition to be thwarted. We're coming out. See that your first-aid stations are ready."

She popped the receiver on the hook and left Mr. Reilly talking into nothingness. Mr. Whalen was informed. World's Fair police were warned. Ticket takers and information clerks were told to keep their eyes peeled for a woman in interesting condition; to get her out of The World of Tomorrow with the utmost possible tact and gentle handling. They received this assignment, generally, with bewilderment. Finding an expectant mother in a crowd of 400,000 Sunday visitors was apt to be difficult.

All morning uniformed personnel on Mr. Whalen's painted meadow pushed through the crowds, staring suspiciously at women who hadn't been too sparing in their diet, or whose clothes just happened to bulge in the wrong places. They didn't find any women they could be sure of and they had been warned mistakes might be costly.

Around two o'clock that afternoon, while doctors, nurses, and ambulance drivers were still waiting tensely, the telephone rang in Mr. Reilly's Special Events office. It was the truculent nurse again. This time she seemed more cheerful.

"We've been out here three hours, now," she told Mr. Reilly. "I'm calling from a booth off the Court of Freedom. My patient's still walking around."

She hung up. Mr. Reilly excitedly consulted the Great

White Father and a special teletype bulletin flashed to all corners of The World of Tomorrow. Policemen and all other available uniformed men hurried to the Court of Freedom which was overrun with pilgrims. They threaded through the throngs, eagerly sizing up women for disproportionate bulges, but didn't find one they could definitely, in a manner of speaking, put their fingers on. Mr. Whalen was distressed. The nurses, doctors, and gynecologists stood nervously at their posts. Three more calls came through, the last at midnight.

The sharp-voiced nurse kept repeating, "Everything O.K. so far. We're still walking around."

At one A.M. Monday morning Mr. Whalen grew weary. The doctor in charge agreed the whole thing must have been a hoax. The grounds were almost empty and nowhere in the vastness of The World of Tomorrow had the cops or information men heard the wail of new life. Mr. Whalen went home.

"The hell with it," the doctors said.

One by one the lights on Melancholy Meadow winked off. Only the Trylon, the Perisphere, and the plaster George Washington glowed through the dark.

The New York Times, next day, rejected this item. The typed story was in my mailbox. Across the top, some stern editorial hand had written: "We turned this down. Motherhood, we'll have you know, is still a sacred institution in this office."

Murder, Inc.

One Christmas Eve in the darkened chapel in Sing Sing Prison I sat with Principal Keeper Sheehey at the annual prison show. The high-vaulted auditorium was crowded with felons. Dim rays from windows near the ceiling pointed the felons' cheek bones, touched their foreheads with pale patches of light, played on blond heads and on gray.

Bill Robinson was guest star. He tapped across the stage, murmuring breathless snatches of oral patter. The prisoners laughed happily. Their zealous hand clapping smote sharply on the ear. A young burglar in smart Broadway toggery sang a sentimental ballad in a thin, high tenor:

> *Your Mother is your best pal after all,*
> *She's always there to help you when you fall,*
> *Though the nights are long and dreary*
> *Mother Dear does not grow weary.*
> *She's always there to answer when you call.*

The audience stirred. Heavy boots shifted on the hard floor with whispering sound. On the long bench to our left you could see tears, like quicksilver, sluggishly rolling down the prisoners' cheeks.

251

The P. K. said, "The way I figure, this is the tip-off on criminals. They lack emotional balance. They are extremists: rocking with laughter one second, plunged in maudlin melancholy the next. No middle or normal stages."

I came to think the Principal Keeper was probably right because he had known and handled countless felons in all criminal categories, but the murderers I met and studied seemed no different from ordinary persons.

There were some exceptions. Vincent Coll, who killed at least fifteen men and two women before he was shot to death in a telephone booth in Twenty-third Street, was one of these. He resembled a clear-cheeked freshman, but his eyes had the texture of cubes fresh from the ice tray. "Legs" Diamond was sinister in another way. He looked ratty.

Mostly, though, murderers of the Volstead period—the ones I knew best—were rather merry-looking fellows. Al Capone, for example, looked like any head barber who hadn't watched his diet. In repose his face was fat and smiling. In anger he would cloud up pretty fast, but so would any man.

The late Dutch Schultz was the dreamy type. I thought Dutch was miscast, that he was meant to be a poet instead of a beer baron in the Bronx. He had literary leanings. Dixie Davis once introduced me to Dutch in a hotel in Syracuse. Dutch started to put out a hand in greeting but stopped in mid-gesture. He squinted at me rather sharply.

"Ain't you the one who wrote I was a pushover for blondes?" he wanted to know, "Didn't you write that in the *Times?*"

He seemed angry. I murmured I had written something like that. I started to defend it.

"I was *told* you are a pushover for a blonde," I said. "Someone told me that."

"That," Dutch said sternly, "is beside the pernt. I only remember it made me feel bad when I saw it in the *Times*. I don't think 'pushover for a blonde' is any kind of language to write for a newspaper like the *Times*."

One morning in May, Sheriff Mangano of Brooklyn delivered "Happy" Maione and "Dasher" Abbandando to Sing Sing prison.

"Two for the back," he told the keeper.

"The back" is the death-cell block. The sheriff removed the gyves from Happy and The Dasher.

"So long," he said. Abbandando didn't answer. The sheriff squeezed Maione's arm. "Well," he said, "so long, Happy."

Maione tried to say "So long, Sheriff," but the words wedged in his throat. His eyes filled.

This emotionalism would have astonished Happy Maione's coworkers in Murder, Inc. Maione had killed at least ten—probably twenty—men, all most untidily. The George Rudnick murder, for example, for which he and Abbandando got their death sentence, had been done with a meat cleaver and ice pick. With Happy, if it wasn't the cleaver, it was apt to be the ice pick or both. He used a gun only on short-order jobs.

Although by now a majority of U. S. citizens have heard of Murder, Inc., the war has undoubtedly deprived it of the attention to which in normal times it would have been entitled. Murder, Inc., killed at least sixty-three men in and around New York in the nine years between 1931 and 1940. As many again were probably accounted for elsewhere by its talented personnel working on call in Newark, Jersey City, Chicago, St. Louis, Los Angeles, and Florida, among other places.

District Attorney William O'Dwyer, a former Brooklyn policeman, was startled by the murder troop's extraordinary scope when he started to research the subject. He found six men dominating Murder, Inc., in New York's metropolitan district. Six more men had a Chicago branch. In Los Angeles the management was made up mostly of expatriate New Yorkers. These big shots did not murder. They assigned the homicide to earnest craftsmen like Happy, The Dasher, Pittsburgh Phil, and Buggsy, who worked on salary. The executives drew their profits from multiple interests. Through dummy fronts, for example, they controlled a great part of the country's liquor distribution. They controlled labor unions through union officers who used their organization to shake down employers. The various branches owned night clubs and many of the busier gambling houses.

Sometimes they operated bawdyhouse chains on the side but there was less of this than most people thought. The organization engaged in many legitimate enterprises and shouldered its way into many heretofore honest firms with years of solid tradition.

Chain-store, or corporate, homicide started in the pre-dawn of Repeal; roughly, about nine years ago. Around this time major big-city bootleggers, labor-union racketeers, and other important criminals realized that under Repeal the public might expect comparative quiet; fewer gang brawls, less freehand killing. In order successfully to apply their liquor profits to new enterprises, the head men from different cities met and created a national syndicate known among its founders as "The Combination."

The name "Murder, Inc.," as applied to The Combination, was a bit of journalistic license. Murder was not The Combination's business. It did no murder for outsiders and did not kill for a fee. Indeed, its revised rules sharply restricted the use of homicide to business needs and reduced rather than increased the total number of U. S. murders committed annually. The new handbook sternly forbade murder for personal or romantic reasons, or even for revenge. Executive heads of The Combination dispassionately debated each murder before causing it to occur, much as a Wall Street syndicate might discuss a maneuver in the stock market.

When The Combination setup was first proposed there was need for a national framework. This was at hand in the Unione Siciliane which was controlled by "Lucky" Luciano, but Lucky and his advisers were concerned about some of the union's older members. These men were conservatives, in a way; they saw no need for modernizing murder. They were inclined to be stubborn about innovations. The more stubborn ones began to die off with remarkable rapidity. Joe ("The Boss") Masseria, who had borne a charmed life, was probably the most ornery. He died in a dingy Coney Island *estaminet* one spring morning of multiple revolver wounds. The other conservatives began to catch on. They moved hastily for modernization.

Complications developed, though, as The Combination began to function. One young Brooklyn trooper, for example, was sent on an out-of-town job. The fellow came back with his assignment unfinished. It seemed the finger man for The Combination's out-of-town branch was of the older Unione Siciliane group. He spoke no English. The Brooklyn gunman made a second trip, this time with an interpreter, and the job came off all right. To keep down the budget, thereafter, The Combination found out beforehand whether a contract called for a linguist.

Because out-of-town kills were expensive, The Combination rarely called for talent from other cities unless the murder subject was someone important and entitled to special honors. Removal of disloyal or untrustworthy punks, eradication of informers, and even liquidation of secondary Combination executives were left to home talent. On exchange kills, spadework was done beforehand in the host city. When the visiting trooper arrived, he was met by a finger man whose only function was to point out the victim. A visiting trooper did not identify himself by name to a finger man. The finger man, by the same token, remained anonymous. If the police grabbed either the visiting trooper or the finger man, neither could identify the other.

Before a kill, the party or parties who had contracted for the murder established an alibi. They went on a short cruise so the passenger list and testimony of fellow passengers would clear them in court. Sometimes they went to some neighboring state and visited public places—night clubs or theaters—where they could be seen. One out-of-town Combination boss, a proud father, arranged a kill to take place while he and his wife attended a benefit performance of his daughter's dancing class.

On out-of-town kills a trooper did not know whom he had murdered until the killing got into the newspapers. Professional pride sometimes tempted a trooper to tarry in a strange city to see how local journals reviewed his work. But this was strictly forbidden under the new rules. When a kill was done the trooper immediately left the city; was over the border and speeding home before the police were rounding up obvious, but alibi-proofed, suspects.

An order to murder in the delicate phraseology of The Combination was "a contract." The order reached the salaried gunman through the troop boss who in turn got it from some Combination executive. (There was method in this indirection. If someone blundered in commission of a contract, the police found it difficult to trace the murder order to its original source.) If a contract called for something special fancy, the troop boss sometimes took it on himself, with or without assistants.

Murderers' apprentices—"punks" to the trade—went on the payroll at fifty dollars a week. They started with piddling chores—stealing cars to transport corpses after murders, swiping extra license plates for these cars to make identification more difficult. They took courses in crowding convoy machines before and behind these murder transports so that policemen at cross streets could not read the license plates. The curriculum covered technique in "schlamming" (severe beating), "skulling" (assault just short of murder), and conduct at police line-ups in event of arrest.

Serious students, who showed aptitude, were privileged in their senior year to attend undergraduate murder clinics; to watch *cum laude* men like Happy Maione or Pittsburgh Phil operate with ice pick, bludgeon, and cleaver. Talented young men advanced rapidly. A hard-working, conscientious trooper, first class, subject to call at any hour of day or night for professional duty, got from one hundred to one hundred and fifty dollars a week. Real artists, like Maione, got around two hundred dollars. Troop bosses, like Strauss, commanded two hundred and fifty dollars and pickings.

Troop chiefs, looking for new murder-school pupils, watched local striplings who were trying their hand at neighborhood stickups, general bullying, and at cutting in on small-time card games and dice meetings. The talent scouts chose those who showed promise. The new pupil gave up extracurricular activities after he went on The Combination payroll because The Combination did not want its punks arrested in nonprofitable holdups, as they easily might be. The new boys, exposed to police massage treatment while they were still greenhorns in homicide, might have babbled about their Combination murder-car stealing.

A freshman in murder school was permitted to take on certain "personal jobs" but these operations were limited. He could, for example, hijack loot taken by independent stickup men. He could strip burglars or street money-lenders of their profits, on the theory that burglars and independent stickup men were not apt to complain to the police. This gave the murder-school student something to augment his Combination salary. The troop boss, or headmaster, if he liked the new boy, sometimes threw him a minor neighborhood slot-machine concession. Early in its history The Combination set up geographical limits for each unit's range of operations. It sternly forbade its troops to murder except on executive contract. While The Combination, like Civil Service, paid pensions to widows of deceased workers, it laid down the principle that no one in The Combination, executive or punk, could retire or withdraw. A trooper's refusal to fulfill a murder contract, once assigned, was designated as disloyal. Double-crossing was written in as a cardinal sin. Misappropriation of Combination profits was defined as one form of double cross. Informers, naturally, were to be put out of the way. To simplify matters, conviction on any count carried a death sentence.

In order to regulate its members, The Combination set up its own judicial system, including a high or supreme court, whose verdicts were monotonously adverse to defendants. Each Combination's executive board was bench and jury. Every offender had the right to a hearing. For punks, troops, and troop chiefs, the local court's verdict was final. Executives were entitled to appeal to the high or national court, made up of Combination leaders from different parts of the country.

Inarticulate defendants were allowed counsel (not a real attorney, but some gifted member of The Combination) to plead their cause. Abe ("Kid Twist") Reles, for example, though he lacked academic background, fancied himself as a mouthpiece. He had, by intently listening to lawyers who had delivered him from justice in the forty-three times he had stood prisoner before city and county courts, acquired an astonishing hash of legalistic flubdub.

He liked to utter courtroom clichés like 'If it please the court," or 'I respec'fully except."

In the role of counsel The Kid pleaded "Pretty" Levine's case before a Combination court. Pretty was a tall, rather handsome man, dark, with pale-blue eyes. He was the son of a quiet Brownsville shop owner. Reles had adopted him as a protégé and had enlisted him in the Brownsville troop. After he had stolen a few murder cars, though, Pretty decided he didn't like the homicide business. He had married and had become a father. He thought he would give up his troop apprenticeship, buy a motor truck, and try a more prosaic way of earning a living. At Pretty's hearing, Kid Twist unloaded his full repertoire of legalistic bombast. Hoarsely fervent, he asserted Pretty's right to leave The Combination. He offered to guarantee, if it pleased the court, that his client would keep all Combination secrets. The Kid was long proud of that dramatic plea, but it was indiscreet. He and his wistful punk were marked for ice-pick and cleaver dismissal. They fled to the District Attorney for protection.

The visit of Kid Twist to District Attorney O'Dwyer was historic. It was this that brought Murder, Inc., to the attention first of the perplexed Mr. O'Dwyer and then to the general public. It led directly to the unhappy plight of Messrs. Maione, Abbandando, Strauss, and Goldstein.

The murder of Puggy Feinstein, an insignificant loan shark, for which Buggsy Goldstein was convicted, was interesting. It shed light on one department of Murder, Inc.'s activities of which the efficiency left something to be desired. Perfectionists on its faculty, headed by a Mr. Albert Anastasia, had worked out to the ultimate degree the cunning business of decoying, fingering, and doing-in murder subjects. Their department for out-of-town, or exchange, murders surpassed anything previously developed. Research men for The Combination had not, however, figured out a perfect method of disposing of victims. They were still hard at work on this when Mr. O'Dwyer interrupted.

Actually, there had been two perfect disposal jobs in earlier murder annals, but these were awkward and could not be adopted by The Combination for routine purposes. The late Jack ("Legs") Diamond, who was a whimsical fellow anyway, is supposed to have figured out one of these. Diamond put the body of Harry Weston, a business competitor, in an unguarded concrete mixer one night and Weston became—and still is—part of Kingston highway in upstate New York. This system had obvious drawbacks. Murder, Inc., never considered it. The other disposal masterpiece was the sinking of "Bo" Weinberg, who had been in Dutch Schultz' entourage. Bo's feet were encased in fresh concrete. When the concrete hardened into a block Bo was put into the East River. This system was too cumbersome. It meant a truck haul, and trucks are too slow for murder jobs.

In their disposal experiments The Combination's homicide staff patiently tried to improve on crude orthodox systems. In the summer of 1937 they used Walter Sage as a laboratory subject. Sage was a Strauss protégé, a reliable worker until he tried to hold out a portion of Strauss' slot-machine profits. Walter fell under the ice pick. The research men surmised that the pick thrusts would puncture vital organs and keep the corpse on the bed of Swan Lake where they dumped it. They chained a thirty-pound rock to the legs and a sixty-pound slot machine to the neck to make sure. The body came up in two weeks. This puzzled the research men. They finally decided they would have to brush up on anatomy and learn how to apply the pick in the proper places.

In April, 1938, the research staff tried another disposal experiment. This time their subject was Hyman Yuran, potential witness against the New York Combination executive, Louis ("Lepke") Buchalter. They dug a grave four feet deep, hard by the mossy banks of Loch Sheldrake in the rural Catskills, and lined it with quicklime. They figured that the lime would destroy all identification marks and leave the state without a corpus delicti, even if police did locate the burial place. The theory was all right but the lime did not act on Yuran's dental work. This established identification.

The Murder, Inc., research department was disappointed but pushed further experiments with scholarly zeal. In September, 1939, they tried disposal by fire. Puggy Feinstein—suspected, as Yuran was, of disloyalty to Lepke—was chosen as the subject of their test. Puggy had no special dental work so the research staff didn't bother to dig a grave. Proceeding on the hypothesis that fire would destroy fingerprints and birthmarks, they used gasoline and, after they left the body in a lot at East Fifty-first Street and Fillmore Avenue in Brooklyn, anxiously awaited results. Anastasia, the faculty adviser, was particularly interested in this experiment and only the best men worked on it. It turned out a failure, though. Police fingerprint experts identified Puggy.

All through the trial for the Puggy Feinstein murder, Headmaster Strauss feigned insanity. He mumbled, shadow-boxed with imaginary little men, loosely pivoted his neck as if trying to shake something off. Buggsy Goldstein got completely out of hand when Seymour

("Blue Jaw") Magoon, his old partner, testified against him. He stood up in the courtroom, his fingers interlocked in extreme supplication. Tears rolled down his cheeks.

"For God's sake, Seymour," he cried out. "That's some story you're telling. You're burning me, Seymour."

Professional murderers, through some perversity of Mother Nature, are also apt to be sentimentalists. They grow starry-eyed over fireside themes and death-house audiences cry when soloists render "Your Mother Is Your Best Pal After All" at prison concerts. Buggsy's tender appeal caused Blue Jaw to weep, too, but Blue Jaw bravely turned his face away and continued his account of how Puggy was put to the torch. Judge Fitzgerald reassured the jurors when they came in with a "Guilty!" verdict. He confided that Mr. O'Dwyer had told him, out of court, that Strauss alone had killed twenty-eight men in ten years.

Murder, Inc.'s troops took inordinate pride in their work. In dull seasons, when there was no schlamming or skulling to do, they sat around their hangouts and gravely discussed homicide technique. It was generally conceded in Brooklyn that Happy Maione was born gifted and had red thumb, so to speak, as one gifted in gardening is said to have green thumb. Even more than those of his confreres, Happy's career can be regarded as a kind of scale model or cameo portrait of Murder, Inc., as a whole.

Maione was christened Harry after he was born in Brooklyn on October 7, 1908. His nickname, Happy, was a misnomer. He was a sneering, sadistic bully even as a kid. His father, a sickly tailor, had died of a heart attack. His mother, a quiet, devout little woman, lives in a five-room third-floor flat where the rent is twenty-seven dollars a month. She gets work relief for the two youngest children and a widow's pension.

Happy did not like school. He left in the seventh grade when he was fifteen. He could read and write, but his academic attainments didn't go much beyond that. He worked for six months as errand boy in a small clothes shop in Manhattan. Later he polished boots in a shoe-shine and hat-cleaning store in Williamsburg. He left this to try his hand at bricklaying, but his heart wasn't in the job. He never got his union card. At sixteen he was arrested for assault and robbery, a neighborhood job. He tried to knock down the cop and take the cop's service revolver. The cop laid Happy out, but this episode gave Happy a sinister reputation in Ocean Hill poolrooms in Brownsville. About this time he ran into a girl who had fled the House of Good Shepherd. He set up as a panderer in partnership with a man quaintly called "Bow-wow" Mercurio. "Maione's sex history," the probation officer sadly wrote after the Rudnick murder conviction, "is very bad." Two rapes were entered against Maione's record.

Happy was arrested thirty-five times before he was thirty-one years old. The record included virtually everything except arson. Happy ran a race-horse book in a small way, shook down shopkeepers, had part interest with one of his brothers in a small florist shop. He and The Dasher met up with Abe Reles twelve years ago and helped Reles wipe out the Brothers Shapiro—Willie, Irving, and Meyer—and other business competitors. They buried Willie alive in a sand pit in Canarsie in July, 1934. Maione performed a series of kills in subjugation of a local plasterers' union.

One of his best jobs was the murder of Anthony Siciliano and Caesar Lattoro in a basement on Bergen Street, Brooklyn, during his plasterers' series. The victims were wary, difficult to approach. A big police dog warned them when prowlers got close. Happy got around the two men on February 6, 1939, dressed as a woman. The clothes belonged to the spouse of Victor Gurino, one of his associates. Happy painted and powdered his face, swished around in front of the plasterers' flat, and was invited inside. He shot and killed both men. Before he left he put two spare bullets in the police dog.

At this point in his career Happy rode high. He kept a mistress, according to a probation report, in the house where one of his married sisters lived, and had another woman in Ocean Hill. The mistress, the report gravely recorded, was a girl named Renee. The other woman was written down as "a concubine named Mildred." Happy was one of the big shots in the troop. He rated second only to Pittsburgh Phil Strauss. Dasher Abbandando and Goldstein rated perhaps a grade lower.

The George Rudnick murder, for which Happy and The Dasher got the death sentence, was one of their earlier Combination contracts. Rudnick, a drug addict, had turned stool pigeon. Around the end of March, 1937, Pittsburgh Phil Strauss met Kid Twist for a business conference in a hangout at Saratoga and Livonia Avenues in Brooklyn. The Rudnick assignment was fresh. Kid Twist and Strauss adjourned to a near-by drinking spot. Strauss outlined the assignment. He said, "Rudnick is a stoolie. We got to kill him." He arranged to do the job, Happy and Dasher Abbandando assisting.

Pittsburgh Phil wanted this to be an extra-fancy bit of

handiwork. He said, "We will put a note in Rudnick's pocket. It will say he gave information to the District Attorney. It will be a favor for Lepke."

Strauss assigned a Combination punk to borrow a typewriter. The machine was delivered to Kid Twist's home. Pittsburgh Phil typed the note under difficulties. Neither he nor the Kid knew how to put in the typewriter ribbon. Kid Twist finally held the ribbon in his fingers and the job was done that way. The note was smudged and untidy. On the face of the envelope Strauss typed: "Mr. George Rudnick." He bogged down on the note. He did not know how to spell "friend." There was a scholarly argument over this. Reles was almost certain it was "friend." Strauss said "No." Finally he started the note: "Freind George." This looked O.K. to him. The note was rewritten three times. The last version said: "Freind George. Will you please meet me in Ny some day in reference to what you told me last week. Also I will have that certain powder that I promised you the last time I seen you. PS I hope you found this in your letterbox sealed. I remain your freind YOU KNOW FROM DEWEY'S, THE DISTRICT ATTORNEY'S OFFICE."

Pretty Levine and Anthony ("The Duke") Maffatore, another freshman in the murder college, were told off to steal a murder car. The punks picked a black Buick sedan. Strauss fetched a set of stolen license plates. The Duke and Levine put these on the Buick. Happy checked the new plates to see if they were on tight. The Dasher smashed the car's original license plates.

Everything now was ready for the kill. Rudnick sensed this. He stayed indoors most of the time. If he had to venture out he would come home just before daybreak.

He always moved close to the building line. He figured they would be less apt to see him in the deep building shadows. Dasher Abbandando and Kid Twist tried to find him but they did not have much luck. On the night of May 24, 1937, they finally got word that Rudnick was out somewhere. They passed the word along. Happy and Pittsburgh Phil, Dasher Abbandando and Kid Twist met, according to testimony, in the Sunrise Garage. They figured this might be the night. By an odd coincidence, it happened that on this night, in a flat opposite the Sunrise Garage, Happy's grandmother lay dying. She was past seventy. She had helped raise Harry. All his family were at her house, kneeling in prayer, but Happy had the Rudnick job and could not go.

A little before midnight, someone screamed in the flat across the street from the Sunrise Garage. Happy's grandmother had died. Happy's brothers and sisters kept on wailing for hours but Happy, detailed to wait at the garage until his colleagues returned, could not leave his post. Meanwhile, at about 4:30 A.M., Kid Twist and The Dasher were still waiting for the stoolie in a little tan Ford car in Saratoga Avenue near Livonia. The Dasher had borrowed the Ford car from a boyhood chum who was not in Murder, Inc. "I want to take out a girl," Abbandando had told him. A few minutes later a little figure moved cautiously along the building line, up Saratoga Avenue toward Livonia.

Kid Twist said: "That's him. That's George."

Abbandando peered into the shadows by the building line.

"You're crazy," he said, but he looked a second time. "You're right," he said.

He started the tan Ford. Rudnick stopped. He tried to run back but the tan Ford caught up with him. They put the gun on him and he crept into the tan Ford. He shook with sudden palsy. Abbandando drove toward the Sunrise Garage and Kid Twist followed slowly, in another car. He did not want to be in on this kill. He was stalling.

The Dasher drove the tan Ford up on the sidewalk, with the front of the hood against the door. The door opened and he rolled in, with Rudnick. When Kid Twist came up, five minutes later, Happy Maione and Pittsburgh Phil Strauss were standing over the body.

Happy said: "The work's finished. You are not needed."

Dasher Abbandando had Rudnick by the shoulders, keeping him in sitting position. Strauss tide a rope around Rudnick's neck. They tied the body in a jack-knife pose. The black Buick was in this case used as a hearse. Strauss and Maione got Rudnick's body by the legs. Abbandando held the head. They put Rudnick on the floor behind the front seat. The body made a noise through one of the wounds. It startled the troops.

Strauss swore. He said: "The sonofabitch ain't dead yet." Strauss used the pick again.

Maione said: "We got to finish him." He hit Rudnick on the head, just under the hair line. He stepped back. "We got to clean up the floor," he said. He filled a water bucket. Abbandando got a broom and swept toward the sewer drain. They washed the broom, the cleaver, and the pick. Maione spoke to a Murder, Inc., chauffeur named Julie Catalano.

"Drive this over into the Wilson Avenue precinct," he

said. "Take it easy over the bumps. Take your time."

Maione got into the back seat in Kid Twist's car. Catalano abandoned the black Buick in front of 1190 Jefferson Avenue, in a quiet residential street. He walked to the corner and got in with Kid Twist and Maione. They let him out at Atlantic Avenue and Eastern Parkway.

Catalano, The Duke, Pretty Levine, Kid Twist, and a whole line-up of witnesses told this story when Mr. O'Dwyer brought Happy and The Dasher to trial. Happy's lawyers put fourteen of his relatives on the stand. They swore Happy was in his grandmother's house all through the night she was dying, but Burton Turkus, Mr. O'Dwyer's assistant, was prepared for this. He proved through the undertaker and the embalmer that Happy was not in his grandmother's house, as they testified.

The jury did not stay out long. On May 27, 1940, County Judge Franklin Taylor passed sentence. On the Maione complaint, under "Disposition," he wrote: "Sing Sing Prison, there to suffer death by electrocution during the week of July 7, 1940." He wrote the same for The Dasher.

On the morning of May 28, Sheriff Mangano called for the prisoners in Raymond Street jail. Happy tried to be debonair when the Sheriff put on the handcuffs.

"You got here early," he said.

When Maione and Abbandando got in the Black Maria in the prison yard, Happy's mother and his married sister, Jennie, were near the gate. They waved to him. Maione tried to stand up. He hollered, "Good-by, Momma," but he choked on the words. His face was wet with tears. At the 10:30 train that takes prisoners out of Grand Central to Sing Sing Prison, Renee was waiting. She kissed him.

All the way up the Hudson, Happy stared at the Palisades. He littered the floor with cigarettes. The Dasher was glumly silent. Maione cursed Kid Twist Reles.

"He is a yella rat," he told the Sheriff. "He is a squealer."

Sheriff Mangano got his charges into the black taxi that always waits at Ossining station. It moved up the serpentine road. The Sheriff walked the two men through the prison reception room to the high-ceilinged room at the left. The Sheriff took off the cuffs. He nodded to the keeper.

"Two for the back," he said.

Tapping the Wires

THE LATE Dutch Schultz loathed wire tappers. "I hope your ears drop off," he'd say bitterly before he put up his telephone receiver, reasonably certain they would hear him. The obsession grew worse in his last years as boss of the policy racket in New York, with Federal agents and city detectives tapping his office and outpost wires, his sister's home line, and his lawyer's phone. Schultz got so that he distrusted all telephones; he would mark the location of an instrument when he entered a room and shy off as far from it as he could. When he was sober he would glare at a telephone and mutter. Drunk, he was apt to lose control entirely, tear out box and all, and smash the apparatus on the floor. Still, he needed telephones in his business and the instruments were always replaced.

Even in ordinary social conversation over the telephone with his men or with his mistresses, the Dutchman would drum on a desk or any other hard surface handy with a heavy gold pencil which he carried for the purpose. He had an idea he could talk *under* the pencil tap and confound the eavesdroppers. He never learned that the felt pads on which telephones rest absorbed the pencil raps, and that his speech came through clearly in spite of his drumming. Even when he hung up the phone in his office, a small microphone hidden in the earpiece of the instrument continued to function and carried his words to the listening posts over wires spliced into the regular telephone cord. This tiny "mike"—the wire tappers have appropriated the radio term—is one of the trade's newest devices. A telephone with the mike already installed is substituted for the subject's own phone. If the detectives can't manage to switch the instruments, they wheedle some telephone man into doing the job for them. He can usually think up some plausible excuse for making the change. The replacement takes only a few minutes.

The Dutchman got so he would never use names in telephone conversations. He taught his men to speak in cryptic phrases. Detectives would sometimes frown for days over these puzzling fragments, but usually figured them out in the end. One day they listened to a call that came into the offices of Dixie Davis, the Schultz attorney.

"Listen," the lawyer said. "He cannot see. He cannot give. Do you understand?"

The voice answered, "I understand."

This has never been interpreted. If a Schultz retainer forgot the taboo he was apt to hear about it.

Wire tappers, for example, heard someone blurt to Davis, "Hey, Dick, did you take that matter up with George?"

"You are about the most stupid bastard I ever saw!" Davis shouted. "I've told you and told you about mentioning names."

When these quotations came out in wire tappers' testimony during the Davis disbarment hearings, Referee John P. Cohalan was incensed. He said that wire tapping was a rotten thing for any government to engage in. "We'd better go back to the British government and give back our Declaration of Independence," he commented.

Most law-abiding people become peevish rather than alarmed when their telephones start to rasp or grow faint in the middle of a conversation. Only the "tap-goofy," as detectives refer to a nervous few, believe a bad connection means that someone is listening in on their wires. Although they probably are wrong, there is always a chance that they may be right. The police sometimes amuse themselves on a job by tapping near-by wires at random. More often, though, when business is dull they pick up calls from restaurants, poolrooms, and other places which they suspect may be criminal hangouts. "Blind angling," they call it, and defend the practice on the ground that you never can tell when something significant in the crime line will turn up. The chances are that even if they should happen to intercept one of your calls, you'd never know it. Professional wire tappers have learned how to work quietly.

Given the proper apparatus, almost anyone could tap a telephone wire. A simple tap involves scraping the insulation from a segment of the two wires required to make a telephone circuit. A receiver is attached to the exposed portions with metal clips and extension wires. The tapper thus is in the position of a gossip silently cutting in on a rural party line. That's the basis of all wire tapping, but the complexity of the modern telephone system and the increasing wariness of criminals like Mr. Schultz have necessitated many refinements in technique.

New York is the center of wire-tapping activity, at least in this country. District Attorney Dewey's office had considerable success with it. In one instance, while Dewey wire workers were listening in on the bakery racket, they accidentally picked up a conversation bearing upon a case entirely outside their province. They turned the information over to Special Prosecutor Todd, who was handling that matter, and he used it in securing the conviction of the Drukman murderers in Brooklyn. A hint of further activity by Dewey wire men came out in the case of Jimmy Hines, the Tammany leader accused of having conspired with Dutch Schultz, Dixie Davis, and George Weinberg to establish lotteries in New York. A man in the office of Joseph Shalleck, Hines' lawyer, expressed the belief that the Hines wires had been tapped steadily for more than two years, and that someone had been cutting in on Shalleck's home and office lines. With customary legalistic caution, however, he refused to venture a guess as to who might have ordered this tapping, though he did refer significantly to a statement made by Mr. Dewey at the Hines arraignment: "We are prepared to prove that at ten-fifteen A.M. today Hines advised a witness in this case to leave his home, go to a hotel, assume a false name, and hide until this case blows over, as he puts it." The inference seemed to be that such evidence, if it existed, could only come out of wire tapping. Later in the arraignment proceedings Mr. Shalleck indicated a suspicion that his wires had been tapped by the District Attorney's office.

Usually Dewey's detectives followed the standard practice of cutting in on a telephone circuit, but for special jobs they used a Speak-O-Phone, a machine typical of the complicated processes developed by the craft. Included in the equipment are small microphones that can be concealed in a suspect's room and a recording device with phonograph disks to take down voices. Stolen conversations thus can be preserved and played back when the occasion requires it. The Federal government uses about a dozen Speak-O-Phone outfits in Washington which, next to New York, is the eavesdroppers' most fertile field. Commissioner Valentine's staff, on the other hand, gets along with homemade apparatus because the Police Department's budget is too skimpy to include fancy models. (A Speak-O-Phone with recording attachment costs about five hundred dollars.)

The Lindbergh case was a wire tappers' holiday. They cut in everywhere. Just before the ransom money was passed, as they were listening on Dr. Condon's wire, they heard Jafsie in conversation with a mysterious "Axel," who announced he was coming to the Condon home. The tappers got the idea that "Axel" was the kidnaper, or one of the kidnaper's aides. They hid themselves around the Condon home until a strange car drove up and were ready to swarm over "Axel" as he stepped from the car. They were stunned when their man emerged. It was Lindbergh. It turned out that he always used the name "Axel" to identify himself to the Doctor.

Wire tapping got its start in New York in 1895 when a former telephone worker who had joined the city police suggested that it might be a good idea to listen in on wires used by criminals. William L. Strong, who was Mayor at the time, gave the project his blessing and for years after that wire tapping flourished secretly. It was something the public of that period wouldn't worry about, anyhow, because in the nineties the telephone was not generally regarded as a household fixture. In those days police wire tappers just walked into the Telephone Company's offices, asked for the location of the wires they were interested in, and got the information without fuss. Lines were usually tapped right in the cellar of the house or at an outside wall box.

There was an uproar when people got wind of the prevalence of wire tapping. An investigation of public utilities in 1916 called attention to it. Those, of course, were war days and eavesdropping of all kinds were widely encouraged. The government was tapping thousands of lines. A complete central-office switchboard had been set up in the New York Custom House, with taps running into it from all parts of the city. Every time a suspected alien lifted his receiver a light showed on this board and a stenographer, with headset clamped on, took a record of the conversation.

Inevitably it was claimed that wire tapping violated a citizen's rights, and a large section of the press cried out against the practice, but nothing came of it. The furor, however, made the wire tapper's job more difficult, because the Telephone Company, finding itself in an uncomfortable position, refused from then on to co-operate with the police in helping them locate suspect wires. Drawing itself up to its corporate height, it assumed a haughty manner toward detectives and since that time the company officially has refused to assist in tapping. To make matters worse, the wiring system grew more and more complicated. Today there are nearly 1,700,000 telephones in the city, and even an experienced wire tapper would be unable to find a particular circuit if he did not know the right people in strategic telephone posts. That is why most police wire tappers, following the precedent of the man who introduced the science in the department, are former employees of the Telephone Company. They have not only the background of an inside view of the system, but friends in the organization upon whom they count for surreptitious assistance. Moreover, an experienced wire tapper who is familiar with the trade terms used by Telephone Company workers is able to pose convincingly as an employee when he wants to learn the location of a particular set of wires. If the specal operator who handles test calls is suspicious and asks "Who's your foreman?" or "What's your order number?" the expert tapper is ready with the answers picked up from his cronies in the company. With the necessary information he can go out, find the circuit, make his tap, run his extension wires to an empty flat or office, and prepare to listen.

Wire tappers are seldom caught at their work. They know they must remove their listening equipment if they hear a telephone subscriber complain to the operator that "something is wrong with the wire." When it is discovered that a line has been tapped, the company for the next five days makes regular inspections of that particular circuit. Detectives are aware of this routine and, when the five-day period has expired, hook right in again.

It's pretty hard to detect a wire tapper by the sound of your telephone. Foreign noises on the line are more apt to be caused by worn-off insulation, dampness in the cables, or some other natural disarrangement. A good wire tapper is rarely guilty of creating "swing," which is the professional term for the crackling noise sent over a telephone circuit by a faulty tap. Wherever possible, he fastens the wires of his instrument to nut-and-washer connections found in panel boxes, the terminals from which extension lines are run. Such connections are practically swing-proof. If circumstances compel him to resort to a "raw" tap, for which he must cut in somewhere in the middle of the line, he uses improved clips with central piercing needles to make a tight connection with the wire.

Police wire tappers are a peculiar, clannish breed, jealous of the good name of their calling. They bridle at the slightest implication that their trade is not altogether manly and sporting. They are happy to have wire tapping referred to by such polite phrases as "bridging" and "censoring"—two expressions used by John L. Swayze when, as general counsel for the Telephone Company, he condoned the practice during the wartime investigation. They were also grateful when one of the instructors in a wire-tapping school conducted by the Treasury Department introduced the term "wire supervising" to describe the work. That gave the calling a new dignity and the phrase is used a lot now when tappers are called upon to testify in court.

Despite these lofty pretensions, the profession has its own little jokes, on a somewhat lower plane. When they find life tedious at the listening posts, wire tappers sometimes entertain themselves by crossing two sets of wires. During a vice-investigation case, several years ago, they played this trick on a simple Irish laborer who was calling his wife from a barbershop where the wires were tapped because the place was considered a likely gathering spot for panderers. The tappers got a quick-witted lady of the town on another wire and joined the two circuits. The bawd caught on and pretended the Irishman was beside her and told his wife he was her favorite customer. The bewildered laborer, who from his telephone could hear the odd conversation, shouted that it was a lie and that he'd have the barber prove it so. His wife would have none of his explanations. "I'll open your skull when you get home, you ape!" she screeched. The wire tappers found this highly amusing.

In the same blunt manner, the police were tickled by a misfortune that upset two of their fellow detectives sometime ago. Both were expert wire tappers and should have known better. They were "planting a bug"—as they refer to concealing a microphone—in a midtown hotel room for a policewoman who was suspicious of the occupant. The detectives completed the job and then went in to visit the policewoman at her listening post. As they entered the room, she stunned one of the wire men with a lusty blow. "Next time," she shouted, "you try to be a gentleman!" It developed that she had been listening with a headset attached to the "bug" while the detectives, busy planting it, discussed the charms of her large person in merrily ribald terms.

As a rule, though, wire tappers are pretty grave fellows. They spend a lot of their own time and money fussing with new listening appliances or trying to improve old ones. Most of them rig up experimental stations in their homes. They shop busily in Canal Street stores which deal in secondhand electrical equipment, buying apparatus discarded by the telephone and telegraph companies. Out of these experiments, in 1930, came the dial detector, an indispensable instrument for tapping wires in a city where few numbers are now called orally. Once it was easy for cops to ascertain the whereabouts of both parties in an outgoing telephone conversation: they knew where the tapped wire led and they could hear the number called by the suspect. But when dials were installed they could not check on the destination of a call. Just when the new instruments were threatening to put a serious crimp in the tappers' usefulness, a detective who had been a Telephone Company mechanic came to the rescue of the craft. His dial detector, which he made out of secondhand telegraph parts, records as a series of dots on a thin paper tape the clicks you hear when you dial. The tapper can read the number called from these symbols.

In most cases the old-school wire tappers prefer their homemade equipment. They find they can duplicate the store sets without much trouble and at considerable saving. This is true even of the newest contraption, an especially powerful induction coil which resembles a five-inch firecracker. It is a magnet wrapped in eight thousand turns of very fine wire—a sinister contrivance that inhales a telephone conversation without being connected to the circuit, the coil merely being placed near the wires leading to the telephone under observation. It will pick up sounds through an eighteen-inch wall.

Police tappers resent newcomers in the business, and are especially bitter toward the graduates of the Treasury Department wire-tapping schools. Few if any of these young men have served apprenticeships with the Telephone Company, which the police eavesdroppers regard as the only worth-while alma mater. The police complain that the Treasury Department rookies aren't taught how to work with telephone linesmen and operators. As a result, they say, the youngsters are always committing blunders which make it just that much harder for the old-timers to get co-operation from telephone men.

The Treasury Department headmasters seldom educate their charges in the technical details of wire tapping. Pupils in the kindergartens—as the selfmade tappers call the Federal schools—are drilled primarily to avoid detection once they have settled themselves at a listening post. They are warned to take their clips off lines when they hear peculiar noises which might mean that the company's wire chief is testing, but never to meddle otherwise with the apparatus, because it is set up for them by older men. This makes a New York detective smile wryly; he always does his own hooking up. The courses in Washington also offer such simple advice as "Don't let strangers into the listening post," "If a janitor or some building official must enter the post, cover the equipment with clothing or a newspaper," "Never leave any notes or reports behind you when you leave your post."

City tappers agree with Federal men, however, on one point. Both consider the practice exclusively a government privilege and look upon wire tapping by private detectives as something illegal and unethical. The private agencies usually get radio men to help them in their telephonic skulduggery. These tappers have one trick, a modification of the wooden horse of Troy, that they use frequently in helping clients who are suspicious of their wives or paramours. The agency tells the man to get his lady a radio; if she already has one they tell him to get her a better set. When the apparatus is delivered it contains a hidden microphone that will pick up a whisper at the far end of a large room. The listening wire is spliced to the aerial lead-in wire which runs to the roof. After that listening in is easy.

The first private detective agency to use wire tapping was the William J. Burns outfit. Early in the World War period they cut in on the wires of a law firm in the Equitable Building, at 120 Broadway, trying to find out whether one of J. P. Morgan's clerks was relaying through it secrets about the Allies' munitions orders. Another agency, a bitter competitor of Burns, learned about the tap and warned the victims out of spite. The information came a bit late. The tappers, suspecting they might be caught, had departed.

No one has ever been convicted of wire tapping, although any layman or private detective caught tampering with someone else's telephone cords is liable to arrest. So are police, for that matter, if they can't prove beyond a reasonable doubt that the tap is being made in the interests of crime detection. That obviously is a pretty easy thing for men in their position to do. The new induction coil, which involves no actual contact with a wire, is described in prospectuses as "entirely legal" and there seems to be no reason for doubting the claim. Criminal lawyers, whose own wires are frequently tapped, have worked hard for Federal legislation against wire tapping, but their efforts have always failed. In 1928 the United States Supreme Court sustained the conviction of a bootlegger on evidence picked up by wire tappers two miles from the defendant's home. The late Justice Holmes dissented, remarking, "Wire tapping is a dirty business." A few years ago the same court decided that Federal prosecutors may not use evidence obtained by tapping wires linking two or more states. The results of intrastate tapping, however, remain admissible. The popular belief that the police would stop tapping wires if evidence obtained by this means were ruled out of all courts is a delusion. Most wire tapping is done to obtain information that may lead to arrests rather than for the purpose of obtaining evidence to be presented in court.

Mayor Mitchel, who was at City Hall when the public first became aware of the prevalence of wire tapping, favored the practice and boasted that he had assigned detectives to listen in on the telephone conversations of the Catholic Charities during a feud he had with that organization. His Police Commissioner, Arthur Woods, conceded that the idea of tapping a wire was "revolting" but defended his men on the ground that "you can't always do detective work in a high hat and kid gloves." More recently, mayors have become tap conscious for personal reasons. In 1929 someone broke into the telephone panel box in the basement of City Hall, located the cords of Mayor Walker's line, and ran out several wires. Detectives traced one of the taps to a spot in the gallery of the aldermanic chamber, where the floor was littered with cigarette butts and matches, showing that a tapper had spent a long and nervous session at his listening post. Another tap ran through the old courthouse in the park to a vacant office in Worth Street. None of the tappers was ever found.

Mayor McKee had tap jitters during his brief stay at City Hall because he used to hear noises on his line. He thought both his home and office wires were tapped. His friends suspected the delicate hand of Tammany Hall, but detectives didn't agree. They offered the theory that, at least as far as the City Hall circuits were concerned, the telephone cords were old and the noises came from natural cable leakage. McKee ordered the City Hall panel box sealed with lead just the same. Since then a newer and stronger panel box has been installed and some of the cables have been replaced. Mayor LaGuardia hasn't complained of tapping, but the problem constantly worries some members of his cabinet—tap goofs, perhaps, at heart.

Tea for a Viper

IT TOOK weeks of dickering to get into a marijuana party, because I was not a viper, which is the Harlem word for a marijuana smoker, but at last it was arranged. Suspecting that I might find the evening a long one, I took an equally uninitiated friend with me. We got out of a cab in front of a gray-stone tenement in one of the darker spots on 140th Street at eleven o'clock on the appointed Saturday night and rang the bell of the right-hand apartment on the ground floor. When the door opened a few inches, escaping marijuana smoke, mixed with the fumes of cheap incense and stale steam heat, came at us like an oven blast. Chappy, the little saddle-colored man who runs the place, led us into the dark interior.

It was difficult at first to make out his friends and fellow vipers in that fetid flat. Hashish smokers (marijuana and hashish, I had learned, are the same thing) dislike strong light. The only illumination in Chappy's place was a blue bulb glowing in the glass case of the slot-machine phonograph. All tea pads, or marijuana joints, use the blue lamps and nickel machines to induce and sustain the hashish mood. They play special recordings of viper, or weed, songs with weird ritualistic themes. One of these was playing when we came in. Big Boo, a long-armed

blackamoor, sprawled on one of the four broken-down
couches in the room and thumped the floor with a bony
fist, in time with the rhythm. Boo was high. The others
were silent.

"Meet the writin' man," Chappy said, introducing my
companion at the same time. Vicki and Fruits, two slender
wenches with high breasts, giggled and the blue light
shone on their perfect teeth and on their oversized imita-
tion-pearl earrings. Big Boo rolled his head to acknowl-
edge the introduction but didn't interrupt his tom-tom
beat. Steel-Haid, a gigantic Negro with bulging eyes,
thrust out a big paw and mumbled something. Duke and
Arthur, a couple of foppish sprigs in their early twenties,
seemed friendly but suspicious. Chappy hurried down
the long apartment corridor to answer the doorbell, while
my friend and I sat in awkward silence, sharing the sofa
with the girls.

I was fascinated by Boo. His eyes were shut tight now.
His thick lips parted and he wailed a low accompaniment
to the dragging tempo of the weed song. The girls swayed
and hummed. The song ended and the record slid back
into the stack. Boo's bullethead perked up as if someone
had worked it with a string.

Vicki laughed. "Boo's high," she said.

"Yea, Momma," chanted Boo. His eyes opened and a vapid grin creased his face.

"Boo goin' blow his top," sneered Arthur. " 'Tain't twelve an' Boo's sent."

"Nay, man," Boo bragged. "Sent, but not spent. Don' high-gyve Boo."

Viper vocabulary changes fast—perhaps to confuse the police. A smoker is high when contentment creeps over him. If he smokes to excess he blows his top; that is, he gets sick. When he reaches a stage of full contentment his body is "sent." "High-gyve" is conversational baiting, or teasing a smoker. Marijuana cigarettes have a dozen names. They are called sticks, reefers, Mary Anns, tea gyves, gauge- or goofy-butts. A pinched-off smoke, or stub, is a roach. Tea pads where inferior cigarettes are sold are beat pads; these places add dry tea leaves or dry grass to supplement the marijuana supply. Pads where semi-conscious smokers are robbed of their money are creeper joints. The automatic phonograph is the piccolo and a detective is The Man.

Chappy's pad is one of four in that particular gray-front tenement. There are hundreds of such places in Harlem —many more of them than there were speak-easies during prohibition. Chappy's suite is a middle-class pad—four rooms with nine couches set against the cracked, cream-colored walls, with a few limp easy chairs to handle the overflow. Some of the upper-class pads have as many as eight and nine rooms, elegant furniture, lots of decorative silk dolls, gaudy hangings, and artistic moonlight scenes painted on dark velvet. Wine is an aid to the hashish smoker and all the pads sell it—a cheap local "ink." A few sell shake-up, too, which is a fierce whisky made by

shaking up straight alcohol and a little coloring: a dangerous combination when mixed with hashish. Chappy won't
handle it. "I don't pour no trouble" is the way he puts it.

Ground-floor pads keep their windows shut tight. This
is an invitation to dioxide suffocation, but Chappy thinks
that's better than letting the sickly-sweet odor of burning
marijuana into the street for the first passing pounder, or
patrolman, to smell. "One whiff," said Chappy, "and we
get a bust." ("Bust" is Harlem for a raid.) They burn
cheap ten-cent-store incense to disguise the marijuana odor.
Vipers don't seem to mind the damp warmth in the sealed
pads. They get quicker action from the weed in that atmosphere. Some vipers get high on a single stick, but
others need three or four. Chappy has one customer, a
Harlem blues singer, who can inhale fifteen in four hours,
but she's unusual. Many swing musicians and chorus girls
are inveterate vipers. The drug acts quickly on the musical sensibilities and gives a weird, indefinable lag to their
rhythm. It's a sexual excitant, too. Canary breeders
learned that long ago. They feed the birds on marijuana
seed in mating time by mixing it with the customary seed.
In Harlem some of the tea pads are bed houses, but not
Chappy's place. "I got my self-respec'," he says.

Fresh customers came dragging into Chappy's at midnight. They kept Chappy busy. Some took off their
overcoats but most of them didn't bother. One group of
well-dressed vipers retired to one of the back rooms.
Chappy served them reefers and wine and closed the French
door with the dirty-white curtains. By this time the main
parlor held about twenty smokers, all sucking at reefers.
The piccolo played without cease. Smoke and incense
snaked through the room in visible layers.

Vicki's cigarette burned a ragged hole in the dark and

her giggling increased. At each puff you could hear the peculiar hissing intake of breath that marks the smoking technique of the viper. Inhaling this way gets the smoke to the brain more quickly. Exhalation is slow and reluctant. The longer the smoke is retained, the greater the effect. The reefers are handmade, half as long as an ordinary cigarette, and thinner. They have double paper wrappers because the weed is coarse and apt to break through. Dry throat and hunger pangs mark the beginning of the high stage in a smoker. That's why vipers sometimes carry a little bag of peppermints or peanuts.

A new arrival called to Chappy across the room. "Deuce me, man," he said. "Deuce for Buck," chanted Chappy, bringing out two reefers and collecting a quarter. An ace is a single stick and sells for fifteen cents. Impoverished customers are served at the door. They pay only ten cents because they smoke "on the walk"—in their own homes or anywhere outside a regular pad. Chappy adds the extra tax on inside patrons to pay for wear and tear on his furniture and for atmosphere and rent. His rent is thirty dollars a month. He pays eighteen dollars a pound for cigarettes and makes about two hundred per cent profit on them. When his stock runs low he calls a dealer at 110th Street and Lenox Avenue and an automobile brings a fresh supply.

Federal agents had told me that vipers are always dangerous; that an overdose of marijuana generates savage and sadistic traits likely to reach a climax in ax and ice-pick murders. They cited the case of a Florida cracker who killed his whole family—five or six people—with a woodshed ax. Robert Irwin, the artist who killed the Gedeons and their boarder with an ice pick, had ten reefers in his room, which the police found when they searched the place. The hairy-chested gun girl who murdered a bus driver in New Jersey a couple of years ago testified that marijuana drove her to it. Detectives in Harlem suspect the marijuana defense may be the latest style with smart criminal lawyers. In their own dealings with hashish users taken in raids, the police uptown never had a tough one. "They just act restless when we get them to the station house," one cop explained. "They never fight."

Medical experts seem to agree that marijuana, while no more habit-forming than ordinary cigarette smoking, offers a shorter cut to complete madness than any other drug. They say it causes deterioration of the brain. Chappy's customers scoffed at this idea. They said reefers only make them happy. They didn't know a single viper who was vicious or mad. Once in a while some smoker gets a bit horsy and overplayful, but they "bring him down" just by talking to him. They say the marijuana makes the blood pound in their veins and gives them the sensation of suspension in mid-air. As they get high, the walls recede, lights back away, and their legs and fingers don't respond. Reflexes go haywire. They get to giggling. Time and sound and distance seem to stretch like a rubber band. It is easy, watching them, to understand why a smoker would feel that he was crawling when his car was doing eighty miles an hour. Chappy said that it was even dangerous for a viper to cross a street when he was high. "You hear a auto horn an' you see the lights," he explained. "You think they a mile away an' they right on top of you."

From the piccolo case, above the throb and beat, came the words of the viper song, low and soothing. The soloist was some husky-voiced woman.

I dreamed about a reefer five feet long,
Mighty, immense, but not too strong.
You be high, but not for long,
If you're a viper.

Boo was thumping the floor again, with his eyes shut tight. Vicki jumped up, and Steel-Haid caught her and crushed her against his body. They jerked to the music's beat, her slender form bending at sharp angles, in perfect rhythm with the tune. Her head shot back in an ecstatic fling. The blue bulb lighted their laughing faces.

"I'm the Queen of Ever'thing," Vicki shrilled. "I gotta be high before I swing."

The magnetic pull got Arthur and Fruits. They met in the center of the dark room in violent contact, locked in amorous embrace, and went into a creepy dance. The recumbent vipers moaned in voodooistic chorus:

Light yo' tea an' let it be,
If you're a viper.
When yo' throat get dry
You know you're high.
Ever'thing is dandy.
Truck on down to the candy sto',
Bust yo' conk on pep'min' candy,
Then you know yo' body's sent,
You don't care if you don't pay rent,
Sky is high and so am I,
If you're a viper.

Chappy's customers danced themselves breathless and rolled on the couches, convulsed with soft laughter. They didn't talk much. By three o'clock most of them were completely under, just able to moan and giggle with the music.

The smokers went through alternate periods of exaltation and exhaustion. They never stopped their silly laughter. Yet none of it was noisy; there was nothing, for example, to compare with the racket and hubbub that come in the later hours of an ordinary cocktail party. As a rule, customers lie around until the stupor leaves them. That may be anywhere from an hour to five or six hours, depending on the individual. When a customer is ready to cut out—the term for departing—Chappy "brings him down" with milk. The milk seems to hasten clearing of the brain.

Marijuana is made from the flowering top and leaves of India hemp plant. It is one of the oldest drugs in the world and has a different name in every country. It is bhang, hashish, or hasheesh, mazra, kef, reefer weed, or cannabis sativa. In the pharmacopoeia it is cannabis indica. In medical practice it is used to induce sleep or hypnosis. Commercially it is used for rope, twine, bags, mats, and canary food. It grows anywhere.

Marijuana growing in and around Manhattan had the Federal agents crazy for a long time. The stuff turned up in empty lots in the best neighborhoods as well as on the city dumps. They even found some under the Queensboro Bridge, near Sutton Place. Federal and city sleuths laid elaborate traps for the growers but never caught anyone. Then someone in the Federal service figured the thing out—the mysterious crops came from the marijuana seed dumped from the traps of canary cages. That was stopped quickly. Under a new law, all marijuana seed intended for birds must be sterilized in 220 degrees of oven heat before it goes on the market. Such seed will not germinate. Right now most of the smokers' supply comes from New Jersey, Staten Island, and Westchester.

The use of reefers has become so widespread that the Federal government has been making a concentrated drive on dealers. Since a Federal law was passed rating marijuana with vicious narcotics—heroin, cocaine, and the rest—the agents' activity has been greatly increased. There are thousands of white vipers in the city, but nowhere are the pads as thick or popular as in upper Harlem and in the Spanish and Mexican quarter around 110th Street and Fifth Avenue. Down that way reefers are sold in candy stores, restaurants, and grocery stores. In Harlem, marijuana is taking the place of whisky. A viper can get drunk on anywhere from one to four or five cigarettes—ten to fifty cents' worth—while it would cost him a dollar or two for a whisky jag. No hangover, either.

By five o'clock the atmosphere in Chappy's place was that of a Turkish bath. The piccolo was grinding out the viper song for the hundredth time. Chappy was high, too. He grinned foolishly, left sentences in mid-air, and when he walked he used the gait that comes from the floating sensation—a slow-motion gliding walk called the seven-foot step. Vicki and Fruits and two new wenches—The Trush and Lili—kept at their primitive dancing in delirious spasms, occasionally dropping back on the sofas, doubled with hushed laughter. Boo thumped. Chappy floated as he served fresh sticks and wine. It was Sunday morning and no one had to go home. No one but my friend and myself. The door of the pad shut behind us. We swallowed the sharp, cold air in grateful gulps.

Murderers Delivered

THE MURDERER sucked so hard on his cigarette that the paper curled and sparks fell. As he was linked to the Negroes on either side of him the handcuff ratchets sounded like grinding teeth.

John Durrant, the gaunt chief Deputy Sheriff, tapped the prisoners for tools or weapons. He even looked under their hats. They stood in awkward submission.

Durrant signed a receipt for the men: Salvatore Didato, forty, murder, thirty years to life; Lloyd Archer, twenty-four, dangerous weapon, one to three years; George Newkirk, twenty-four, burglary, two to five years.

"O.K.," Durrant said.

The keeper said, "O.K., John." He opened the heavy iron door and Durrant nodded to the prisoners.

He said, "Let's go."

Behind bars and wire mesh silent prisoners watched the shackled men down the long corridor. The murderer kept losing step. He was small—five feet five inches. He had to hold his wrists high.

Raymond Street Jail yard was deserted; concrete glaring in bright morning sun. The murderer's eyes watered. He had gone into the gloom of a cell in August when he shot and killed Paul Moncuzzo, his friend, in Carroll Park. They had fought over a woman. Now it was spring.

The prisoners climbed into the van. Durrant went to sit with the driver. Walter Prendergast, the other deputy, climbed in with the men. He locked the grilled door. "O.K.!" he called.

The van bounced in the street ruts. The prisoners swayed. They stared back at the receding jailhouse. Men and women stared at the prisoners as the van passed. They blinked in the strong light. Archer, the burglar, seemed anxious to talk. He shuffled his broken shoes. His shirt was soiled. He had no collar, no vest. At St. Felix Street he craned his fat neck to look down the block. He said to Prendergast, "That's my block." He grinned. "Sho' looks pretty."

The other men were silent. The little murderer's eyes still watered. He stared straight ahead. When his jaws flexed it reminded you of caterpillars. He had not shaved for days.

As the van rumbled over Manhattan Bridge the Negroes looked wistfully back toward Brooklyn. The one with the broken shoes finally turned away. He called out the names of the streets that flashed by.

"Do I get out," he said, vaguely, "no mo' jailhouse fo' mine. No, suh."

No one answered. The van moved up Second Avenue, across to Lexington. It pulled up at Grand Central Station on the Forty-second Street side. Men and women stopped to stare. Prendergast and Durrant followed the shackled prisoners down the ramp to the lower level. Here no one seemed to notice the handcuffs. The prisoners' coat sleeves hid them.

Durrant arranged the seating in the Ossining train. Archer and the murderer faced forward. Newkirk rode backward, leaning over to ease the handcuffs' strain. The

Negro prisoners looked wistfully on Harlem. When the train clacked northward by the river, Archer talked of his boyhood when he worked on boats.

"That's my life," he said. "I like to set on a boat an' look an' look. I like boats." He talked of spring. He pointed to the Palisades with his free hand. "Putty soon all the trees bus' right out," he said. "Putty soon I'd be up there, of a Sunday, a-ridin' a bicycle."

Newkirk and the murderer stared through the window on the sunlit water and on the trees. They did not talk.

Prendergast had been taking prisoners to Sing Sing for more than eighteen years. He figured at least 135 of them went to the death chair.

He said, "I kid with them. I tell them they'll get out soon. They eat that up."

Once Prendergast took up an opera singer, a fellow named Ricci. He sang *Pagliacci* all the way up. A few weeks later a Negro prisoner, one of ten in a consignment, sang "Mexicali Rose" in the train. The deputy shook his head.

"Boy," he said, "they went for that. You should have seen the linen break out."

The broken-shoed unfortunate put a diffident question. Could he get in the prison band, Boss? Prendergast said he thought so. The fat Negro grinned happily.

"Sho' like to get me to play the gee-tar," he said. "Sho' would."

The murderer seemed astonishingly meek. He smiled a furry smile, sort of sad. He was a painter. He said this would be his season, spring. He spoke of his boyhood. He was born in Melilli, a little place in Sicily. He had a chance to get back in 1937, but didn't go. His thick lips tightened with emotion, but he smiled again.

"No more," he said. "No more."

The fat boy turned to Prendergast as the train rolled past Scarsdale. He wanted to know if their pictures would be taken for the papers.

Prendergast said, "No, no pictures. You ain't big enough."

The fat one indicated the murderer by a nod of the head.

"How about him, Boss?" he said. "How 'bout this gen'lmen?"

"No," Prendergast said.

The fat boy lapsed into puzzled silence.

At Ossining the train screeched noisily to a stop, moved on again. The countryside was still. Birds piped in the trees. Durrant and Prendergast got the prisoners into a taxicab and the car wound slowly up the long hill to Sing Sing Prison. Durrant walked the three men to a thick-barred gate. He was admitted by a guard. He took off the men's handcuffs. The door clanged behind him when he came out again. A prison keeper opened the front door for him and the room flooded with sun.

"Swell day, John," he said.

Durrant nodded. He said, "Swell day."

The last thing you saw, as the door slowly shut, was the little murderer. He was staring into space. He was rubbing his wrists.

Junkies and Fellow Gentlemen

IN FRONT of Lincoln Hall's marriage canopy, a bower of stiff artificial calla lilies entwined in intensely dark-green leaves, the fervent chairman of the United Junkmen's Association of Brooklyn, Inc., thundered for justice for the trade. Antinoise laws, he bellowed, had ruined the calling. The microphone tinnily protested his ardent assault, set up a metallic whine at every syllable. Two hundred tired-looking, middle-aged men in work clothes listened in bewildered silence. The bull-voiced chairman darted a finger at the fifth row back.

"Mr. Friedman," he cried, "how many years you are in the junk business?"

A tall, thin man, sunken cheeks gray with stubble, stood up. He seemed embarrassed in the sudden limelight.

He mumbled, "Twenty-two years. Twenty-two years I am in the junk business."

A murmur breathed through the wedding chamber. Other junkmen twisted in their seats to face Mr. Friedman. The chairman thundered another question.

"Was you ever stopped in the streets by policemen, Mr. Friedman?"

The thin man said, "Please, Mr. Chairman. I am an honest junkman."

With eager passion the stertorous chairman pressed his point.

"Why are they stopping you now, please, Mr. Friedman, if you are an honest junkman?" he demanded triumphantly.

"Because I am ringing bells," the thin man said bitterly.

An angry undertone rumbled from the swart throats. The craggy-browed chairman caught the undertone at the crest. The microphone plates danced again under his tirade.

He shouted, "Eighteen years I am hollering junk in the streets. Eighteen years I am ringing my junk bells. Last week in our meeting we had five tickets in here. Why?" No one answered. "Why?" he persisted. "Because illegitimate junk peddlers steals a bicycle. It's a sickness with these illegitimate fellas. A disease what you call. For them illegitimate fellas we catch the blame."

Someone stood up to put in a word. The chairman sat him down with a magnificent wave of his hand. The chairman spoke with heavy dignity.

"Please," he said. "Please give me the courtesy. I am talking. In this city," he rumbled, "you got maybe 8500 junkmen with license. Eight hundred—it could be one t'ousand—are bad and they are ruining you. Ain't you are ashamed of your sweethearts and wives when you read a junkman took off a bicycle or maybe a suit of clothes off a line hanging? This thing we must correct. If you stick with us you will be recognized as decent gentlemen. You will be able to make maybe a couple pennies and bring home a loaf bread, a bottle milk to support your family."

Hardened, work-soiled palms thundered applause. The chairman's brow was dewy. He glared fiercely down the side lines, emotionally caught by his own eloquence and

the applause. During a brief recess a young peddler explained about the Junkmen's Association. He said it means to fight the antinoise ordinance.

He said: "If we can't holler 'Junk, rags, furniture, old clo',' how can the housewives know we are there? If we cannot ring on our junk bells, how can they hear us?"

The association, he said, had caused to be made for its

members large white buttons bearing each member's likeness. It wanted the men fingerprinted. It wanted to do away with unscrupulous dealers who send men out to steal, rather than to buy.

He said: "We want the peddlers should be polite to the housewife. We want the housewife to know we are for her protection."

Another earnest young man said the yearly turnover in junk came to $1,000,000,000. More, now, with the war. The market kept changing. South America at the moment was a good market for secondhand sewing machines. It used to be China and Japan. Scrap metal for battleships. Old furniture was a staple seller in the South. Old vacuum cleaners sold well in the Midwest. Egypt was the only clothes market that would buy vests or coats without the rest of the suit. Blue overalls made blotting paper. Old tires made blowout patches. Old rugs made "roofing," tar paper mostly. Old newspapers made cardboard. Over-issue newsprint—what the trade called "new news"—was used for wrapping. Cotton mattresses made gunpowder. Rags made high-grade paper, wipers, shoddy. It depended on the grade of rags.

Sometimes a peddler accidentally made a good buy. One man paid thirty-eight cents for brass that turned out to be $28.50 worth of gold. A Negro junk man found $73 in an old suit lining. Another peddler found $200 in an old hair mattress. One fellow bought an iron statue of President Garfield at the Vanderbilt estate on Long Island and it turned out to be bronze, worth, maybe, $200.

The energetic chairman ended the meeting with a lesson on politeness to customers. He picked his words carefully to make the lesson sink in.

"If a housewife has got an item wort' three dollars," he

said, "and she wants, maybe, six dollars, be always a gentlemen, a credit to the profession. Don't say to this worm, 'The hell wit' it.' Don't do this. Tip your hat. Be nice. Don't even slam the door. Say, 'Lady, t'ank you just the same.' This you got to do if you don't want the public to look on us like low class. We must be gentlemen, and we'll make money, even in a crisis."

The class in politeness roared noisy approval. Boots thumped the floor. Rough hands pounded heartily. The chairman beamed.

"Fellow gentlemen," he said, "the meeting is adjourned."

The Beggars

THE PROBLEM of handling the city's beggars has perennially been one that particularly bothers the police and the welfare agencies. The police try to keep them off the streets, and the social-service workers condemn almstaking and would like to apply enlightened theories of rehabilitation to all mendicants, whether crippled or able-bodied. It is a problem of long standing, and is no nearer a solution now than it ever was.

People concerned with the problem estimate that our local beggars have been taking in around $2,000,000 annually for a good many years past.

A very small proportion of the cripples who offer shoelaces and pencils in return for handouts and of the blind musicians who play in the streets are licensed by the city. After Mayor LaGuardia took office, the number of licenses was cut considerably. Special efforts were made to get the public to co-operate in doing something about beggars. Through his Welfare Commissioner, the Mayor asked New Yorkers not to give money to street mendicants of any sort. LaGuardia's point is that those who give handouts have already paid heavy taxes so that the city can provide for the destitute; he thinks that by giving money to a beggar, the individual is not only encouraging a hit-or-miss sort

of charity but is placing an unnecessary additional tax upon himself. A plea to this effect, signed by the Mayor, was printed in most theater programs for well over a year, and posted in subway cars, but the beggars still take in more in the theatrical district than anywhere else. Beggars do not like the relief which the city offers as an alternative. For an unmarried panhandler it is likely to be only food and a cot in the Municipal Lodging House; for a family man who is not crippled it means home relief or, at best, the pay of a WPA job; and for the physically disabled it will probably turn out to be life in an institution. Beggars prefer to beg.

Unlicensed mendicants are always liable to arrest for vagrancy, but apparently they are not much bothered by this threat. Some officials estimate that there are between six and seven thousand persons now begging in the city. No one knows the proportions of professional beggars and of itinerant panhandlers, nor can it be said with any certainty how many of the beggars who appear to be blind or lame or otherwise physically handicapped are really able-bodied. There are a large number of "phony crips," as the fraudulent cripples call each other, and there are many beggars known as "blinkies," who have good vision but pretend to be blind. Some of the sham cripples and blind men are so expert that only a doctor can detect their fakery.

Arresting beggars is the business of the Police Department's Mendicant Squad, and one cop with this assignment told me that it is a meaner job than Vice Squad work, which most cops detest. A policeman who attempts to take a cripple off the street knows that he probably will be heckled and abused by emotional citizens. If the cop does his duty and drags his deformed prisoner into court, he can be reasonably certain of having wasted his time. Magistrates usually do not bother to try to find out whether a cripple's affliction is real or feigned and are inclined to give the prisoner the benefit of the doubt. Even when there is no question of physical disability, a magistrate will hesitate to lock up a panhandler who may be a decent sort of chap temporarily down on his luck. So, although the courts occasionally send a confirmed vagrant to jail, they usually dismiss the case and let the chronic and faking beggars as well as the needy return to the street as fast as the men of the Mendicant Squad bring them in.

This futile procedure has been described as "revolving-door justice." To help cope with the problem, a group known as The Beggars' Clinic, supported by Federal relief money, was started in 1934 and was operated for about a year before it had to be closed because Congress cut down the relief budget.

The Clinic placed a doctor with a staff of assistants in Night Court to examine every beggar brought in by the police and sift the malingerers from the truly disabled. The pupils of a blind man's eyes will not dilate and contract, while a faker can't prevent his eyes from reacting to light and dark. Blinkies, therefore, were exposed by lights flashing in their eyes. The expert turned up many types of phony crips. Some beggars had encased sound legs in form-fitting shells that looked like artificial limbs. Others distorted the position of their heads or bodies by wearing steel braces. Some rolled their eyes and shook like an aspen leaf, but though their palsy resembled Parkinson's disease, the tremor that follows sleeping sickness, the medical men were not fooled. There were beggars with no physical defect who, by leaning on crutches of uneven size, achieved a grotesque twisting of their bodies. One such beggar, having heard of the Clinic and knowing that he would undoubtedly be shown up, dropped his odd-sized supports and escaped by outrunning a young cop who had just arrested him.

Some of the prisoners, it was found, should have been in institutions for mental defectives, and while the Clinic was operating, that's where they landed. One of these was a cheerful Negro who called himself the Safety-Pin King because of his ability to eat safety pins. He could eat a good many other strange things as well. He was arrested in front of the Hotel Edison one day while amusing a crowd by swallowing razor blades and broken electric-light bulbs. The Clinic's doctor suspected that the fellow didn't actually swallow the stuff at all, but he changed his mind when the Negro, with no trickery, gulped down a mouthful of pins as if he enjoyed doing it. The man then offered to eat some of the courthouse light bulbs, but the startled doctor was convinced. He sent the prisoner to a state asylum for mental cases, where he is now. Abusing the stomach in this fashion frequently does not impair the patient's health as much as might be imagined and the Negro is likely to live a long while.

Magistrates knew just what to do with each beggar brought to court as long as they had the Clinic to guide them. They sentenced to the workhouse phony crips and confirmed panhandlers, who are called "Chronickers." The really needy were put up in municipal lodgings until they could find jobs. A good many war veterans who were found begging were turned over to the American Legion, which presumably took care of them somehow. Other types were sent to hospitals and charitable organizations for treatment or rehabilitation. When the Clinic was closed, however, the courts reverted to the old system of turning the beggars loose.

Rehabilitation of bona fide cripples who have become confirmed professional beggars is not a simple thing. Blind men and "joyriders," as the legless who push themselves around on little wheeled platforms are known, are stubborn about giving up their trade. A good spot at an express station on the subway, or a busy corner in midtown, or in Coney Island during the season, may yield anywhere from forty to eighty dollars a week and the cripples argue that they can't do half as well as that caning chairs or turning out knickknacks in an institution. Some of them support families in a fair degree of comfort with the income from their tin cups. They are hard workers and usually put in from twelve to eighteen hours a day when the taking is good. A few of them are extravagant, and the police even found one joyrider who hung around in a Broadway bar in his off hours, paying for his drinks, but the general run of them are inclined to be penny pinching and manage to save quite a bit.

There are rich beggars, but they are never quite as rich as the newspapers say they are. The Beggars' Clinic discovered that one mother and son had $6000 between them. The son, who was in his early thirties, scraped at a violin and pretended that he had palsy and a paralyzed neck. The mother was his pilot. One beggar, who posed as blind and crippled but was neither, was exposed by his former wife, who sued to recover back alimony. He had $10,000 in banks around town. The Clinic found that one handsome young man who had nothing the matter with him made fifty dollars a week singing love songs on subway trains four hours a day, five days a week. He had romantic black hair and went in for white sports shirts open at the neck. He admitted that he got most of his money from middle-aged women. A number of the beggars brought to the Clinic had cash pinned or sewed to their inner garments. One old woman had $4000 in hundred-dollar bills attached to her chemise with safety pins. She explained that whenever the bills began to weaken and tear around the pinholes she went to the bank and exchanged them for new money. She did that about once every three months.

Blind beggars seem to like to stick together and most of the blind mendicants you see around Times Square and in the shopping districts have their homes in a community of their own extending several blocks along Cooper and Decatur Streets in the Bushwick section of Brooklyn. Many of them are men who have been through high school or further and the majority of them learned music or some trade at the Indiana School for the Blind in Indianapolis. They even have a lobby of sorts that is constantly agitating at Albany for a pension for the sightless. They would like to have something around $1200 a year apiece. Many of these men used to be licensed street performers. Some of those who lost their permits when the Mayor cut down on the number issued have continued to play in the streets with very little interference from the police. Others have found jobs on WPA projects.

Nearly three per cent of the city's mendicants have had some college education and one per cent are college graduates. Engineers seem more apt to descend to panhandling than other groups of college men; no one could say why. The police brought in one beggar, a gray-haired man of sixty-nine who was once a Deputy Collector of Internal Revenue. He had studied law at the University of Virginia and was an auditor for the Shipping Board on Hog Island during the war. As an undergraduate he had been voted the best-dressed man on the campus and the most likely in his class to succeed. One of his sisters was the wife of a Southern state legislator and another was married to a member of the faculty of a Midwestern university. When the magistrate heard the probation officer's report on this case, he dismissed the vagrancy charge on condition that the prisoner apply for an old-age pension, for which he was eligible.

The beggars' cant has names for all types of practitioners. There are the "nibblers," who gaze wistfully into a restaurant or bakeshop while they gnaw at a prop bread crust. They never speak to prospects and depend simply upon their attitude to appeal to passers-by. In the same category are the "divers," who dig hungrily into ashcans when they see a prospect approaching. The "flickers" are beggars who throw fits or pretend to have fainted from hunger. One of these once told a detective that he had pretended to have fits thirty-seven times in one month and usually collected enough after each act to pay for a day's food and lodging. It was easy, he said, except when the public insisted that he lie on the sidewalk until an ambulance surgeon arrived. When that happened he had to go through the routine of being taken to a hospital and being dismissed after an examination. "Pillinger" (the etymology is obscure) is the name for beggars who operate in front of big shops and public buildings, and "P.D.s" are punch-drunk prize fighters who beg at the doors of places like Madison Square Garden. The Jamaica Kid, a Negro pugilist who was a pretty good boxer some years ago, belongs in this class. Fight promoters occasionally put "P.D.s" on small allowances to stay away from their clubs. They sometimes make ambitious young fighters think too much.

Once in a while, a beggar hits on a new dodge and does pretty well at it. One posed as a leper. He would emerge from a shadowy areaway on a side street late at night and walk toward a prospect with arms raised above his head to show that he wasn't carrying a weapon. In a hollow voice he would warn the passer-by not to come close because he was a leper, and then entreat him to drop money on the sidewalk. This was frequently good for a quarter and sometimes for as much as a dollar. The man who worked this game kept shifting his ground and the cops never caught up with him. They were sure he was a fraud, however, and classified him as what beggars call a "weeper"— a panhandler with a hard-luck story.

In a class by themselves are the "dingoes," who really are small-time confidence men rather than beggars. They take pride in their work and like to get together to brag about the sly ones they have put over. One dingo got a dollar and one of the President's best cigars by "putting

the arm" on Mrs. Roosevelt at the entrance of her own
town house. Another is a well-dressed, dignified man who
carries an empty violin case and shows prospects a few
coins. His story is that he has been out of work, but that
at last he has a job to play in a concert if he can get to
Newark within an hour. All he needs, he says, is a few
more pennies to make up the carfare.

One type of beggar keeps strictly within the limits of
Jewish communities in the city. He is the *schnorrer,* a
bearded mendicant who begs at the doors of the syna-
gogues, at the gates of Jewish cemeteries, and wherever a
Jewish wedding is being held. On the East Side a good
many storekeepers leave outside the door a handful of
pennies in a small container, the *pushke,* from which the
schnorrer takes his mite—a single cent. This type of beggar has tradition behind him; he survives chiefly because
of the ancient Oriental belief that the giver is blessed for
his generosity and by it stores up heavenly credit. Shopkeepers know the beggars operating in their neighborhoods and are rarely imposed upon by outsiders. The
newer generation of Jews tends to ignore the *schnorrer,*
but up to five years or so ago his take was fairly high. One
bank in Grand Street even used to have a separate counter
for *schnorrers* where they could make up their coppers,
nickels, and dimes in rolls for deposit without delaying the
lines at the regular tellers' windows. There were a great
many women *schnorrers* among the Jews in the old days.
Some of them would hire a neighbor's child and take it
with them to increase their appeal, particularly in the
shopping and market districts. The usual rental for a
baby was twenty-five cents a day. Another trick was showing a landlord's dispossess notice, generally faked, to entice
larger contributions.

A detective who has had a lot of experience on the Mendicant Squad says that slightly more than half the beggars who appear blind or crippled are frauds. He knew of one blinkie who tapped his way around Times Square for years, doing pretty well at begging until he took to supplementing his income by picking pockets at night. When he was caught at it in a bar at Seventh Avenue near Forty-seventh Street, he explained that, being blind, he thought his fingers were in his own pocket. He wasn't blind and he got six months. Another blinkie simulated blindness by pasting his eyelids down with collodion before he left his flat each morning. He carried with him a small vial of alcohol and a cotton swab, with which he removed the collodion at the end of the working day. In the halfway-phony class are "sitters," one-legged men who beg at fixed posts and leave their wooden legs at home when they are on the job because an empty trouser leg has more appeal.

Most city officials seem depressed when you bring up the beggar question. "New York will always have them," they tell you gloomily, "Just as honey will always draw flies."

Mom, Murder Ain't Polite

ANNA LONERGAN came to our house for dinner one night. She brought her fourteen-year-old son. Between the soup and the chicken courses, Anna fell into a dreamy mood and started talking about her brother and her husbands and all the nice fellas she had known and how hardly any were left, now, what with all the shooting in her neighborhood.

The boy grew restless. He said, "Mom, it ain't nice to talk about murder when you're eating. It ain't polite."

Anna's clear white skin ebbed red. She glared at her son. She turned indignantly to us.

"You got an encyclopedia?" she said.

We had the *Britannica.* Anna seemed highly pleased. She ordered the boy to leave the table.

"You go in the next room," she told him in sharp maternal reproof. "You stay there and read the encyclopedia and you don't get no dessert."

The boy sullenly left the table.

Anna turned back to us happily. "I always do that," she explained. "When he talks back to his mother I make him go out and read the encyclopedia. That's the way to train children."

And Anna eagerly took up again the story of how many men her husbands had killed.

It is not often that Anna yields to the philosophical mood, but sometimes she talks wistfully of what a funny thing life is; how, when she was a little girl in yellow pigtails, she used to trot around the religious-goods store on Barclay Street with the sisters from St. James' because she wanted to be a nun, and how she turned out, instead, to be Queen of Brooklyn's Irishtown Docks.

This mood never lasts very long. Anna would rather tell about the sixteen years' dock war and how she won dower rights to the queenly title through the strong arms and the good trigger work of her two husbands, Wild Bill Lovett and Matty Martin, and her brother Richard ("Peg-Leg") Lonergan. She estimates that before they died (all three of them of bullet wounds) they killed about twenty men between them in order to gain and hold the water-front leadership and the graft that went with it. This esti-mate may sound extravagant but it is really conservative. Records in the Medical Examiner's office show, for in-stance, that in the ten years from 1922 to 1932 there were seventy-eight unsolved murders in the section of Brooklyn called Irishtown—the rough-cobbled area between the Brooklyn Navy Yard and Fulton Ferry, under and around the approaches to the Brooklyn and Manhattan bridges. The prosecuting officials always fretted about this but were never able to do anything about it. The police usually knew who the killer was but they could never get any witnesses, and without witnesses an indictment was not ob-tainable, much less a trial. Exactly how many of the seventy-eight unsolved murders in that decade are attrib-utable to dock wars, and how many to incidental motives, nobody really knows.

Anna's men were hard-working fellows who kept pretty regular hours. Six mornings a week they would go down to the docks for the stevedores' roll call. They had to be there to make sure that no stevedore was working who was not paying a share of his salary to the dock leadership. Sometimes a stevedore would argue about paying tribute and he would have to be beaten up or maybe his skull would have to be cracked. Men like that were not shot unless they were exceptionally obstinate. But when some superstevedore, with a gang of ten or twelve supporters, would try to take the leadership away from Anna's men, somebody usually got killed.

When Anna claims that Wild Bill, Matty, and Peg-Leg murdered about twenty men between them, she does not count neighborhood killings attributable to such things as honor, bad temper, and misunderstanding. Murders di-

rectly attributable to the racket of extorting a portion of
stevedores' salaries were discussed at her dinner table, and
she remembers most of them distinctly. She recalls only
the more spectacular of the family murders that fall within
the noncommercial or amateur category. Back in the
twenties, every time there was a killing in Irishtown, the
newspapers would label it "dock-war murder," but Anna
says that was a lot of journalistic prittle-prattle. When
Jim Gillen was killed on Jay Street in 1921, for example,
his death was attributed to dock trouble, but the motive
was something entirely different. Wild Bill Lovett killed
Gillen for pulling a cat's tail. "Bill always hated to see
anyone hurt a animal," Anna says.

It has been Anna's experience that you become accustomed to murder if you see enough of it. She didn't like it
at first, but as time went on it became more or less routine.
Sometimes a sensitive ear may detect a bit of pride in
Anna's voice as she tells how many times she has gone to
the morgue to identify her own dead or the neighbors'.
She started when her father was killed by her mother, and
went again when Bill got his. When her brother Peg-Leg
was shot to death with Aaron Harms and Needles Ferry,
his pals, Anna identified the three of them at one time.
Later, Charlie Donnelly disputed the dock leadership with
Matty Martin, who was Anna's second husband, and she
made another trip to the morgue as a friendly gesture to
Mrs. Donnelly, who was afraid she couldn't stand the
ordeal of identifying her own husband. Eddie McGuire,
murdered on the docks on May 16, 1928, was officially
identified by Anna, too, and finally she did the honors for
Matty, who had been accused (wrongfully, according to
Anna) of the McGuire killing. Anna probably has an all-
time record for morgue identifications, but she hasn't

checked up on it. She never dreams about any of the killings and never cries when she thinks of them. Detectives say the only time they ever saw her cry was when she claimed Peg-Leg's body.

Anna was the first of fifteen children. Her father, John Lonergan, was red-haired, six feet two inches tall, a second-rate prize fighter when he married Mary Brady over on Cherry Hill on the East Side of Manhattan in 1898. There is some family legend that he once sparred with John L. Sullivan, but Anna wouldn't swear to it. Anna was born with a caul, which is supposed to bring good luck, but her Uncle Nelson, who was a captain on one of Jay Gould's yachts, bought it from Anna's mother. Sailors, you know, believe you can't drown if there's a caul aboard ship. Uncle Nelson had three, which he'd picked up here and there, just to make sure. He couldn't swim.

As a little girl, Anna attended St. James' parochial school on the East Side, the same one that Al Smith went to when he was a boy, and Al's wife sponsored Anna's enrollment in the Sacred Heart sodality. Anna admits, though, that the children were sponsored in groups and that she didn't know Mrs. Smith "real well." The Lonergans moved to the Brooklyn water front when Anna was about ten years old and took a house on Johnson Street. During this period Anna was extremely devout, trudged everywhere with the sisters, and, to use her own expression, "was in church morning, noon, and night." At about this time, too, she had her first contact with murder. Margaret Doran, one of her classmates, asked her one day after school to visit the Doran home on Pacific Street, in the same neighborhood, and in the basement they stumbled over the body of Margaret's mother. Margaret's pa, a motorman on the Smith Street trolley line, had chopped off Ma Doran's head.

Some dock workers found his body in the river next day. He had jumped off the wharf, after the killing, in a fit of remorse. Anna doesn't remember any other details, and she doesn't think the incident bothered her for any length of time. She says most people have a wrong idea about murder from books and movies, and it doesn't really haunt you and affect your sleep.

Anna is close to forty now, by her own count. She is still fussy about her blonde, bobbed hair, never misses a Saturday appointment at the neighborhood beauty parlor, and is extremely proud of her white hands. She is careful with her fingernails, too. She never uses red nail polish because she thinks it's cheap and vulgar, but she does do a rather professional job on her face with lipstick and eyebrow pencil. Her experience as a Broadway show girl is responsible for that. She danced at Rector's and Churchill's when she was eighteen and had a nonspeaking part with Fay Bainter in *The Kiss Burglar*. Since leaving the stage, she has been shot twice and stabbed once, and when she mentions these things she always crosses herself and thanks God that none of the scars show. Dressed for the street, she is still a good-looking woman. "My mother was beautiful, too," she'll tell new acquaintances. "She was the pitcher of me when she was a girl; a natural blonde, the same as me, only her hair turned gray overnight after Richard [she hates to have her brother called Peg-Leg] got his."

The first casualty in the Lonergan family was Boy, the family's pet spaniel. Boy was a cop hater, like most of the residents of Irishtown. The elder Lonergan had a special trapdoor in his bicycle-repair shop on Bridge Street, leading into a hole in which the dog could hide after he had nipped a patrolman, but one day a mounted officer, quick on the draw, fired a shot at the Lonergan pet and Boy died in what was to become the traditional Lonergan manner.

Anna was out walking with Laura Rich at dusk on April 16, 1923. She was still in the show business then, and so was Laura, who was from Irishtown too. As they passed the bicycle shop, they saw two other Irishtown girls ("tramps," Anna calls them) talking with old man Lonergan and Peg-Leg. Anna told her mother about it when she got home, and then forgot about it.

But Anna's mother didn't forget about it. She went down to the shop, and before she got through telling John Lonergan what she thought of him and the loose women he was entertaining, the cop had to come in off his beat to restore peace and quiet. A half-hour later Mrs. Lonergan went back to the bicycle shop and within a few minutes after she got there, her spouse was dying from bullet wounds. Anna heard about it and rushed down to the store. She pushed her way through the crowd and got in before the cops came. The old man was sprawled out on the floor and Mrs. Lonergan was kneeling over him, screaming. Anna sent for a priest and got her mother into a chair. "Mamma," she said, "what have you done to Papa?"

Peg-Leg wasn't in the store when the old man was killed. He showed up at the station house as his mother was being booked for murder, and tried to take the blame. That's why the rumor got around, later, that he actually committed the murder. Anna admits that Peg-Leg told the desk lieutenant, "The old lady didn't do it; I did," but she says there was no truth in his confession. "It was Mamma done it," she says explicitly.

The two girls who started the whole business came to John Lonergan's wake and made Anna furious, but she

restrained herself until they left her house. Then she
went after them with a boy's baseball bat which had been
parked in the umbrella stand in the hall for some years.
She caught up with one of them, a girl named Kate, and
knocked her out cold. Anna thinks now that perhaps it
wasn't ladylike, but, as she says, "I was berling mad at the
time."

Big Ed Reilly, who was famous in Irishtown as a de-
liverer of oppressed gunmen and beautiful ladies with
homicidal tendencies long before the Hauptmann case, was
hired by Bill Lovett as Mrs. Lonergan's attorney. Reilly's
oratory at the trial made short work of the case against
Mrs. Lonergan. It pictured Anna's mother as the patient
drudge, beaten and kicked by her brute of a husband every
day of their married life. With a quavering voice the
lawyer depicted Mrs. Lonergan moved to great anger when
the old man sent Anna home from the bicycle shop bleed-
ing at the mouth because she had asked him to give her
money for the family supper. Mrs. Lonergan had gone to
the shop to reproach her husband for this and in the course
of the argument which resulted the elder Lonergan had
pulled a gun. Mrs. Lonergan, naturally, had tried to take
it away from him and had shot him, accidentally. Anna
was the star witness for her mother. She talked convincingly, and the jurymen seemed sad and turned Mrs. Lonergan loose.

Sometimes when Anna recalls her wedding to Bill Lovett, on July 28, 1923, she grows melancholy. She would
have liked a church wedding with a misty veil and long
train, and maybe some orange blossoms and organ music,
but she had to stand up before City Clerk McCormick in
ordinary street clothes. A formal wedding would have
been out of place, in the circumstances. The ceremony

came off only a month after Anna's mother had been freed of the murder charge; Peg-Leg, her brother, had just been arrested in connection with another killing (the murder of Eddie Hughes in a Sands Street speakeasy), and the bridegroom himself was out on bail on a charge of carrying concealed weapon.

Anna had known Bill since they had been kids together on Catherine Street on the East Side, but had never thought much of him. He was shy around women and he was short—only five feet seven inches in height—and his face was a peculiar gray, owing to a lung condition. His black hair accentuated the pallor. The family had liked Bill, though, and the elder Lonergan had encouraged the match. Peg-Leg was for it, too, because he and Bill had been in Cumberland Hospital once at the same time—Peg-Leg with a bullet wound he'd acquired in a brawl in a Gold Street speak-easy, and Bill with five bullet wounds inflicted by the Frankie Byrnes gang of Irishtown.

Bill's courtship was almost mute. He used to sit around the Lonergan home by the hour, pretending he was calling on Peg-Leg, and he would stare at Anna. The old man pleaded with Anna to talk to Bill. "I don't talk to fellers who go around shooting people," she said one time.

That made the old man mad. "Your brother shoots people, too," he argued.

"Yeh," said Anna, "and he ought to be ashamed of himself."

Bill finally compelled Anna's admiration, though, by assuming ownership of a loaded .25-caliber automatic that was found on the elder Lonergan when detectives raided a Greenpoint speak-easy where he and Peg-Leg and Bill were having some of their favorite needle beer. "It was only a little gun," Anna says when she tells about it, "but I always thought it was a swell thing for Bill to do."

Bill promised to give up homicide as soon as he and Anna were married. They moved out to Ridgefield Park, New Jersey, to a little house with a garden around it, and Anna buckled down to the mean job of reforming Bill completely. It was even harder than she thought it would be. He was to have gone to work in a Paterson silk mill, but never quite got around to it. He had a few hundred dollars left after the house was furnished, and coasted along on that. They had been married about a month when Bill came home late one night, sat down in a parlor chair, and yanked out his automatic. (Anna had let him keep that one, out of his collection, for self-protection.) He told Anna to get into the far corner of the room. "I want to see if you can take it," he said. She had an idea what was coming, but she started for the corner, hoping he'd change his mind before she got there. He didn't, though. If Anna knows you well enough, she'll take the shoe off her left foot and show you where Bill shot away part of her big toe.

Anna was proud of Bill's marksmanship, of which the toe shooting is an example, but he did embarrass her sometimes by showing off with his automatic. He never did any shooting unless he was very drunk. Once, before they moved to New Jersey, he shot out all the lights in a Smith Street trolley car. Anna was humiliated, to hear her tell it, but she got a laugh out of the passengers. They all looked so scared. Another time, when Anna and Bill were visiting friends in Irishtown, Bill shot two pork chops out of the friend's frying pan. It was good shooting, but it was a social error. They were never invited to that house

again. On another occasion, at an Easter Sunday party in
Bridge Street, before they were married, their host put on
a derby hat and gave an imitation of Charlie Chaplin. It
wasn't a good imitation, and Bill fired a shot at the hat.
Someone jiggled his arm and the slug caught the host in
the shoulder. Bill was all for a second try, but he was
talked out of it.

Bill was very proud of Anna and bought her the best
clothes he could find. He liked to be seen with her, and
was pleased when other men eyed her, but was apt to get
nasty if they looked at her too long. He shot one man just
for that. It was over on the Chelsea docks, in Manhattan,
where he'd gone to visit his father, who was a stevedore
there. An inoffensive French chef on a liner stuck his
head out of a porthole for a breath of air. Anna came into
his line of vision and he let his eyes rest on her for a few
seconds. This annoyed Bill. "He thought this Frenchman was trying to make me," Anna explains, "so he gets
his gun out and shoots the poor feller's right ear off."

During the courtship period in Brooklyn, Anna could
always tell when Bill was primed for a killing. A spot in
the center of his pale forehead would grow dark when the
urge came on. His stevedore pals knew that spot, too, and
would excuse themselves from Bill's presence when they
saw it blooming. Still, to hear Anna tell it, Bill wasn't
really vicious, because the fiercest dogs would make up to
him, and in her opinion that is an infallible sign of something basically gentle in a man's nature. Bill liked babies,
too. He proved that the night of March 31, 1920, when
he killed Dinny Meehan, who was Irishtown dock leader
at the time. As he walked through the Meehan flat on
Warren Street, Brooklyn, he stopped in the parlor to pat
little Dinny, Jr., on the head before he went into the bed-

room and put two slugs into big Dinny. One of the shots ricocheted and wounded Mrs. Meehan, who was sleeping with her husband, but she recovered. Three years later Mrs. Meehan showed Anna the scar as an argument against her marrying Bill, but it didn't change Anna's mind.

Outside of shooting off Anna's big toe to see whether she could take it, Bill made an ideal husband, for a while. He stayed in the Jersey cottage at night and read a lot. Anna says he was a sucker for anything penned by Arthur Brisbane, and for all kinds of history. He was a great Bible reader, too, and could quote long passages from the Scriptures. He didn't care much for the movies, but he knew they were Anna's favorite form of entertainment and he'd take her whenever she asked. Today Anna prefers Wallace Beery and John Barrymore films. She likes Broadway shows, too, but not as much. She seldom comes to Broadway now at all. Stage pathos leaves her cold unless a child is involved; the spectacle of kids getting a dirty deal, on the stage or off, always makes her cry.

Three months after she started to reform Bill, Anna noticed that he wasn't paying much attention to his history books, his solitaire, and two-handed pinochle. He was off form in his checker game, too, and seemed tired of Paterson. He sometimes spoke wistfully of Irishtown. One night, when he couldn't bear the nostalgia, he blurted that he was going to Brooklyn. "Just for a little visit, Doll," he told Anna. She decided to go over, too, and he arranged to meet her later that night near her favorite Irishtown beauty parlor, at Jay and Fulton Streets. When he didn't come, Anna went to his mother's house on Bath Beach and asked Bill's brother George, who was studying for the priesthood, to help her search for Bill. George didn't like the idea, but he agreed to go along. When they had made the round of all the water-front speak-easies and home-brew joints, George suggested they try the Dockloaders' Club at 25 Bridge Street, but Anna vetoed that.   She said Bill had been shot once at that address, and was superstitious about returning to any place where he'd once been hurt.   They gave up the search then, but it was at the Dockloaders' Club that Bill was found by the police some hours later, filled with bullets, his head bashed in with a stevedore's bale hook.

Bill was buried in the National Cemetery in Cypress Hills with full military honors.   He had served with the Seventy-seventh Division in France and had won the D. S. C.   After he got back from the other side, he had been shot on five separate occasions and had been formally arrested seven times (but never tried) for killing people. His death left Anna penniless.   The insurance companies had considered him a poor risk.   Anna closed the house in New Jersey and moved back to her mother's.

She was rather proud of the long homicidal record of her first husband.   A newspaper reporter once asked her how she ever came to marry a man who, during his career, had been officially accused of seven murders.   Anna bristled so fiercely that the journalist shrank.   "The papers only gave Bill credit for seven," Anna said bitterly.   "He killed nearer twenty-seven in Brooklyn."   In her indignation, Anna went on to say that Bill never got credit, either, for the half-dozen murders he added to his list during the two years that he was hiding out in Chicago after he had killed Dinny Meehan, the dock leader.   The Chicago murders were strictly amateur, though, she says now, and perhaps deserve only a footnote in his record.   He did the Chicago jobs as a favor to friends who gave him shelter.

Another thing that stirred Anna to anger was any news-

paper reference to her as "gun moll." She has never fired
a revolver or automatic, and is a little afraid of them. It
isn't that she's a softy. She has taken loaded weapons from
many a truculent drunk, and she often had to pick guns
up during house cleanings at home. But she has never
really used one in her life.

Anna doesn't consider herself tough. As a young girl,
she shied away from the more raucous neighborhood ele-
ments because the he-men of the Irishtown section along
the Brooklyn water front didn't conform to her ideals of
what true gentlemen should be. She has been arrested
only once. When she was fourteen years old, she was
shopping one night with some older Irishtown girls when
an Italian storekeeper, as she puts it, "made passes at us
with his eyes." All Italians—called "ginzoes" by the
'Towners—were poison to an Irish girl like Anna. She
fished a slab of liver off the street counter of a butcher
shop next door and smacked the shopkeeper's face with it.
It splashed his shirt with red stains and he thought he had
been stabbed. His screams brought the police, and Anna
and her friends were taken to the Poplar Street police
station. She might have gone free because she was a
minor, but a sort of grim loyalty is one of her virtues, and
she gave her age as eighteen. She and her friends were
released next day after a night in jail.

After that the only fighting Anna did was in behalf of
Peg-Leg, her brother, who was red-haired and pugnacious
like her father. Anna loves to recall how Peg-Leg held on
to the groceries and change the night he lost his left leg
under a Smith Street trolley car. The accident happened
when he was stealing a ride on the way back from the
store, she remembers, and he was carried into Conley's
saloon. He wouldn't get into the ambulance until he had

handed the package over to his mother. Anna likes to tell the story because it illustrates what stuff the Lonergans were made of. Papa Lonergan gave the boys free rein as they grew up, but was strict with the girls. Until she was eighteen, Anna had to be in bed every night before the Navy Yard bells bonged at nine o'clock, or feel her father's horny hand. Later, when she was in show business, the curfew didn't apply. The family needed the money. Even Mrs. Lonergan worked, scrubbing offices in the Borough Hall district, to keep the family going.

While Anna was light-footing it on Broadway, Peg-Leg was helping his father run his bicycle shop. They had the Telephone Company trade. In those days, the repair men rode bicycles instead of Fords. Peg-Leg had a lot of interests outside of the shop, too. Despite his wooden leg he managed to get around, and became pretty handy with an automatic. He was a good man in a speak-easy brawl, and got an early start on his long string of homicides. He never went to prison for any of them, but neither did Anna's husband, Bill Lovett, or any other Irishtown trigger men. That seems to puzzle most people when they hear about it, but it's quite simple, as Anna explains it. Most of the killings were done when there were no witnesses around. Even when there were witnesses the cops couldn't get anything out of them. The neighborhood code forbade squealing, and in Irishtown an informer was rated twenty degrees lower than an Italian policeman.

By the time he was twenty, Peg-Leg was a holy terror along the docks and in the Irishtown speak-easies, but Anna will not admit it. She will concede that he killed a lot of men, but will insist that he was good at heart. He took up homicide, she contends, not from choice but by accident. It seems that when Peg-Leg was seventeen,

Giuseppe Bonanzio, a Navy Street drug peddler, tried to get him to handle narcotics in the bicycle shop as a sort of sideline. Peg-Leg refused and Bonanzio pulled a gun. Peg-Leg grabbed the weapon, according to Anna, and it went off. Bonanzio dropped with a bullet in the heart. The killing made Peg-Leg a neighborhood big shot, and pretty soon he was taking on killing jobs for his friends on the docks. "He wasn't a professional killer," Anna says. "He'd just do these jobs to help his friends out."

Peg-Leg figured in so many shootings that the magistrates got sick of seeing his face in court. His official record shows three arrests for assault and three for homicide, but Anna says the records don't begin to reflect his activities. "You can't go by the police records," Anna says.

After Bill died, Peg-Leg teamed up with Matty Martin, who was to be Anna's second husband. Matty was what might be called the coleader of the Irishtown stevedores. With his partner, Charlie ("Cute Charlie") Donnelly, and a gang of supporters, he dominated the docks and exacted tribute from all the dockworkers. Peg-Leg would meet Matty on the docks every day and help him with his work. Then the two of them would go to Anna's house for dinner and relaxation.

It wasn't long before these evenings took on a romantic tinge. Like Bill, Matty went in for mute courtship. Anna has found that rather a common trait among men who do a lot of shooting. They're hard-boiled and fearless among men, but practically tongue-tied around women. "It used to be real pitiful to watch Matty trying to get out a word, every now and then," she remembers. It took every bit of courage he had. Matty was taller than Bill, but, like Bill, he was a heavy drinker. He could hold even more than Bill could, though, and no one could ever tell when he was drunk. Bill had liked publicity, but Matty hated it. When Matty finally proposed to Anna, he persuaded her to get married at Saugerties, New York, so the newspapers wouldn't make a fuss about it. They were married in February, 1924, three months after Bill had been killed and buried. Right after the wedding they returned to Brooklyn to live with Anna's mother in the Bushwick district, which is a long way from the water front.

It was Anna's idea the family should move out of Irish-town. She thought people were getting to know too much of the family affairs, what with the publicity that came with every fresh shooting. Besides, she hoped Bushwick would be a safer place for Matty. They moved, but it didn't turn out that way. Two weeks after the wedding, when she was walking down the street with Matty, not far from the house, one of the aspirants for the stevedore crown on the Irishtown docks stepped out of a doorway with a revolver and aimed at Matty. Anna jumped for him, caught his shooting hand, and tried to pull the weapon away from him. One shot went off, and the powder burned Anna's right temple. It left no scar, for which she is grateful. She thinks that if the burn had left a mark people *would* think she was a gunwoman. She never tells the name of the man who tried to shoot Matty, which may be taken as indication that he is still alive.

Anna found that Matty didn't care much for food. He lived on booze most of the time. The only thing he really cared for in the way of solids was home-baked bread. His poor appetite didn't bother her, however. Bill hadn't been much of an eater, either. Matty was more easily domesti-cated, on the whole, than Bill had been. He preferred tinkering with radios to going out and he bought every new gadget for eliminating static or getting more distance. At one time, he owned and tinkered with five radio sets. None of them worked very well.

The chief reason for Matty's radio tinkering late at night was insomnia. Sometimes, when he did get to sleep, he would wake up screaming. It wasn't conscience, Anna says; Matty's mother said he used to do it even when he was a baby. Besides being an insomniac, Matty was a somnambulist. One hot night, when the Lonergans were asleep on mattresses on the parlor floor, he got up and walked to the rear window. Anna, who happened to be awake, was amazed at the ease with which he stepped between the sleepers in the dark. On another of his walks in his sleep Matty went downstairs, ate everything in the icebox, and took up the *Brooklyn Daily Eagle* that lay on the table. An hour later Anna went down with her mother to look for him. When Mrs. Lonergan became convinced that Matty wasn't shamming, that he was actually reading in his sleep, she told Anna to get him out of the house. "Take him away," she ordered, terrified. "He gives me the horrors."

Anna and Matty then took up housekeeping in a one-family frame house in the Bushwick district. Anna never liked apartment houses, because she has found apartment-house dwellers nosy. Another advantage of the one-family house was the flower garden. Anna had always been fond of flowers, and she found Matty was, too. He had a "green thumb"—a way with plants—as well as a supple trigger finger. He was tender with guppys, too, and in sentimental moods played the zither well.

Peg-Leg, while Anna and Matty were living in the quiet life in Bushwick, didn't find enough activity or competition on the docks to satisfy his craving for target practice, so he ventured into the Gowanus area for frequent ginzo-baiting expeditions. He focused his attention on the Adonis Social Club, an Italian cabaret in Twentieth Street where Al Capone, as an unknown dance-hall bouncer, had perfected his marksmanship by shooting necks off beer bottles when there was nothing else to do. Peg-Leg and two of his stooges, Needless Ferry and Aaron Harms, swilled and guzzled liberally in the cabaret the night before Christmas, 1925, sneered at Jack ("Stickem") Stabile, the bartender, and insulted Italian patrons individually and in groups. They chased all the Irish girls out, just as they used to do in Fort Greene Park, and told them to "come back with white men." Then Peg-Leg and his friends went on drinking.

On Christmas morning, Anna made another excursion to Kings County Morgue and identified Peg-Leg, Ferry, and Harms. All three had been shot through the back of the head as they stood at the Adonis bar. Detectives made twenty arrests in the case, but ran into the customary thing —none of the men or women who were in the club when the shooting started knew who had fired the shots, and no amount of persuasion by the police, physical or oral, could convince them that they did. Among the twenty prisoners was Capone, and he was turned loose along with the others. Anna says she knows who did the job in the Adonis Club and that she knows who killed Matty and who killed Bill, but she says she won't tell.

Anna arranged Peg-Leg's burial. She was in the habit of taking charge of all family burials. She has always been the family spokesman, too, whenever any member of her family figured in a shooting. She never tells the police much. "The way I look at it," she says, "is this: those who live by the gun, they die by the gun. It's in the hands of

God." Anna is extremely religious, and always has been. Through all the shooting and the frequent murders in which her husbands and brother figured, she never missed a Mass. Her mother, who is still living, is just as steady in church attendance. Anna makes special novenas to pray for her mother's health. Her favorite saint is Saint Teresa, the Little Flower, to whom she pleads for safe guidance for her brothers and sisters. "I always pray they'll have good company and not go bad," she says.

Things stayed quiet for Anna a long time after her brother Peg-Leg was buried. Matty was arrested at Peg-Leg's wake for carrying a loaded revolver and did six months on the charge. After he finished his prison term, he went back to the docks, and resumed his coleadership. He would come home from the docks every night around six o'clock and fiddle with his rheostats and verniers, and his life seemed secure and relatively peaceful. He gave Anna all she needed to run the house and a liberal clothing allowance besides. He even took her to the movies once a month, much as he disliked the cinema. But by the end of 1929 Matty's share of the money extorted from the stevedores and truckmen on the water front had dropped from an average of two hundred dollars a week to around fifty. The depression had hit shipping hard. Anna noticed, however, that "Cute Charlie" Donnelly, who shared the leadership of the stevedores with Matty, was still able to keep his wife in good clothes and seemed to have as much money as ever. She must have mentioned it to Matty. On the morning of January 29, 1930, Matty had a business conference in the loaders' shack on Dock Street and flatly accused Donnelly of double-crossing him. After the conference, Donnelly was found dead on the floor of the shack. No witnesses. Anna felt sorry for Mrs. Donnelly. She

identified the body at the morgue and helped with the
funeral plans.

After the Donnelly killing, for which Matty had to make
the customary trip before the magistrate to get his usual
dismissal, Anna kept hearing rumors that Matty was
marked for the next "out." The night of December 13 she
had a bad dream, and with it her first and only premonition
that death was in the offing. She explains it now as "a
funny kind of feeling" and clutches in the general vicinity
of her heart when she tells about it. She awakened Matty
and told him about the dream, but he wasn't impressed.
He didn't come home to dinner the next night, though.
A police car called instead, and took Anna to Cumberland
Hospital. Matty had been wounded in a De Kalb Avenue
speak-easy. He lived two days. When the cops asked him
who had shot him, he wouldn't discuss it. They had three
men in custody, they told him—were they the ones?
"Turn them guys loose," said Matty, and died.

There is every reason to believe that Matty told Anna
who had shot him before he died.

Anna is especially proud of the confidence reposed in her
by her husbands and their friends in all matters pertaining
to homicide. Whenever there was a fresh killing, the men
would tell her about it immediately. That wasn't true in
the homes of other warring dock loaders. Few women
could be trusted as Anna was. She did not, however, get
all her information about the murders from her immediate
family. The underworld has a system all its own, called
"the kite," which brings murder bulletins to those who can
be trusted with them. Anna used to get them long before
the police or newspapers did. Sometimes they would come
by telephone, sometimes by messenger. "It's like a magazine subscription," she says. "You don't ask for it, but it

keeps right on coming." Anna has an idea that she is cut in on the kite line because occasional newspaper articles and a mention, now and then, in some book (there's a whole chapter about her, for instance, in ".Not Guilty," the book about Sam Leibowitz) keep her name fresh in the minds of people along the water front who are close to the warring stevedore gangs and who get murder news while it's hot. *By Fred D. Pasley. 1933*

Anna is quite proud, too, of her popularity at Sing Sing. She has made several trips to the death house to console friends, and all the boys up there seem to like her. The late Leonard Scarnici, bank robber and murderer, was, in spite of being an Italian, one of her friends. After he was put to death in the electric chair, she felt pretty bad about it. "Maybe he buried a man alive up in Connecticut, like they say he did," she said recently, "and maybe he did all the killings they gave him credit for, but I knew him and I still think he had a heart of gold."

Anna lives alone, now, in a little one-family house in the Bushwick section. She devotes a lot of time to keeping the place neat. She is fussy about little details; it makes her uncomfortable if a guest so much as nudges an antimacassar out of place. She keep about two hundred books in the house, most of them slightly out of date. She has read all of Victoria Cross, and her favorite novel is *One Night of Temptation,* by that author. There is a copy of Herbert Asbury's *Gangs of New York* in her collection, but she keeps it only out of sentiment for Matty, who liked it. Anna never cared for it very much, because it's about tough people. At least that's what she says. In the next breath, though, she's apt to point out that both Bill and Peg-Leg are mentioned in it, as well as her Uncle Yake Brady, who was a noted brawler on Cherry Hill.

Anna doesn't think she will ever marry again, although she has had some attractive offers. She says she may, of course, change her mind any day. There was a report, after Matty died, that she intended to marry Edward (Red) Patterson, a South Brooklyn holdup man who had done time in Sing Sing Prison, but that was not true. Anyway, Patterson is dead now. He was killed in a brawl by Jim Cahill, an ex-cop.

Anna keeps hoping for better times. She has an idea she may find a future in politics, and to get started in the right direction has joined a Democratic club in her neighborhood. She thinks she might be coleader someday. She learned how to smoke at the club, and picked up a passing knowledge of bridge there. She hasn't been near the docks for a long time. She cut down her water-front visits after one of the lads stabbed her in the left arm because she demanded a cut on the meager, present-day graft. For a time after Matty's death the boys who inherited the water-front leadership saw to it that she got thirty dollars a week, but later they cut that off. "There's only a few of the old crowd left down there, anyways," she says, "and they're a bunch of heels."